AF560328

WHITE-COLLAR CRIMES
Causes, Prevention, Law and Judicial Trends

WHITE-COLLAR CRIMES

Causes, Prevention, Law and Judicial Trends

DR. SHAILESH KUMAR SINGH
LL.M., M.Phil. (Law), Ph.D. (Law)
Shriji Institute of Legal, Vocational Education and Research,
Bareilly
(M.J.P. Rohilkhand University, Bareilly)

REGAL PUBLICATIONS
New Delhi-110027

WHITE-COLLAR CRIMES
Causes, Prevention, Law and Judicial Trends

ISBN 978-81-8484-374-3

Reprint : 2019

Typeset by
S.S. COMPOSERS
3190, Mohindra Park, Shakur Basti, Delhi-110034.

Printed in India at
MAYUR ENTERPRISES
WZ Plot No. 3, Gujjar Market, Tihar Village, New Delhi-110018.

Published by
REGAL PUBLICATIONS
F-159, Rajouri Garden, New Delhi-110027.
Phone: +91-11-45546396
E-mail: regalbookspub@yahoo.com

There is sufficiency in the world for man's need,
but not for man's greed.

—Mahatma Gandhi

Contents

Preface

"अभिवाक्षशीलस्य नित्यं वृद्धोपसेविनः।
चत्वारि तस्य वर्द्धन्ते"।।

Today's society is more active and mobile than that of the past. In today's world man has become a money-making machine. The basic need theory is now outdated. The acquisitive tendency of man has devalued the value of money. Growth of industrialization and population explosion has degraded the social, cultural and moral values of the society. Growing need and conflict in various interests of the society have made the man greedy. Consequently, societies have become more complex in which more and more problems are being generated. In this complex society, the definition of crime and criminal has also taken a considerable change. Today, crime is not a phenomenon to be associated only with the activities of the people who are economically weak or living in slums or who commit crimes because of mental deficiency, but it is highly surprising that even people who are economically sound and enjoy high social status are engaged in various anti-social activities. Through most of their activities are not crime in the real sense because they are not covered under the strict requirement of an offence, even then they are crime because they are injurious and harmful to the society and the social values. These anti-social activities are causing great damage to the established values of the society, which is a dangerous trend that might darken the future of the future generation.

The scope of white-collar crimes is expanding day-by-day and has reached to its peak. Unlike other offenders, white-collar offenders enjoy various social and economic advantages. They are well educated, better equipped and gain favour of the society. White-collar crimes more or less, are not different from traditional crimes so far as the criminality is concerned, but they differ in their modus operandi. Traditional crimes can be expanded on the line of means-rea or the intention behind them, social attitude, poverty oriented or emotional disturbance but white-collar crimes can be expanded, if not fully at least partly, on the line of moral degradation, selfishness and high ambitions of wealth earning, without taking any care of the social values and ethics. They cause injury to the community and to the country as a whole.

This book will help all the law students who are pursuing graduation, post-graduation and research. In presenting the book I acknowledge with gratitude the various works of great jurists, judges, law professionals without whose help it would not have been possible to complete the work.

I am also thankful to the publisher for printing and publishing the book and also those who have helped me in making my dream come true.

DR. SHAILESH K. SINGH
(Assistant Professor)
Shri Ji Institute of Legal and
Vocational Education Research
(MJP Rohilkhand University, Bareilly).

1

White-collar Crimes

Meaning, Concept and Historical Development

"Justice has always evoked ideas of equality, of proportion of compensation. In short justice is another name of liberty, equality and fraternity"

—Bhim Rao Ambedkar

Criminologist and sociologist Edwin Sutherland first popularized the term "white-collar crime" in 1939, defining such a crime as one "committed by a person of respectability and high social status in the course of his occupation." Sutherland also included crimes committed by corporations and other legal entities within his definition.[1]

Sutherland's study of white-collar crime was prompted by the view that criminology had incorrectly focused on social and economic determinants of crime, such as family background and level of wealth. According to Sutherland's view, crime is committed at all levels of society and by persons of widely divergent socio-economic backgrounds. In particular, according to Sutherland, crime is often committed by persons operating through large and powerful organizations. White-collar crime,

1. Edwin H. Sutherland, White-collar Crime: The Uncut Version 7 (1983). Sutherland used the term in a 1939 speech, entitled "The White-Collar Criminal," he gave to a joint meeting of the American Sociological Society and the American Economic Association. For a further discussion of the definition of "white-collar crime," see J. Kelly Strader, *The Judicial Politics of White-collar Crime*, 50 Hastings L. Rev. 1199, 1204-14 (1999).

Sutherland concluded, has a greatly-underestimated impact upon our society.

Sutherland's definition is now somewhat outdated for students of the criminal law. As white-collar crime began to capture the attention of prosecutors and the public in the mid-1970s,[2] the term came to have definitions quite different from the one Sutherland used. Indeed, studies have shown that crimes we generally consider "white-collar," such as securities fraud and tax fraud, are committed not just by persons of "high social status" but by people of divergent backgrounds.[3] Thus, although the term "white-collar crime" is a misnomer, it continues in widespread use.

This is probably so because "white-collar crime" provides a convenient moniker for distinguishing such crime in the public mind from "common" or "street" crime.

The citizens of India are in broad agreement regarding the basic values and fundamental principles of a socialistic society. Since the achievement of independence there has been a tremendous change in the structure of Indian society. This change is visible in social, cultural, political and economic values on one hand and a shift in the values of life on the other. White-collar crimes, which were unknown to the Indian society, have become a regular feature of rich and powerful sections of modern Indian society.

Today's society is more active and mobile than that of the past. In today's world man has become a money-making machine. The basic need theory is now outdated. The acquisitive tendency of man has devalued the value of money. Growth of industrialization and population explosion has degraded the social, cultural and moral values of the society. Growing need and conflict in various interests of the society have made the man greedy. Consequently, societies have become more complex in which more and more problems are being generated. In this complex society, the definition of crime and criminal has also taken a considerable change. Today, crime is not a phenomenon to be associated only with the activities of the people who are economically weak or

---

2. William J. Genego, *The New Adversary*, 54 Brook. L. Rev. 781, 787 (1988) ("In the mid-1970s federal prosecutors became increasingly interested in white-collar offenses . . . ."); Peter J. Henning, *Testing the Limits of Investigating and Prosecuting White-collar Crime: How Far Will The Courts Allow Prosecutors to Go?*, 54 U. Pitt. L. Rev. 405, 408 ("Beginning in the mid-1970s . . . the federal government began targeting white-collar crime as a high-priority prosecutorial area.").
3. John Braithwaite, *Crime and the Average American*, 27 Law & Soc'y Rev. 215, 216–224 (1993) (reviewing David Weisburd, *et al.*, Crimes of the Middle Classes: White-Collar Offenders in the Federal Courts (1991) ("white-collar" defendants are much like non-white-collar defendants).

living in slums or who commit crimes because of mental deficiency, but it is highly surprising that even people who are economically sound and enjoy high social status are engaged in various anti-social activities. Though most of their activities are not crime in the real sense because they are not covered under the strict requirement of an offence, even then they are crime because they are injurious and harmful to the society and the social values. These anti-social activities are causing great damage to the established values of the society, which is a dangerous trend that might darken the future of the future generation.

This type of activities (crime) of the rich and powerful is not new to the society but they have not been brought to the record because of some historical reasons, and even social negligence. Criminals of this category always dominated the will of the society. The concept, since the time immemorial has been that "King can do no wrong" or that *"Samrath ko nahi dos gosai"*, so these criminals have always been side tracked they could not be brought on record because of their social dominance and money and muscle power. So people are of the view that these crimes are not new to the society but have been prevalent in almost all the time.

These anti-social activities (crimes) are done by the persons who are engaged in doing their legitimate business according to the law of land and under the grab of a valid license. These activities are managed in such a planned manner and with such a skill that they remain beyond the reach of common man and social recognition, despite continuous exploitation. These so-called criminals run their activities successfully as most of their acts are in accordance with the existing law. So, they are in fact, the licensed robbers. Besides these licensed robbers, there are unlicensed robbers too in the present time. Those who are engaged in various mal-business activities, manipulation of storks and prices according to the law of land are licensed robbers but there are others also who violate the existing law in robbing the people and public exchequer. In recent years, various scams in India are the examples of such robbers. The people involved in these activities violate the faith of the people, which is a foundation of nation and without which we cannot survive.[4]

It is also a matter of great concerns for us that most of our material resources and wealth is flowing to foreign banks in a planned manner. According to the news published in "*The Times of India*" (Delhi Education: 30 January, 1997); "An unofficial estimate by the International Monetary Fund saying, Indians have stashed away at least $ 100 billion in foreign banks. The findings of a research study by three US

4. Girish Mishra and Braj Kumar Pandey; White-Collar Crimes; Gyan Publishing House, New Delhi (1998), p. 15.

economists are that the capital flight from India to the United States alone in 1994 and 1995 must have ranged from $ 3875 million to $ 11300 million". The people involved in these activities are not ordinary criminals, but they are the pillars of the society. They are well-educated; reputed people who enjoy very high social, political and economic status in society. They are the ideals of the society. They travel by air and in-conditioned coaches. Their views become the headlines of newspapers. They deliver speeches in public meetings like ideal leaders. They live in palatial buildings. Their society is very high. Their interviews are flashed by the media very enthusiastically. So, they are more dangerous to the society than the ordinary criminals.[5]

This really shows, how gave the problem is in India, the stream of scams continues to flow without any check, and corruption has assumed wide-ranging dimension. In recent times various scams like Hawala scam, Tehelka episode, Petrol Pump and gas agencies allotment case, Fodder scam of Bihar, Telgi's stamp scam and many more, are all cases in which powerful and influential people of the society are involved. So, the speedy social changes in today's world have added new dimension to the nature of crime. Crime committed by rich and powerful persons—economic crimes, political crimes, political violence, poll rigging, environmental crimes, cyber crimes, and consumer frauds and many more—are the new outcome of this change. These are traditional criminals on one hand, who are less educated and poor and commit crimes like theft, robbery, etc. and on the other hand, there are criminals of high social and economic status, whose crimes are not easily traceable. Such people commit crimes for enjoying wealthy and luxurious life. These people may be national or state leaders, representatives of some association, capitalists, professionals, industrialists, persons in power or public officers, etc. They commit crimes for their selfish ends and they can even influence a change in the existing law to serve their own purpose. So, the concept of crime has taken a considerable change in recent years. Crimes reported in recent years are qualitatively different from those reported in the past. Traditional crimes are fast getting replaced by new types of crimes in which economic advantage is the prime concern of the people. Such crimes of these rich and high status persons of the society are not visible on the surface but remain underneath and are deep-rooted. They are not only injurious to the individual but to the society as a whole and cause pressure on the national economy and the exchequer. These crimes largely include cheating, counterfeiting, criminal breach of trust, tax evasion, etc.

5. *Ibid.*

Another important phenomenon which has further aggravated the problem of these criminal activities in recent times is the concept of economic globalization. Globalization is the growing reality of the modern time. The concept of globalization has changed the social, economic and political relations among the countries of the world and world have become a global village. The phenomenon of globalization has caused increase in trade, more mobility, opening up of economy, removal of control structure and braining in liberalization. Technology advances and innovation have greatly accelerated in recent times and we have been affected by such changes. Consequently "trafficking in narcotics, trafficking in arms and explosive, fraudulent financial deals, foreign exchange manipulations, etc. are adding new dimensions to the emerging crime scenario. These have led to the recognition of new criminal activities such as 'Money Laundering' and 'Dealing in proceed of crimes' which generate the black money or parallel economics, thus, undermining the financial security of the nation."[6]

It is clear that "the falsity of the traditional theory of crime, which attributes criminal behavior to backward socio-economic conditions, has been exposed beyond doubt in view of the presence of crimes committed in large number by powerful and resourceful forces in the area of business, politics and bureaucracy. The reports of the enforcement agencies of government as well as of Commissions of Enquiries are revealing the perpetration of a great variety of crimes by the people of upper socio-economic group. This type of the criminality is on the increase in view of the current rapid social and economic changes. Modern practices of automation, mechanization and development of new and more complex financial schemes have opened new avenues for criminal exploitation."[7]

The study of analyzing the nature of such crimes of the high status people of the society was taken up first by American sociologists in the beginning of 20th century. However, some indications of such crimes can be traced back in the works of 19th century novelists like Honore de Balzac and Charles Dickens.[8] These crimes are, thus, prevalent in the society since long but they have never been treated as crime. It was only in the 20th century that more attention was given to these crimes committed by people of upper-strata. Sutherland later on called them as 'While-collar Crimes'.

---

6. Crime in India (1994); Published by National Crime record Bureau; (M.H.A.) Economic Offences, p. 327.
7. Gurpal Singh; Problems of Whit-Collar crime in India and its control; published in Punjab University Law Journal (1977), p. 51
8. *Ibid.*

Meaning and Scope of this Offence

As an alternative to the socio-economic definition, many define "white-collar crime" based instead upon the manner in which the crime is committed. In 1981, the United States Department of Justice described white-collar crime as non-violent crime for financial gain committed by means of deception by persons whose occupational status is entrepreneurial, professional or semi-professional and utilizing their special occupational skills and opportunities; also, non-violent crime for financial gain utilizing deception and committed by anyone having special technical and professional knowledge of business and government, irrespective of the person's occupation. This definition focuses on the use of deception as the criminal means. The defendant, however, still must be at least "semi-professional" or have "special technical and professional knowledge." Thus, in some ways, this definition is still too narrow. Not all defendants in white-collar cases have professional or semi-professional status, nor do they necessarily possess special skills. A defendant in a tax fraud or false claims case, for example, might have neither of these characteristics.

Perhaps a better way to look at white-collar crime is to focus on the ways that practitioners and judges distinguish white-collar crime from common or street crime. A "white-collar" prosecutor or defense attorney, for example, would more likely define "white-collar crime" as crime that does *not*:

(a) Necessarily involve force against a person or property;
(b) Directly relate to the possession, sale, or distribution of narcotics;
(c) Directly relate to organized crime activities;
(d) Directly relate to such national policies as immigration, civil rights, and national security; or
(e) Directly involve "vice crimes" or the common theft of property.

Sometimes the criminal statute itself will render almost all crimes charged under that statute "white-collar" by definition. For example, charges brought under the securities fraud and antitrust criminal statutes are generally "white-collar" crimes under the above definition. On the other hand, under some criminal statutes charges can be brought for both white-collar and non-white-collar offenses depending on the nature of the defendant's conduct. For example, conspiracy, extortion, and obstruction of justice are charges often brought in both white-collar and non-white-collar cases. The most common and notable white-collar crimes are covered in the chapters that follow. These include crimes committed both in the corporate and governmental settings, and crimes committed by individuals. It is important to note that not all court cases relating to white-collar crime are criminal cases. As discussed more fully below, some statutes, such White-collar Crimes may be divided into Occupational Crime and Organizational Crime but in common parlance there exist 10 popular types of White-collar Crimes as :—

1. **Bank Fraud.**—To engage in an act or pattern of activity where the purpose is to defraud a bank of funds.
2. **Blackmail.**—A demand for money under threat to do bodily harm, to injure property or to expose secrets.
3. **Bribery.**—When money, goods, services or any information is offered with intent to influence the actions, opinions and decisions of the taker, constitutes bribery.
4. **Cellular Phone Fraud.**—Unauthorized use or tampering or manipulating cellular phone services.
5. **Embezzlement.**—When a person who has been entrusted with the money or property, appropriates it for his or her own purpose.
6. **Counterfeiting.**—Copies or imitates an item without having been authorized to do so.
7. **Forgery.**—When a person passes false or worthless instruments such as cheque or counterfeit security with intent to defraud.
8. **Tax-Evasion.**—Frequently used by the middle-class to have extra-unaccounted money.
9. **Adulteration.**—Adulteration of foods and drugs.
10. **Professional Crime.**—Crimes committed by medical practitioners, lawyers in course of their Occupation.

If there is an industry in which India has surpassed the developed west then it is the field of White-collar crimes. White-collar crimes in India is not in total based on the theory propounded by Prof. Sutherland but partially on the concept by Prof. Hugh Barlow as "Crimes committed by the people of lower strata in their occupational status".

Following are some of the other ***definitions*** of white-collar crime given by different criminologists:

Larry J. Siegel in his book on Criminology said, *"White-collar crimes are illegal acts that capitalize on a person's place in the market place and which can involve theft, embezzlement, fraud, market manipulation, restraint of trade, false advertising, etc."*[9]

---

9. Rohinton Mehta; Crime and Criminology; Snow white Publication Bombay, 1st

Clinard and Quinnery (1973) says, "*Occupational crime consist of an offence committed by individuals for themselves in the course of their occupation and the offences of employees against their employers-corporate crimes are the offences committed by corporate officials for the corporation and the offences of the corporation itself.*"[10]

Edelhertz (1970) has expressed his views about white-collar crimes as "*an illegal act or series of illegal acts committed by non-physical means and by concealment or guile, to obtain money or property, to avoid the payment or loss of money or property, or to obtain business or personal advantage.*"[11]

According to Albert Reiss and Albert Biderman, Data sources on white-collar law breaking (1980), "*white-collar violations are those violations of law to which penalties are attached that involve the use of a violator's position of significant power, influence or trust in the legitimate economic or political institutional order for the purpose of illegal gain or to commit an illegal act for personal or organizational gain.*"[12]

These definitions make it clear that with the advancement of the time, the definition of a white-collar crime was also modified by various criminologists so as to be included in it the changing new dimensions of these crimes. Sutherland originally applied the term in a limited sense because his focus was mainly on corporate criminality but gradually it opened new frontiers with the advancement of science and technology. The central theme of these crimes has been the persons of upper world. So white-collar crimes as sometimes also called 'upper world crimes' committed during their course of business or profession.

The scope of white-collar crimes is expanding day-by-day and has reached to its peak. Unlike other offenders, white-collar offenders enjoy various social and economic advantages. They are well educated, better equipped and gain favour of the society. White-collar crimes more or less, are not different from traditional crimes so far as the criminality is concerned, but they differ in their *modus operandi*. Traditional crimes can be expanded on the line of *mens-rea* or the intention behind them, social attitude, poverty-oriented or emotional disturbance but white-collar crimes can be expanded, if not fully at least partly, on the line of moral degradation, selfishness and high ambitions of wealth earning, without taking any care of the social values and ethics. They cause injury to the community and to the country as a whole.

White-collar crimes, which are the result of social disorganization, competitive tendencies and a lust of money and power, cause greater financial loss to the society than the loss suffered by society from other

10. *Ibid.*
11. *Ibid.*
12. *Ibid*

crimes. These offences cause irreparable damage to the economy of the nation, thereby affecting the growth and development of the country. Some of the major impacts of these offences can be illustrated as "increase in inflationary pressure, distortion of developmental work, uneven distribution of resources and creation of elitism, marginalization of tax-base, generation of black money, creation of paralled economy, country's economic equilibrium is shaken, breeding ground of corruption, illicit business and public office corruption thrive and affect normal business activities, resources of financial and commercial institutions are diverted and distorted, moral and commitment of citizen is weakened, the poor/weakest continue to be poorer and are at risk and so on."[13]

In recent globalization era, these offences have reached to their climax. Almost every alternative day a new scam or racket is reported on the front page of newspapers but nobody bothers; rather they take them for granted. We have become habitual of these activities. People remember them for a short span of time and forget. Who bothers if that a public bridge is constructed and is demolished in two months? Roads on which crores of public money has been invested, does not bear the impact of very first rain of the season. Huge public buildings and offices are constructed and their roofs are not able to withstand even a few drops of rain. The question is how the bills of these substandard public works are passed by senior public officers? How the approval is done and payment made? Who is responsible for this? The vigilant custodian of public safety and security remains in deep sleep. Whether some one has thought of it, or is thinking of it, or will think of it? These social culprits are flourishing under the protective umbrella of political leaders, public officers and investigating agencies and their activities are going on without any check. When will our nation get up from this deep sleep? When will a voice be raised against these activities? When will the awareness come to our society? We are eagerly waiting for that day. Every body seems to be watching the situation helplessly without any flutter even. Need we be merely silent spectator! What a pity?

One of the most burning problems that the world is facing today is to control the epidemic of white-collar crimes and to save the society and the nation from their disastrous effects. White-collar crime is a topic that must draw immediate attention of thinkers, academicians and criminologists of modern time; and they must evolve a workable theory of controlling these crimes. It is a matter of common experience that the business community is perhaps more criminalistic than slum-dwellers. It has also been experienced that white-collar crimes are found in almost

13. Crime in India (1994), *op. cit.*, pp. 327-28.

every occupation. The crimes committed by the people of slums are direct but white-collar crimes are indirect and so they are not easily detected or identified and hence are increasing day-by-day. The society is infected very much by the virus of this epidemic of white-collar crimes.

In the modern capatilist system the white-collar criminality has gained peculiar impotence. The monetary loss caused of the public by these crimes may be so great as the loss caused in other ways. The financial losss, in fact, is one side of the coin, the potential danger is the damage it causes to our social structure and to social relations. These highly placed anti-social elements are responsible for moral degradation of society, corruption in public life, devaluation of ethical and social values and creation of an environment of dishonesty and disintegrity. Common man is loosing faith in existing social set-up and thinks in a different way. Hence, there is an atmosphere of chaos all around in the society. Money and muscle power is the status symbol of today, corruption is deep-rooted, doctrine of trust has lost its importance and legal institutions and laws are frequently disregarded by disobedience. White-collar crimes are, thus, parasite, which are eating up the very foundation of social structure and are causing irreparable loss to moral and social values.

The most unfortunate aspect of white-collar crimes is that despite wide ranging economic and social effects, there is no organized social agitation against them. The possible reason perhaps is that unlike ordinary criminals, white-collar criminals belong to the high society and the community does not easily organize itself in initiating action against them.

Due to the increasing trend of white-collar crimes, it is high time to recognize the importance of the impact of these crimes. These crimes are committed with the connivance of the highly placed people, the authorities and innocent public is being exploited because it is uneducated and unskilled to recognize the gravity and impact of these crimes. In the world of computers, globalization, technological advancement, scientific development and environmental awakening, the competition among business, growth of monopolies, less social awareness and small controlling elite have again aggravated the problem. Corruption and kickbacks are at the peak and they are so complex in nature that no existing law can stop them and no remedy can cure the malady completely. Our existing law and procedure is deficient in many ways to control the epidemic of these crimes. Our investigation and enforcement machinery is not properly equipped, skilled and trained so as to deal with the techniques adopted in these crimes. Our government and judiciary are also not serious in dealing with these crimes.

There is a continuous increasing trend of white-collar crimes and society is still unaware of the dangerous effects of these crimes. Then the question arises as to what these white-collar crimes are in the changing scenario? What is the nature of these crimes? What steps should be taken to bring awareness to the society about these crimes? Have to save the society from their dangerous effects? How to check the degradation in public moral from their adverse effect? How to regenerate confidence in society?

Media and communication agencies are not sharing their responsibilities properly in bringing awareness in the society and exposing the guilty. The reason, perhaps, is that newspapers and media, which might publicise white-collar crimes, are controlled by big business establishments. So white-collar criminals, who hold a very high social status are met with deferential treatment accorded by courts, administrative authorities and media. Then, how to check this differential treatment? What effective measures should be evolved to make responsible courts and commissions? How can our media and communication agencies be made more responsive? It is there any need of making some code of conduct for these agencies?

White-collar crimes being the outcome of clever and skilled technique, our investigating and law enforcement agencies are lacking in trained and skilled staff to do their job effectively. So the problem is as to how to gear up the investing and law enforcement machinery? What our government and law enforcement agencies are doing about it? How to curb the growing trend of these crimes? Is there any need of some training or orientation programmes for these agencies?

In India, corruption has assumed wide-ranging dimensions, while these crimes signify the plundering of the people's resources for the selfish enrichment of powerful persons, the existing law, the judicial system and law enforcement agencies of the country exhibit their helplessness to eradicate these crimes from society. Then the question emanates how corruption is to be dealt with iron hands? Is there any need to make necessary changes in the present legal system for prevention and control of these crimes? Whether there is any need of formulating a new and comprehensive criminal code to deal exclusively with these crimes?

HISTORICAL DEVELOPMENT OF WHITE-COLLAR CRIME IN INDIA

E.H. Sutherland was the first American sociologist who used the term "White Collar Crime" for the anti-social activities of the persons of upper class of society done in their occupation.[14] There are many

14. Sutherland's Research Paper on White-collar Criminality, Published in *American Sociological Review*, Vol. V, No. 1.

occasions in business or profession for immoral behaviour but people generally overlook them. Many professionals and traders engage themselves in various anti-social activities in their day-to-day business but people do not take note of it. Prior to Sutherland, no sociologist or criminologist tried to give any name to this type of criminal behaviour of business community. The reason, perhaps, was lack of social awareness and money and muscle power of these rich and powerful persons of the society. He studied them systematically on scientific basis, because these activities and persons engaged in such crimes are dangerous to the society and mankind.

One of the main reasons for not bringing this type of behaviour in the definition of crime was that "early criminologists viewed crime in terms of deviant behaviour, which was itself considered to be an outgrowth of poverty."[15] According to this view (which prevailed in the eighteenth and nineteenth centuries), the social and physical conditions of the poor gave rise to anti-social behaviour. However, Marxist scholars of the nineteenth and twentieth centuries viewed crime as an outgrowth of the class conflict. These two positions, the traditional and Marxist, still influence many of the studies in criminology.[16]

In the 1930s, the traditional approach came under attack as a result of earlier developments in this area. During the latter part of the nineteenth century, many laws had been enacted to deal with the anti-social behaviour of the rich and powerful. Further, new policing agencies had been established to control abuses in the business world. The scope of illegality was expanded to include offences of the wealthy.[17]

It was in this environment that Edwin H. Sutherland began to attack traditional concepts and theories of crime. He noted that the explanations for crime could not be found in poverty alone; that criminality was much more complex phenomena. For example, he noted that poverty is no explanation for the crimes of the rich and the professional segments of the society such as, manipulation of stocks, price fixing, both commercial and political bribery, and false and misleading advertising. According to him, "crime is, in fact, not closely correlated with poverty, and that an adequate explanation of criminal behaviour must proceed alone quite different lines. The conventional explanations are invalid principally because they are derived from biased samples. The samples are biased in that they have not included vast areas of criminal behaviour of persons not in lower class. One of these

---

15. James Q. Wilson; Thinking about Crime (New York/Basic Books, 1975), p. 38.
16. August Bequai; White-collar Crime: A 20th century crisis by; Lexington Books, Toronto, 1978, p. 1.
17. *Ibid*, pp. 1-2.

neglected areas is the criminal behaviour of business and professional men."[18]

On this background of anti-social activities of rich and powerful persons of society as discussed by Ross "The Criminaloid", that lay foundation of the concept of "White-Collar Crime" given by Sutherland. "The treatment of the crimes of the rich and influential remained for more than three decades where Ross had left it. A major break through could come only in 1939 when the doven of US sociologists, Edwin H. Sutherland, as President of the American Sociological Society brought in the term "While-Collar Crime" to encompass criminal activities in corporate, commercial, professional and political spheres within its purview. He called it as a new class of crime: the crime with the multi-victims and the uncertain victims."[19]

The concept of white-collar crime was employed in relation to the crimes of the "upper world", as distinguished from those conventional crimes committed by the lower classes. In his view, white-collar crimes are not new to the society as they can be found on all occasions. The following illustrations for some of the most common illegal practices within business and the medical profession support this view.

"White-collar criminality in business is expressed most frequently in the form of misrepresentation in financial statements of corporations, manipulation in stock exchange, commercial bribery, bribery of public officials directly or indirectly in order to secure favorable contracts, embezzlement and misappropriation of funds, short weight and measures and misgrading of commodities, tax frauds, misapplication of funds in receiverships and bankruptcy. These are what Capone called "the legitimate rackets". These and many others are found in abundance in the business world.

In the medical profession, which is here used as an example because it is probably less crimanalistic than some other professions, we find illegal sale of alcohol and narcotics, abortion, illegal service to underworld criminals, fraudulent reports in testimony in accident cases, extreme cases of unnecessary treatment, false specialists, restriction of competition and fee splitting."[20]

Sutherland delivered his first written paper titled "White-Collar Criminality" in 1939 and it was his first published statement on white-

---

18 Edwin. H. Sutherland, "White-collar Criminality," Gilbert Gies and Robert F. Meher; White-Collar Crime; (offence in business, politics and professions) ed. (New York; Free Press, 1977), pp. 38-39.

19. Girish Mishra and Braj Pandey; *op. cit.*, pp. 24-25.

20. Sutherland; 1949 as Quoted by Geis, 1968, p. 42.

collar crime, though he reported later that he had been at work on the subject for more than a quarter of a century.[21] Because of his pioneer work in this field, a noted British criminologist has suggested that if there were a Nobel Prize for criminology; Sutherland would surely merit it for his white-collar crime work.[22] Till this time no criminologist or sociologist focused his attention towards white-collar criminals who were of rich, wealthy, cultured and educated background and were engaged in earning lots of money and wealth by illegal and unusual means. So the credit goes to Sutherland for developing and defining the concept of 'white-collar crime' in a systematic way and calling those persons who commit them "White-Collar Criminals". He was successful in attracting the attention of society towards dangerous results of these crimes.

It should not, however, be concluded that there was no awareness of it until Sutherland focused his attention on these types of crimes. As observed by Barnes and Tatters:

> "There has always been crime among businessmen. There have always been instances of violation of trust. Most of us have read of chicanery and plunder in the history books and such acts have often constituted the central theme of the fiction of earlier times. But American people seemed to believe that anyone who betrayed a trust or who mulcted the widow's mite in a shady but legal deal, would eventually suffer, if not here, surely here-after. Existing practices, however, were generally accepted as being within the canons of good business. Business, therefore, was justified in pulling a shrewd deal. The victim either did not report what was done for fear of being ridiculed, or receiving little sympathy because he has been fleeced in a social by approved and even legal deal-caveat-emptor (let the buyer beware) expressed the prevalent attitude."[23]

The object of this study is to study white-collar crimes in Indian perspective. It is, therefore, necessary to search the roots of these crimes in Indian society. White-collar crime is a particular type of behaviour of a particular type of section of society. So, before discussing the historical development of these crimes in India it is necessary to look into the structure or environment of Indian society in which particular type of behaviour is inflicted. For this purpose historical development may be divided into two categories:

---

21. Gilbert Geis and Robert F. Meher; *op. cit.*, p. 25.
22. Hermann Mannheim; Comparative criminology (Boston, Honghton Mifflin, 1965), p. 470.
23. Barnes and Terrers: New Horizons in criminology, 3rd ed., pp. 43-44.

1. Early concept, and
2. Modern concept

Crime in general and white-collar crime in particular, is nothing but a particular type of behaviour of the individuals in the society. So, it is essential to study the behavioural change of the Indian society from time to time.

Early Concept

In India, the source of Hindu Jurisprudence or the legal system is the early concept of Dharma as propounded in the Vedas, Puranas, Smrities and other works on the topic. Dharma was considered as righteous conduct for the welfare of the individual in the society. Originally Dharma was founded as the solution to the eternal problems of the individual, originating from natural human instincts.

The act of the individual in the society is primarily governed by his impulse or desire. Pursuance of some desire is the main source behind every action of the man. In 'Manu Smriti' it is said:

अकामस्य क्रिया केचिद् दृष्यते नेह कर्हिचित्।
यद्यपि कुरूते किंचित तत्कामस्य चेष्टितम्।।[24]

—Manu II:4.

According to Manu there is no act of man which is free from any desire; whatever a man does is the result of an impulse or desire. In this verse, it is stated that the force behind every action of a human being is his desire. Thus, the source of all evil actions of human beings is his desire for material pleasure which causes conflict of interests among individuals.

These desires of human being are influenced by other impulses inherent in human beings such as anger, passion, greed, infatuation and enmity. These impulses have to be controlled by an individual in order to pursue his rightful conduct according to Dharma. But if these impulses are allowed to act uncontrolled, it may cause evil thoughts in the mind which might instigate him to cause injury to others for fulfilling his own selfish desires. This is the basis of all evil action of human beings in the society.[25]

24. Pt. Hargovind Shastri; Manusmriti; (The Kashi Sanskrit Series-114) IIIrd ed., 1982, p. 36.
25. M. Rama Jois; Legal and Constiutional History of India; Volume-I, (Second Printing, 1990), p. 5

The rules of Dharma or righteous conduct were evolved to control these conflicting eternal desires (impulses), arising out of natural instinct of man. People generally deflect from the path of 'Dharma' and commit 'Adharma' when they are overpowered by these desires, passion and greed. Stronger persons then began to harass the weaker ones. The rules of Dharma were laid down as a remedy to deal with this situation for the welfare and happiness of the people and the king was entrusted with the responsibility of enforcing the rules of Dharma.[26]

One thing on which the propounders of Dharma were agreed was that the fulfilment of desires of human beings was an essential aspect of life, for his satisfaction, but that must be regulated according to Dharma (Law) otherwise it would have undesirable results. Therefore, for an orderly society, the desire of individual for material gain (Kama) and pleasure (Artha) must conform to the norms of Dharma. So in ancient times in India Dharma (Law) laid down a code of conduct covering every aspect of human behaviour, observance of which was considered a must for peace and happiness of individuals and the society. Every act or conduct which was in disobedience to rules of Dharma (Law) was called Adharma (Sin) and was declared to be injurious to society and individual.

The necessity to act according to the rules of Dharma, for the peace and happiness of the society has been forcefully expressed by Manu in the following verse:

धर्म एव हन्ति अधर्मो रक्षति रक्षितः।
तस्माद्धर्मो न हन्तव्यो मा नो धर्मो हतोऽवधीत्।।[27]

—Manu VIII:15

Manu states that Dharma protects those who protect it. Those who destroy Dharma get destroyed. Therefore, Dharma should not be destroyed so that we may not be destroyed as a consequence thereof. Thus, Manu stressed that protection of Dharma was essential for the peaceful co-existence of individual and society both.

So in ancient India there was an ideal stateless society run according to Dharma (Law) and both were protecting each other. But when powerful individuals, overpowered by their desires, began to encroach upon the life, liberty and property of other weaker individuals, the concept of state with King as its head came into existence. The King was given power to protect Dharma and run the society by protecting the interests of the individuals and punish the guilty. It was at this stage that

26. Mahabharata Shanti Parva—Ch. 59.
27. Manu Smiriti; *op. cit.*, p, 361.

the system of legal proceedings for enforcement of the right and punishment of the wrong was established and the King was given power to decide suits by enforcing principle of Dharma (Law) and punish the wrong doer. It was also at this stage of the evolution of human society that Civil Law, Criminal Law and establishment of courts started with their powers, functions and procedure, as part of Dharma, was laid down which marks the commencement of legal and constitutional history in ancient India.[28]

The institution of kingship was believed to be the creation of some spiritual power in ancient India because he was the protector of Dharma. This is evident from the following verses of Manu:

दुराजके हि लोकेऽस्मिन्सर्वतो विद्रुते भयात् ।
स्वार्थमस्य सर्वस्य राजनमसृजत्प्रभुः ।।
इन्द्रानिलयमार्काणामग्नेश्च वरूणस्च च ।
चन्द्रवित्तेशयोष्चैव मात्रा निर्हृत्य शाश्वतीः ।।[29]

—Manu VII: 3-4

In this verse Manu states that without the King there was no order in the society. People were running and departing here and there due to fear of powerful persons. So in order to save the society (world) from their fear, God has created the King.

Manu further states that with the extract of Indra, Vayu, Yum, Surya, Agni, Varun, Chandra and Kuber, God has created the King.

Thus, it is clear that institution of King was treated as most pious because it was the creation of God for an orderly society to enforce the rights, duties, power and liabilities (Rajdharma) in the society.

Vedas also have a mention of the view that the King is the creation of some spiritual power and he holds the highest place due to being protector of the society from all evil actions (Adharma) of the wrong-doers.[30]

After the evolution of the concept of enforceability of the law through the institution of kingship, ancient Indian jurists took up the cause of define law, Law was recognized as an instrument to protect the rights and liberties of individual in the society. Whenever the rights and liberties of an individual were encroached by another, the injured could seek the protection of the law with the assistance of the King. The power of the King (State) to punish the wrong-doer was recognized as the sanction behind the law to compel obedience to the law.

---

28. M. Rama Jois; *op. cit.*, p. 9.
29. *Ibid.*, pp.. 306-07.
30. Rigveda: 12:24:1, Yajurveda: 37:8, Atharva Veda: 8:14:10.

Among the various recognised sources of Law in ancient time, Shruties (Vedas) stand as the first source, then comes Smritis and thereafter the concept of good conscience.

श्रुतिः स्मृतिः सदाचारः स्वस्य च प्रियमात्मनः।
संगस्य अल्पजः कामो धर्ममूलमिंदं स्मृतम्।।[31]

—Yajnavalkya: 1-7

The Shrutis (Veda), the Smritis and the good conscience are the recognised sources of law. Veda are not very specific about the concept of law. Smritis, which are actually the collection of legal principles scattered in Vedas, Dharma Sutras and Custom or usage accepted by the society at that time, are the main sources of law. Among the various Smrities, Manu Smriti or the Code of Manu has been recognised as an important and authoritative source of law in the development of legal history of India. All the later law writers based their legal literature on Manu Smriti and so Manu has been regarded as the first law-giver. Manu Smriti is divided in eighteen sub-divisions covering various aspects of Civil as well as Criminal Laws. It is divided in twelve chapters and consists of 2694 verses.[32] Out of eighteen sub-divisions of Law five exclusively belong to the branch of Criminal Law. Next to Manu Smriti, Yajnavalkya Smiriti acquired a high position in the development of Hindu jurisprudence. This Smriti is divided in 3 chapters and consists of 1010 verses. Next comes Narada Smriti which has its important place in the development of Law in ancient India. This Smriti deals with the courts and procedural law. Katyayana Smriti deals with substantive civil and criminal law and also with procedural law. Thus, smritis had their important role in the development of Hindu jurisprudence in India.

The object of the Law of Crimes in ancient India was to impose penalty by the State against offender when it was proved that he had committed an offence punishable in law. The concept of offence under the ancient Indian Criminal Law had its origin in the word Adharma or Pataka (Sin). As to what acts are offences (sin) I depends upon the social values that existed in a particular society. The concept of Pataka had its origin in the Shruti (Vedas) and was developed in Dharmashastras. Any act or omission in violation of the rules laid down in the Vedas was considered as Pataka (Sin).

The meaning of Pataka (sin) can be gathered from Chapter XII of Manu Smriti in which he has classified the qualities of human beings:

31. Hari Narayan Apte; Yajnavalkya Smriti (1904).
32. Manu Smriti, *op. cit.*

यत्कर्म कृत्वा कुर्वंश्च करिष्यति चैवन लज्जति ।
तत्ज्ञेयं विदुषयं सर्व तामसं गुणलक्षणम् ।।[33]

—Manu XII: 35

When a person, while doing an act or while doing it in future or after having done an act in the past, feels ashamed, those acts must be treated as quality of darkness (Tamoguna).

In this verse Manu has explained the dark qualities of man (Tamoguna). These dark qualities of man were treated as Sins since long back. The concept of Pataka (Sin) in the ancient society was used for all wrongful acts (social, cultural, religious or moral) of the individual. Wrongful acts were the acts which were contrary to Dharma. Manu stressed that the King must inflict severe penalty or punishment on those persons who commit great Sins (Mahapatakas)

ब्रह्मश्च सुरापानश्च स्तोर्य च गुरूतल्पगः ।
एते सर्वे पथज्ञया महापातकिनो नराः ।।[34]

—Manu IX: 235

In this verse Manu has referred to four great Sins (Mahapatakas) including murder of Brahmin, drinking intoxicant, theft of ornaments of Brahmins and maintaining sexual relations with Guru's wife.

चतुर्णामपि चेतेषां प्रायश्चित तत् कर्मणाम् ।
शरीरं धनसंयुक्तं दण्डं धर्म्य प्रकल्पयेत् ।।[35]

—Manu IX: 236

These four sinners if they do not ask for a pardon, the King must punish and fine them in accordance with the law. This shows that an act of sin (offence) was condemned. If the sinner (offender) after committing an offence, admits his offence and makes a Prayaschitta (laments) voluntarily, he was to be exempted from the severe penalties. If he did not do so, the King (State) was under a duty to punish the offender.

Thus, the concept of crime and criminal administration emerged from the ancient concept of 'sin' and the power of King (state) to punish. The offences were classified under the three heads: Aparadhas, Padas and Chalas. There were 10 (ten) offences coming under the head

33. *Ibid.*, p. 638.
34. Manu Smriti, *op. cit.*, p. 512.
35. *Ibid.*

of Aparadhas,[36] offences falling under the head of Padas,[37] and 55 offences under the head of Chalas.

The important distinction in civil disputes and criminal offences in ancient times in India was that, the King could act on mere information in case of offences but in case of civil law, an aggrieved party had to initiate the proceedings. The information of the offence committed could be made by any citizen and not necessarily by the injured party; but this was not the position in civil wrongs. So, the King was under no duty to act on his own in case of civil wrongs, but in case of criminal offence he was under a duty to act on mere information.[38] Thus, the King (State) had the special responsibility in matters of controlling crimes and punishing offenders.

This work is undertaken to study white-collar crimes only; so my prime concern is to search and research the roots of white-collar crimes in ancient times. Therefore, the list of all offences falling under the head of Aparadhas, Padas and Chalas is not given. Under the head of Aparadhas, the offence of theft and under the head of Padas, the offence of misappropriation of property are enumerated as some of the important offences.[39] It is actually the ancient concept of theft, which is the root from which concept of white-collar crimes has emerged. White-collar crimes are the outcome of greed of earning more and more wealth by any means; This is not possible with limited means of earning. The fulfilment of all these desires can be met only through some unusual methods adopted by people in their profession. So white-collar crimes are nothing but an extension of the old concept of offence of theft or it can be said that earning wealth through unauthorized or illegal means in the process of pursuing their legitimate business is nothing but a licensed robbery.

In ancient Law, theft was defined in various ways by different writers:

तमब्रवीतथा भाषस्तेय समन्वितः।
स्तेयं त्वया कर्तुम् इदं फलान्याददता स्वम्।।[40]

36. L. Srinivasacharya (ed.); Smriti Chandrika of Devanna Bhatta; Translated by J.R. Gharpure, (1914), p. 63—The list of Aparadhas is given.
37. R. Rama Sastri, Saraswati Vilasa (1927), p. 73, the list of these offences under the head Padas and Chalas is given.
38. Smriti Chandrika: Gharpure., *op. cit.*, pp. 48-49.
39. The list of these offences is also given in Narada Smiriti and Saraswati Vilasa.
40. S.D. Satvalekar (ed.): Mahabharata Shanti Parva, 23-25. (Sanskrit to Hindi translation) (1952).

It means that taking a thing belonging to another without being given anything is called. Steya (theft) you have committed Steya (theft) of fruits, as you have taken them without being given to you:

प्रच्छन्नं वा प्रकाशं वा निशायामथवा दिवा।
यत्परद्रव्यहरणं स्तेयं तत्परिकीर्तितम्।।[41]

In this verse it is said that depriving a man of his wealth either clandestinely or openly, either during night or daytime, is known as theft.

The offence of theft has been referred to in all the works of Dharmasastras right from the Vedic texts. Out of eighteen topics of Law laid down by Manu and Yajnavalka, the five topics deal with the law of crimes and out of these five, one of the category is the category of the offence of theft.

The offence of theft is divided into two categories.

द्विविधास्तस्करान्विद्यात्पर द्रव्यापहारकान्।
प्रकाशांश्चाप्रकाशांश्च चारचक्षुर्महीपतिः।।
प्रकाशवश्चकास्तेशां नानापण्योपजीविनः।
प्रच्छन्नवश्चकास्त्वेते ये स्तेनाटविकादयः।।[42]

—Manu IX: 256 and 257

Manu in these verses has divided thieves in two categories:

1. Aprakasha (Concealed) Thieves

The persons who take away property, money, wealth or any article of another by adopting secret methods are known as Aprakasha thieves.

2. Prakasha (Open) Thieves

Traders who employ false weights and measures while selling gold, cloth, etc. and thereby extort money from the people openly belong to this category.

Similarly, gamblers, fortune-tellers, persons who make imitation articles and prostitutes, who extort wealth from others by deceiving them are also open thieves.[43]

उत्कोचकाश्चौपधिका वृश्चकाः कितवास्तथा।
मग्डलादेशवश्त्ताश्च भद्राश्चेक्षणिकैः सहं।।

41. P.V. Kane; Katyanana Smriti: 810: (Sanskrit to English translation) (1933).
42. Manu Smriti; *op. cit.*, 516-17.
43. Brihaspati Smriti: Published by Sacred Books of the East series, Vol. LXXXV (1965 reprint) p. 360.

असम्यक्कारिणश्चैव महामात्राश्चिचिकित्सकाः ।
शिल्पोपचारयुक्ताश्च निपुणाः पण्यमोशितः ।।[44]

—Manu IX: 256 and 257

Manu further states that the person who extorts money by seeking bribe through coercive methods by making false prediction of profit or birth of a male child, or by hiding his misdeed under the cover of Sadhus or Sanyasis or without having any knowledge predicting any result are open thieves. Similarly, uneducated elephant coach, physician, painter, shilpi and prostitute, who extort money through deceptive methods are all thieves and liable to be punished.

From this classification it becomes clear that the persons who deceive people in several ways listed under Prakasha thieves are also deemed as persons committing the offence of Steya (theft), and they were made punishable in the same manner as for an offence falling under Aprakasha category.[45] So in ancient times no distinction was made between Aprakasha thieves and Prakasha thieves.

The gravity of the offence of Steya (theft) depended upon the value of the article stolen. Regarding amount of penalty, there was a clear distinction that habitual thief will be given heavy punishment but first offender and ordinary thief will be treated leniently. Before giving punishment the King (State) was supposed to take into consideration all the circumstances and the effect of the crime. Another notable point was that it was clearly laid down in Smritis that if a person who is learned and had full knowledge of Dharma (Law) commits the offence of theft, the gravity of the offence is higher than in the case of one without such knowledge. Manu classified the amount of penalty according to caste. He said that if a person after knowing the effect of theft, commits Steya he is liable to be given a heavier punishment. In that case the gravity of offence of theft by a Vaisya is double than that of Sudra, and that by a Kshatriya four times than that of a Sudra, and that of a Brahmin eight times than that of a Sudra, or if he is a Brahmin learned in the Dharmasastras, it was sixty-four times.[46] This rule is similar to the maxim that "Ignorance of law is no excuse".

Thus, it is evident from this discussion that even family background or social status is very important in case of committing a serious offence like theft. White-collar criminals are the criminals who belong to a reputed family and they carry a good reputation in society. So according to ancient version white-collar criminals, since they belong

44. Manu Smriti; *op. cit.*, 516-17.
45. Narada Smriti; SBE Publication Vol. XXXIII (1965 Reprint), p. 223.
46. See Manu Smriti; VIII-337-38, *op. cit.*, p. 437.

to a noble family (as society thinks of them), deserve a serious punishment. They are the serious type of criminals and a threat to the existence of society. The gravity of their offence becomes more serious again, due to the fact that they commit open robbery under a valid license and in such a way, as not to loose their image in the society. In other words, they are the open (Prakasha) thieves.

It is also to be noted that not only those who took away any, article belonging to another by whatever methods were considered as having committed the offence of theft, but every illegal gain made by persons adopting deceptive methods while practising their trade or calling was considered amounting to theft and persons indulging in such acts were called open thieves. So even in ancient times the persons who commit crime by adopting fraudulent and deceptive methods in earning wealth in pursing their legitimate callings (white-collar criminals), were considered a subject for being given serious punishment.

In this context if we judge the criminal liability of white-collar criminals, it is clear that they are the persons who hold upper status in the society. They are well-educated and have full knowledge of Law. They know very well what they are doing. Hence the effect of their crime is more on the society than that of the ordinary crime committed against any individual. They degrade moral and legal values of the society openly, so gravity of their offence is greater than that of the ordinary criminals.

In ancient India, various provisions in ancient literature regarding theft, concealment, misappropriation of property, fake weights and measures, trade and commerce, failure of duty towards society, offences committed by public servants, irregularity in maintaining accounts, cheating and professional or trade misconduct or negligence and fraud are the basis in which the concept of white-collar crime is rooted. Following are some of the specific provisions which clearly indicate that even in ancient times in India, professional or trade misconduct and fraud by persons of upper social status were taken seriously and special provisions for their treatment were made.

By Physicians

In 'Brihaspati Smriti' it is said—

अज्ञातौषधिमन्त्रस्तु यश्च व्याधेरतत्ववित्।
रोगिभ्योऽर्थं समादत्ते स दण्डयत् चोरवत्।।[47]

If a physician, without any knowledge of drugs and their effect

47. Brihaspati Smriti; 360: *op. cit.*, pp. 179-80.

or without knowing the nature of disease, gives treatment and. takes money (fees) from the patient, he shall be punished like a thief.

In 'Manu smriti' also, wrong committed by a physician was treated as a serious offence. In this context it is said—

चिकित्सकानां सर्वेशां मिथ्या प्रचरतां दमः।
अमानुषेषु प्रथमो मानुषेषु तु मध्यमः।।[48]

—Manu IX: 284

A physician who does not treat his patient in a proper way shall be liable to be punished by payment of fine. In the case of wrong treatment of human beings, the fine shall be double than that of treating an animal.

By Goldsmiths

A goldsmith deals with the public, so he has a greater responsibility to perform his duties. If he commits any wrong in his profession, that must be taken seriously. In Kautilya Arthasastra it is said—

स्वर्णकाराणा अशुचिहस्तद्रव्यं स्वर्णमनाख्याय।
सरूपं क्रीणतां द्वादशां पणो दण्डः।।

A dishonest goldsmith who cheats people by misappropriation of gold while weighing or melting or by mixing inferior metal, shall be punished to pay fine of twelve Panas.[49]

By Merchants or Traders

Adulteration of Marketable Commodities

Adulteration of goods has been treated more seriously because it affects our day-to-day dealings, causes health hazards and brings moral degradation in society. The following provisions show that adulteration of food and other articles was considered a social and economic offence and punishment was provided for them.

In 'Yajnavalkya Smriti' it is said —

कूटस्वर्णव्यवहारी विमांसस्य च विक्रयी।
अंगहीनस्तु कर्तव्यो दत्वा भचोत्तमसाहसँम्।।[50]

—Yajnavalkya II: 297

48. Manu Smriti; *op. cit.*, p. 522.
49. R. Shamasastry; Kautilya Arthasastra (Eng. Ed.) (1967), p. 231.
50. Yajnavalkya Smriti, *op. cit.*

A merchant who sells false gold and unclean meat shall be liable to pay the highest fine.

Manu is also of the view that a person shall be punished for adulterating (marketable) commodities by payment of fine.[51]

मेषजस्नेहलवणगन्धधान्यगुडारिशु ।
पण्येशु प्रक्षिपन् ट्टीनं पणान् दाप्यस्तु षोहुष ।।
मृश्चर्य मणिसूत्रायः काष्टवलकलवसनम् ।।
अजातौ जातिकरणे विक्रेयाश्टगुणो दमः ।।[52]

—Yajnavalkya II: 245-246

A person who adulterates medicines, oil, salt, perfumes, grain, sugar, etc. and keeps them for sale shall be fined 16 Panas. When land, hide, gem, yarn, wood, bark or cloth, etc. are misrepresented as, of good quality though they are not of good quality, the person concerned shall be liable to pay fine which shall run eight times the amount for which it was sold.

Using False Weights and Measures, etc.

तुलासनमानानां कूटकान नाणकस्य चं ।
एभिश्च व्यवहर्ता यः स दाप्यो दण्डमुत्तमम् ।।[53]

—Yajnavalkya II: 240

He who tampers his balance (tula), measures (weight), and standard coins, and also the person who uses them shall be liable to the highest punishment of fine.

तुलामानप्रतिमान प्रतिरूपकलक्षितैः ।
चरन्नलक्षितेर्वापि प्रान्पुयात्पूर्वसाहसम् ।।[54]

—Katyanana: 812

If a trader deceives his customers by tampering his balances, measures of weight and measures of capacity, or by any other method, shall be punished to pay fine.

Similar views are also expressed by Kautilya, Manu and Yajnavalkya and they have made these offence punishable.

---

51. Manu Smriti: IX: 286: *op. cit.*, p. 523.
52. Yajnavalkya Smriti; *op. cit.*
53. Yajnavalkya Smriti; *op. cit.*
54. Katyanana Smriti (1993), *op. cit.*

Cheating in Price, etc.

A trader who dishonestly cheats his customers who pay the same amount of money by giving good quality things or more in quality to one and bad quality or less in quantity to another or cheats by discrimination in regard to price shall be punished with a heavy penalty of fine.

It is evident from the above analysis that in ancient India we can search roots of white-collar crime. It is seen that if the educated and upper class persons of society by their crooked behaviour do some evil in the course of their profession or take money under a false pretence or extort money by threat or receives some advantage by deceiving others, they are subject to a heavy penalty. Similarly, various provisions regarding offence against administration of justice in which liability of judges and witnesses is imposed, offence by public servants and so on are all examples that in ancient times people of high social and economic status were treated at a different footing and if they committed an offence in pursuing their legitimate business they were subjected to a heavier penalty, because they had full knowledge of the existing law and so they were treated as great danger to the society.

From the foregoing discussion it can be concluded safely that in the "development process of Criminal Law in India many criminal codes had come into existence and were replaced due to need of the time. Veda was the ancient authoritative text which first of all recognised immoral conduct of people as 'sin' (crime) and prescribed 'Prayaschita' as form of punishment to eradicate the same. Later on, Hammurabi framed the Criminal Code in 2100 B.C. in which crime was recognised as a punishable factor and people were threatened by fear of punishment by God or God-Kings to conform to the approved pattern of conduct. In 200 B.C. another Code was prepared by Manu to deal with criminal offences. According to him the source of law was long lasting custom. During the reign of Chandra Gupta at about 300 A.D., the famous Code 'Arthashastra' of Kautilya came into existence. This Code carried principles of Manu and other great Rishis and provided a complete criminal administration system in India."[55]

Modern Concept

With the advancement of time, India came under Muslim rule. Mohammad Ghori defeated Prathviraj in 1192 A.D., which marked the commencement of the Muslim rule in India. On April 21, 1526 Babur defeated Ibrahim Lodhi in the famous battle of Panipat and became the first Emperor or founder of the famous Moghul Empire in India. Except

---

55. Prabhat Chandra Tripathi; The Menance of White-Collar Crimes and Need for a New Code; published in *Criminal Law Journal*/3-III of 1997, p. 33.

from 1538 to 1556 Moghuls ruled the vast territory of India for more than 300 years until 1858 when Bahadur Shah II was the last ruler.

Muslim rulers ruled the country according to the tenets of Quaran. Muslim Law of Crimes was introduced in India during Moghul rule. Aurangzeb, prepared a comprehensive digest of Muslim Criminal Law entitled 'Fatawa-i-Alamgiri'.[56] Their criminal law was based on the principle of deterrent punishment to maintain strict discipline in the society.

Britishers came to India for the purpose of trading but gradually their commercial interest got transformed into political interest. Under the Charter of 1600, power to make law or to issue orders for regulating the management of the Company and the affairs of its servants was given to the general court of the Company. The legal system which they applied in India consisted of both English law and personal laws of Hindus and Muslims and it continued till India got freedom. Thus, after 1600 Britishers introduced their legal system in the country and even after independence we are still guided by the laws enacted by the English in many respects.

During British rule in India, codification was started in England. Bentham was the Chief architect of codification, to whom the word codification owes its origin.[57] Under the idea of codification, the laws on several topics regulating rights and liabilities of the individual were collected together in a compact manner. During the nineteenth century, pursuant to the idea or codification, important legislative reforms were undertaken in India.[58]

Consequently by the Charter of 1833, a central legislature for India was established in 1833 for the codification of laws in India. The first Law Commission was appointed in 1835 and McCauley, the then member of House of Commons and barrister was appointed as the Chairman of the first Law Commission. This Commission first of all took up the cause of codification of criminal law in India. Under the able guidance of McCauley, a draft of Indian Penal Code was prepared. Subsequently, Indian Legislative Council enacted Indian Penal Code, 1860 which was the first authentic code on criminal law in modern India based on English criminal law. Subsequently in 1872, the Indian Evidence Act and in 1898 the Criminal Procedure Code came into existence and it provided a uniform legal system in India. By this time the concept of 'crime' and 'criminal' had gone a radical change.

56. History and Culture, Vol. VII, p. 544, quoted by M. Rama Jois; Legal and Constitutional History of India; (Second printing, 1990) Volume II, p. 10.
57. Ilbert; Legislative Methods and Forms (1901), p. 122.
58. *Ibid.*, p. 129.

After the second World War, fast social and economic changes occurred in the world. Population explosion, industrial revolution, development in science and technology, development in means of transport and communication, electronic media and computer systems, etc. are the outcome of this change. This made the world smaller and day-by-day new type of crimes came into existence. Among these new crimes white-collar crime is one of the most serious crime affecting the society in the modern time. The rise of white-collar criminality in most of the countries is due to economic and industrial progress and is connected directly or indirectly with the production and distribution system of wealth.

Commenting upon the various factors responsible for rapid growth of white-collar crimes, Friedman has observed:

> "The industrial revolution had initiated great social changes having far-reaching consequences. The changes in the economic and social structure of property, comprising the transformation of an increasing proportion of wealth from property intangible, visible and mainly immovable goods into ownership in intangible and invisible powers and rights such as shares, trade marks, patents and copyrights, coincided with the growth of large-sized corporations replacing individual entrepreneurs. This development, *inter alia*, led to concentration of economic and consequent political power in a few hands, absentee ownership and impersonal monopoly, emphasis on money and credit and decline in the sense of social responsibility on the part of large property."[59]

The Law Commission of India has also taken a note of the various contributing factors for the growth of white-collar crimes and has made the following observations:

> "The advancement of technology and scientific development is contributing to the emergence of "mass society", with a large rank and file and a small controlling elite, encouraging the growth of monopolies, the rise of a managerial class and intricate institutional mechanisms. Strict adherence to a high standard of ethical behaviour is necessary for the even and honest functioning of the new social, political and economic process. The inability of all sections of society to appreciate in full this need results in the emergence and growth of white-collar and economic crimes...."

59. Friedman; Law in a Changing Society (1951), p. 186.

> The two World Wars also had made a great contribution in the growth of white-collar criminality. "The traditional values of the society were vitally affected due to the scarcity of things and mounting demands. The end of the Second World War almost coincided with the independence of India and the emergence of the concept of a welfare state in the country. In a welfare state, the government tends to control a vast number of means of production and distribution of goods and material services. Assuming that such controls are in the interest of the community, the fact remains that the governmental controls provide a fertile source of white-collar criminality in a society infested with chronic shortages, corruption and endemic inefficiency in the administration of State activities."[60]

This was a transitional period for India in which great social and ethical changes occurred. India was facing the challenge of organising the society of post independence era at the one hand and providing necessities of day-to-day life on the other hand. Another important task before India was the distribution of economic resources to keep the movement of the wheel of growth of nation on a smooth footing. Consequently, the provisions were made under Article 39(b) and (c) of the Constitution for imposing obligation on the state regarding the ownership and distribution of national wealth and resources. It states that "the State shall in particular direct its policy towards securing that the ownership and control of the material resources of the community are so distributed as best to sub-serve the common good; that the operation of the economic system does not result in the concentration of wealth and means of production to the common detriment."

In order to bring this policy into effect and control the virus of white-collar criminality, various steps have been taken by our legislature in the form of enacting various Acts such as: Essential Commodities Act, 1955; Industrial (Development and Regulation) Act, 1951; Imports and Exports (Control) Act, 1947; Companies Act, 1956; Foreign Exchange (Regulation) Act, 1973; Central Excise and Salt Act, 1944; Income Tax Act, 1961; Customs Act, 1962, etc. In spite of these controlling measures, the white-collar crimes have shown their increasing trend which has proved the inefficiency of the existing Law in India to prevent and control these crimes. Unfortunately, no serious study of white-collar crimes has yet been undertaken in India. It is, thus, a great challenge for the present government to stand up to its constitutional promises.

Globally, in the development of the concept of white-collar criminality, three readings are found most useful. The first one is an

60. Girish Mishra and Braj Kumar Pandey; "White-Collar Crimes".

article written by Edward A. Ross (1866-1951) which stands as the earliest major statement by a sociologist regarding the kind of behaviour which was later on classified as "white-collar crime". The second one is the initial public use of the term itself by Edwin H. Sutherland (1883-1950) in his Presidential address to the American Sociological Society in 1939.[61] The final is the article by Donald J. Newman which reviews some of the major contributions on the topics regarding a satisfactory and meaningful definition and limits of the "White-Collar Crimes".[62]

Ross's early writing on this newly emergent concept opened new horizons in the field of sociology. Until the time of Ross, there was an era of dark sayings in the field of white-collar crimes. His contribution as a sociologist was unmatched and his book 'social control'; not only brought great respect for him but was appreciated by President Theodore Roosevelt. Ross always adopted an attitude in exposing to public view, the illegal acts of respectable business and political persons.[63]

Edward Alsworth Ross through his paper titled 'The Criminaloid', published in the Atlantic monthly, 99 (January 1907) pp. 44-50, focused for the first time on these new type of crimes of the respectable persons of the society, affecting the American Society. Ross was afraid with the society's attitude which was very lenient towards white-collar crimes in comparison to the traditional crimes and criminals. He described this type of the attitude of society as "the quasi-criminal", which was not correct. The society regards them as most successful persons. Their image and status remains very high in the eyes of the people. They project themselves as if they are the ideals of the society. Though, in the real sense, they are worse than the ordinary thieves and robbers because they commit great loss to the society. Despite all this, they remain respectable and even praised by the society. Ross, through his masterly work in this field, tried hard to brought them on record and expose them in the public. He, for the first time called them as criminal and tried to convince the society to think in the same direction.[64]

Ross used the term criminaloid for those persons, who earn their prosperity through underhand dealings and illegal ways and means, which public generally do not take notice in first instance. They may be guilty in the eyes of law but general public opinion remain in their favour. Consequently, society does not treat them as criminal. So, they escape punishment easily and keep their image intact in the society. It has rightly

61. Edwin H. Sutherland, "White-collar Criminality", *American Sociological Review* (February, 1940), pp. 1-12.
62. Gilbert Geis and Robert F. Meher, *op. cit.*, p. 23.
63. *Ibid.*, p. 24.
64. Edward Alsorth Ross; The Criminaloid; Gilbert Geis and Robert F. Meher, *Ibid.*, pp. 29-37.

said that, "unlike their low brow cousins, they occupy the cabin rather than the steerage of society. Relentless pursuit hems in the criminals, narrow the range of success and denies them influence. The criminaloids, on the other hand, encounter but feeble opposition and since their practices are often more lucrative than the authentic crimes, they distance their more scrupulous rivals in business and politics and reap an uncommon world of property."[65]

There are many white-collar criminals around us who are reputed persons of the society and flourishing due to their connections with political persons, bureaucracy and , many more. They are running many legitimate business, institutions, both charitable and, commercial. They are earning lots of money and wealth, through illegal means, under the garb of these legitimate business. They donate lots of money to charitable institutions. They distribute clothes and food to poor and orphans. They publish many religious books at a low price just to attract the attention of religious minded people. They donate lots of money for the welfare and development works of society. By these works, they earn sympathy of the society. Society think them as their well wisher, though they are more dangerous and harmful to the society. By the power of their financial resources and influence, they enjoy and political respect, which no common criminal can dream of it. Thus, these criminals are more dangerous than ordinary criminals because they causes irreparable damage to the nation and adversely affect the ideals of the society. This can be illustrated by some of the common activities that are frequently done in our day-to-day life—distribution of party tickets for contesting election for monetary considerations, exempting tax liability of a person for monetary considerations, selling sub-standard goods under a blended title, bribing public authorities to seek their favour, seeking order for supply of goods in different government departments by money power, bribing the authorities for passing tender in their favour, making adulterated drugs and food items, these and many more can be cited as an example of such persons. These persons are in hurry to acquire more and more wealth within a short span of time. They want to become rich by any means and without any hard labour and waste of time. They apply every trick to reach to the height but still wants to remain innocent and reputed persons of the society. So, these persons are morally insensible, as they are degrading the standard of morality in the society and making society more and more corrupt.

Despite wide ranging effects of their activities, the interesting thing is that, they escape their identity very easily. The reason is that, they generally work through middlemen. The act of smuggling, supply of

65. *Ibid.*

intoxicated drugs, booth capturing, instigating strikes, hoarding, black marketing, selling of duplicate drugs and articles, are such crimes which are done through others and not personally. In these acts, main culprit remains behind the door. He buys the people to commit these crimes on his behalf. He is, thus, a mafia-don or God-father. It is rightly commented, "Look at their faces, they are perfectly normal, nothing of the wolf or vulture. Nature has not foredoomed them to evil by a double dose of lust, cruelty, malice, greed or jealousy. They are not degenerates, tormented by monstrous cravings. They want nothing more than we all want, money, power, consideration in a word 'success', but they are in a hurry and they are not particular as to the means."[66]

Earlier Prof Albert Morris in his paper entitled 'Criminal Capitalists' read by Edwin C. Hill before the international congress on the prevention and repression of crime at London in 1872 noted the "growing significance of crime as an organised business required the cooperation of real estate owners, investors and manufacturers and other honest people."[67] In 1934, Professor Morris called sharp attention to the necessity of a change in emphasis regarding crime.[68]

It is, thus, clear that the earlier works of Prof. Morris and Ross's concept of criminaloid provided a strong base on which future study of white-collar crimes and white-collar criminals could become easier. Sutherland, later on, studied them on more scientific basis. His contribution is remarkable in the sense, that, he extended the frontier of criminology by including in it, the study of the white-collar crimes. "But his definition of white-collar crime is too restrictive, because it fails to recognise that many such crimes bear no relation to the offender's occupation. These crimes include, making fraudulent claims for unemployment insurance, filing false personal and non-business income tax returns, making numerous credit purchases with neither the intention nor the capability of ever paying for them and so on. This definition also fails to include those businesses in which crime is the central activity of the operation; e.g. Pyramid clubs, fraudulent land sale, corporations, bogus home improvement companies and phony accident rings."[69]

It is thus, clear that Sutherland did not sufficiently thought of difficulties arising in developing the concept of white-collar crime. "The definition of white-collar crime, for instance, has always represented something of an intellectual nightmare. This is probably because Sutherland desired to employ the concept of buttress his theory of

66. Girish Mishra and Braj Kumar Pandey; White-collar crimes, *op. cit.*, p.22.
67. Ahmad Siddqui, *op. cit.*, p. 372.
68. Barners and Tetters; New Horizons in Criminology, 3rd Ed., p. 41.
69. Vetter and Silverman. *op. cit.*. p. 234.

"differential association", an aggregation of theorem (of highly unequal power) about human learning attempting to explain not only white-collar crime, but all criminal behayiour. In fact, the definitional water was so muddied that today it sometimes appear wiser to move upstream than to attempt a purification project. The difficulty of such a move lies in the fact that the term 'White-collar crime' and the spirit it represents were magnetic enough to draw the concept deeply into criminological and popular thought."[70]

Sutherland's concept of white-collar crime was influenced by his earlier research regarding the concept of professional theft.[71] According to him white-collar criminals were the upper world counterparts of the professional thieves. He maintained that illegal activities of both the groups were the integral part of their occupational efforts. Both required a particular training and specialised skill in order to pursue their activities successfully. Both are regarded as prestigious by their colleagues. The only difference lies in self-conception of the violators. "Professional thieves when they speak honestly, admit that they are thieves, white-collar criminals think of themselves as honest men."[72]

Donald J. Newman further advanced the concept by providing a sense of research which was followed after the formulation of the concept of white-collar crime. He discussed the matter that sparked a controversy regarding the concept and tried to explain the theoretical implications of these works. Through his masterly researches he also made certain observations regarding the quality of thinking and difficulties felt by the scholars in the area of white-collar crimes. He observed that, "White-collar crime rather than white-collar criminals been the basic orientation in research."[73] He also observed that, "Corporations, like nations, often act in response to others and within intricate framework of interaction. To view corporate and business white-collar crimes as simply the behaviour of greedy people in a greedy world is to stereotype much too simply a highly complex social process."[74]

---

70. Gilbert Geis and Robert F. Meher *op. cit.*, pp. 25-26.
71. Edwin H. Surherland, The Professional Thief (Chicago, University of Chicago, Press, 1937).
72. Edwin H. Sutherland, Crime of Corporation, Gilbert Geis, *op. cit.*, p. 25.
73. Gilbert Geis; *op. cit.*, p. 26.
74. Donald J. Newman; Corporate and Business White-collar crime, Published in Gilbert Geis; *op. cit.*, p. 69.

2

Causes of White-collar Criminality

If you once forfeit the confidence of your fellow citizens you can never regain their respect and esteem. It is true that you can fool all the people some of the times, and some of the people all the time, but you cannot fool all the people all the time.

—Abraham Lincon

Crime is a deviant behaviour of an individual, which is prohibited by society. Criminology is therefore a societal study, which seeks to discover the causes of criminality and suggests measures to be adopted to curb the incidences of crime. The concept of crime and social structure are inter-dependent. There is no society without the problem of criminality. The concept of crime is essentially concerned with the conduct of an individual in society. It is well-known fact that man by nature is social and his interests are best protected as a member of the society. The activities of an individual, which are not approved by the society, are known as activities and they are generally associated with the concept of crime. Besides the traditional crimes such as assault, robbery, dacoity, murder, rape, kidnapping and other acts involving violence, there are certain anti-social activities, which the persons of upper social status carryon in course of their occupation or business. These activities for a long time were accepted as a part of usual business tactics necessary for a shrewd businessman, and any complaint against them often went unheeded. The result is obvious that the study of the white-collar crimes could not be carried on scientific basis for a long time.

The research in the field of white-collar crimes has been a long-neglected relationship between criminal behaviour, criminal law, penal sanctions, and social norms. This neglected attitude of the society caused great increase in the magnitude of the white-collar crimes. It is, therefore, our primary duty to look into the various causes of white-collar criminality. These causes are divided in the following four categories:

WHY ARE THEY NEGLECTED?—THE HISTORICAL REASONS

There are various reasons as to why so little research has been undertaken in the field of white-collar crimes that these crimes continue to rob the society at present as well as in the past. In all societies, crime was regarded as a personal matter between an offender and the offended and State had nothing to do with it. But with the advancement of time, the concept of the welfare state emerged and it became a duty of the State to protect the society from crimes. In modern societies criminals are now prosecuted and punished in the name of the state.

Like other European Countries, India also has been ruled by various dynasties at various times including British, in the past. So our legal development is an outgrowth of British system of laws. These dynasties had their own views and ideologies in. ruling the country. But one thing on which they had common views was that the State was their domain. They thought that they were the State and State was theirs. The King (monarch) and Royal families saw themselves as being above the law. They used the State according to their own wishes and found nothing wrong with their actions.[1]

Similar things have been experienced in the European Societies where the concept of deviant behaviour came in the criminological approach and spread all over the world. "Thus, after the World War-I, the upper classes in many countries of the world viewed themselves as being above the law. So, the modern law enforcement apparatus that began to take shape in the 19th century addressed itself to the poorer, more visible criminal element. The upper class being above the law, got *de facto* immunity from prosecution for their criminal acts. The law enforcement machinery concentrated only on the traditional offences committed by the lower classes."[2]

The mid-nineteenth century witnessed the rise of Marxism and its impact on the world fora. During this period a new thought emerged in

1. August Bequai; White-Collar Crimes, *op. cit.*, p. 6.
2. *Ibid.*, p. 6.

the European Societies that the law is a tool in the hands of ruling party to suppress the lower classes. This new thought fused the study of criminology with political ideology and consequently slowed down its progress. Since the ruling class used the laws to suppress the lower classes by force, it resulted in the breaking of revolution by the lower classes which ultimately, established communism in the form of dictatorship of proletariat. This new ideology again politicized the study of criminology because they thought that criminals were prosecuted for their political opposition to the State. They also used the law as a tool of the ruling class to oppress the lower classes of the society. "According to this view, white-collar felon is acting out the frauds of his class; the answer is not to imprison or study him, but rather to destroy both him and his social group. It appears that those who attempted a serious study of white-collar crimes were hampered by their counterpart and also by conservative elements of the society. This impeded the study of white-collar crime in the 20th century."[3]

In this background of social structure and *de facto* immunity of upper class from prosecution, the legal scholars of the 18th century onward concentrated their studies on lower classes. Another reason for this was that development in the field of industry, commerce, finance and banking was unknown to the people of that time. The politics and ideologies of the time overpowered the thoughts of many writers to think in that direction. They saw crimes of upper classes in the mirror of politics rather than in terms of law. They were justified to the extent that the upper classes thought themselves as being above the law. This ideology influenced the thought of criminologists of the 20th century and they also viewed the crimes of professionals and upper sections of the society through a political prism. So it is rightly said that "the rising ideologies of the 18th and 19th centuries muddled the waters of criminology".[4]

Due to this unfortunate situation, the anti-social behaviour of persons of upper social status could neither be taken seriously by the society nor by the academicians of that time. So, among various studies in the etiology of criminal and delinquent behaviours, the study of white-collar crime remained an example of missed opportunities. It was only the result of the research done by Sutherland in the middle of the 20th century that modem concept of white-collar crime was developed on the scientific basis. Although the selection of white-collar crime as a field of research is a real achievement of the time, it again had an unfortunate slant in the study of these crimes when a controversy was raised whether

3. *Ibid.,* p. 8.
4. *Ibid.,* pp. 7-8.

white-collar crimes are really crimes.[5] This has given rise to a futile terminological dispute, which was clouded by class identifications and ideological convictions that unnecessarily delayed the research in the file of white-collar crimes.[6]

So, the fundamental reason in the increase of white-collar criminality has been the long sustained confusion regarding the concept of white-collar crimes. This confusion was built from the very beginning when the term 'white-collar crime' was introduced in the criminological research. Thus, the problem lies in the continuing absence of conceptual clarity and consensus with regard to white-collar crimes. This confusion left the door wide open for a speculative attempt to define and redefine white-collar crime. Because of this confusion and misconception neither white-collar crimes could be treated as crime in the real sense nor did a creative research start for a long time, which resulted the increase in frequency of these crimes going ahead unabated.[7]

The definition of white-collar crimes again caused great confusion and disagreement among academicians and they contended that the definition was not exact but approximate. The first element in the definition of white-collar crime is that the conduct in issue must be a crime. The nature or seriousness of the conduct is irrelevant so long as it is a crime. So, non-criminal activities, however unacceptable or anti-social, should not be treated as a crime but in fact, they often are treated as crime. This definitional drawback has been criticised by many criminologists. Tappan (1947) has criticized this concept on the ground that there were no definite criteria for determining white-collar criminality.[8]

It is contended that business and professional persons commit crimes, and so their wrongful behavior must be brought within the theories of criminal behavior. In order to support his views, Sutherland studied various decisions of courts and commissions against the 70 largest industrial and mercantile corporations of the United States under four types of laws; namely, anti-trust, false advertising, national labour relations and infringement of patents, copyrights and trademarks. 547 adverse decisions were found against the corporations out of which 49 were handled by the criminal courts. Though the courts found that in all cases behavior was unlawful, but since all unlawful behaviours are not criminal behaviour, in strict of criminal law so confusion prevailed

5. E.H. Sutherland; "Is 'white-collar crime?", *American Sociological Review*, 10 (April, 1945), pp. 132-39.
6. Gilbert Geis and Robert F. Meher; *op. cit.*, p. 170.
7. *Ibid.* pp. 253-54.
8. Katherine S. Williams, Criminology, 3rd edition, First Indian Reprint 2001, p. 61.

whether such a behaviour can be treated as a crime regarding which these decisions were made.[9] An act is crime if it is socially injurious and there is a provision of penalty for the act. Since both the requirements are met in these decisions, so it was concluded that a crime was committed. But this conclusion was questioned mainly on two grounds. First, that the rules of proof and evidence in these decisions were not used with the same frequency as in case of other crimes. For example, requirement of proof of criminal intention and presumption of innocence in favour of the accused were not taken care of, and secondly, in all these decisions, the penalties for the crime have been limited to fine, imprisonment and punitive damages as provided in the laws on which these decisions were based. This differential implementation of the law as applied to the crimes of corporations eliminates, or at least minimizes, the stigma of crime. It has rightly been commented by Wendell Berge, "While civil penalties may be as severe in their financial effects as criminal penalties are, yet they do not involve the stigma that attends indictment and conviction."[10]

So, civil penalty is different from criminal penalty because the former is lacking in additional penalty of stigma of crime. In fact, stigma of crime itself is a penalty which is associated with the crime. "A civil fine is a financial penalty without the additional penalty of stigma while a criminal fine is a financial with the additional penalty of stigma. When the stigma of crime is imposed as a penalty, it places the defendant in the category of a criminal." There are three main reasons for this differential implementation of laws: (1) the status of the white-collar criminals, (2) the trend away from punishment, and (3) unorganised resentment of the society against these criminals.[11]

As to the first factor, the white-collar criminals are persons of high social status, so they have social and cultural homogeneity with legislators, judges and administrators. Thus, the persons who are responsible for the administration of criminal justice belong to the same category. Legislators are political persons and are dependent on the funding of businessmen for their election campaign, so their attitude is always in favour of businessmen and they don't conceive them as criminals, despite the fact that in a society based on the principle of socialism, all are equal in the eyes of law.

As regard to the second factor for the differential implementation of the laws there has been a trend away from punishment in case of

9. E.H. Sutherland; "Is 'white-collar crime?" Published in Gilbert Geis and Robert F. Meher; *op. cit.*,, p. 260.
10. *Ibid.*, p. 266.
11. *Ibid.*,, pp. 267-70.

white-collar criminals. This trend can be seen in the attitude of the courts and various enactments in which conventional penal methods have been supplemented by non-penal methods. The law of probation can be cited in support of this view. It is also to be noted that procedure of criminal law is also modified, so that stigma of crime will not be attached to the white-collar criminals. It is because of this departure of criminal procedure in case of white-collar criminals from conventional criminal procedure that white-collar crimes have generally not been included within the theories of criminology.

The third factor in the differential implementation of the law is the difference in attitude of society in showing resentment, which remains unorganised in case of white-collar criminals. Business community violates its ethics in such a way that their effect is not direct, as in case of ordinary crimes. They can be appreciated only by persons who are expert in the occupations in which they occur. A corporation violates a law for a longer period before it comes to knowledge of the administrative agencies, in the mean time the violation becomes an accepted norm of the business world. The effect of a white-collar crime upon the public is diffused over a long period of time and over a large number of people in such a way that no individual person suffers much at a particular time. The communicating media or agencies also do not perform their duty in organising public sentiments as to white-collar crimes, not because the nature of crime is complicated and it cannot be easily presented as news, but probably because these agencies are owned or controlled the businessmen and in many cases these agencies themselves are engaged in violations of the same laws.

From this discussion it is clear that the concept of white-collar crime has evoked sharp criticism on many fronts. Another important criticism was raised on the ground that most of the white-collar crimes are handled by commissions and tribunals and not by ordinary criminal courts so their decisions cannot be held convictions in the legal sense and a white-collar offender does not acquire the status of a criminal in the real sense. In this regard Tappan has raised a doubt that the inclusion of administrative decisions as the basis for defining non-conformists as criminals will open the door for the extension of the concept of crime to cover behaviour as crime and the moral values of the administrator would be substituted to the legal definition of crime.[12]

Further, the inclusion of white-collar offences has also been criticised on the ground that according to social view, a person is criminal only when he regards himself as a criminal and is so regarded by the society. Since in most of the cases of white-collar crimes, the offenders

12. Paul W. Tappan; Who is the criminal? *American Sociological Review*, 12, pp. 96-102.

do not regard themselves as criminals and neither society treats them as criminals, they should not be included in the category of criminals.[13]

It is, however, not safe to conclude from the above discussion that white-collar crimes are not crimes merely because of the civil penalty or handling of them by tribunals or commissions. In fact, civil fines are the same as criminal fines except that the stigma of crime has been removed from them. It is also not fair to make an inference that because of some technical flaw in the definition, white-collar crimes cease to be a crime. "It must be understood that definitions are only ways of organizing phenomena; they are neither "correct" nor "wrong". Their adequacy can be judged only in terms of how satisfactorily they serve to advance the specified ends, ends which themselves may change with changing social or personal values. Definitions may also be judged in terms of their ability to stimulate research; to fit coherently into larger framework of knowledge; to serve as vehicles for change; to carve out comfortable realms of inquiry, or in terms of a variety of other purposes. The non-scientific implications of definitions should never be underestimated."[14]

So, it is clear that the definitional controversy and absence of conceptual clarity initially obstructed the research in the field of white-collar crimes and even today this confusion persists in many societies. This was a serious setback for the growth of the concept of crime and criminology which ultimately resulted in enormous increase in the incidences of white-collar crimes.

CRIMINOLOGICAL ASPECT

The earlier concept that a crime is committed by a person out of the influence of some external forces like demon and devil and a criminal is treated for sin by torture and Prayaschitta, was slowly modified by criminologists and sociologists.

While psychiatrists developed their theory that crime is rooted in emotional frustration, Roscoe Pound and Jerome Hall have traced the social origins of the concept of crime and Sutherland opined criminology as a body of knowledge and crime as a social phenomenon.[15]

The theories of classical school and neo-classical school propounded by Beccaria, the father of modem criminology, was based

13. Parank E. Hartung; White-Collar offences in the wholesale meat industry in Detroit, *American Journal of Sociology,* 56 (1950-51), pp. 29-30.

14. Gilbert Geis and Robet F. Meher; *op. cit.*, pp. 254-55.

15. Prabhat Chandra Tripathi; "The Menance of white-collar crimes and need for a new code", An Article Published in *Criminal Law Journal,* 3-III of 1997, p. 34.

on the principle of 'Free-Will'. He advanced his theory by placing reliance on "pain and pleasure theory" and pointed out that punishment must be awarded to the individual keeping in view the pleasure derived by the criminal from the crime and the pain caused to the victim therefrom. So credit goes to Beccaria who exploded the earlier myth in the field of crime and criminals that it is the result of influence of some external forces. The "free will theory" was famous till the eighteenth century.

Thus, thrust of Beccaria (1738-93), was reform oriented. He was of the view that the law should be applied equally to all classes of society whether poor or upper classes; however, he had no specific views as to how the upper classes; should be brought within the purview of the law. Edward Livington (1734-1836), a disciple of Beccaria, spoke that crime is an outgrowth of idleness, unemployment and poverty, and criminal behaviour, is learnt by a defect in family background. According to him, environment and subsequent associations of the individual are responsible for criminal behaviour. He observed that laws had been made oppressive and unjust by the upper classes.[16]

John Haviland (1792-1852), had also played an important role in the development of modern criminology. He worked for the reformation of criminals. Once again his study was aimed at the lower classes of the society. Other scholars also had shown their concern for the problem of crime. Karl Roeder (1806-1879) suggested that a criminal is like a child and must be put on the moral path once again. According to Issac Ray (1807-1881) there was a close relationship between crime and mental element. He formulated that crime was the outgrowth of some mental defect. Henry Mandsley (1835-1918) saw criminality in the degradation of individuals and their social values for which he blamed the early education of the individuals.[17]

Then Casare Lombroso focused a new light on the concept of crime that a crime had a close relationship with the personality of the criminal. This theory projected that few persons are born criminals and tried to prove that heredity and biological factors are responsible for criminal behaviour. This concept tried to establish the relation of body structure with criminality, i.e. how the personality of the individual leads him to commit crime.[18]

The two greatest Greek philosophers that the world has ever seen—Plato and Aristotle—had shown their great concern about crime in the society, Aristotle observed that poverty endangers revolution and

---

16. August Bequai; White-collar, *op. cit.*, pp. 6-7.
17. *Ibid.*
18. Prabhat Chandra Tripathi; *op. cit.*, p. 34.

crime generates from poverty. Plato was of the opinion that human greed is the potential factor responsible for crime. Voltaire, Rousseau and Bentham were of the opinion that economic factor had a close bearing on criminality. According to them economic imbalance or unequal distribution of economic resources in the society is the main cause of criminality. They were of the view that crime is the product of reaction against economic injustice. Similarly, William Bonger imposes liability of crime to the capitalistic economy. In the capitalistic economy, economic resources are concentrated in the hands of the few and so the poor become more poor and the rich become richer and this process continuously goes on. So they expressed that the crime is nothing more than the reaction against this economic injustice and is generated due to unequal distribution of material resources in the society.[19]

Thus, it is clear that the explanation of why the upper classes enjoyed, for so long, *de facto*, if not legal, immunity from prosecution can be found not only in the history but also in the writings of criminologists. They also associated criminal behaviour with the lower classes. In fact, many writers were heavily influenced by the rise of new ideologies and political schools of thought of the time. So, the ideological turmoil of the eighteenth and nineteenth centuries and association of crime with poverty led to a side-stepping of any serious study of white-collar crimes and the law enforcement apparatus, that grew failed to address this area, because scholars of crime could not take up the cause to deal with these crimes of upper classes. This trend impeded the study of white-collar crimes in most of the societies.[20]

White-collar crimes occur as a part of the violator's occupational role and generally laws involved are not part of traditional criminal code, and secondly, most of the violators are cut above the ordinary criminal in social standing. The vast bulk of white-collar legislation is regulatory rather than penal in philosophy, is administrative in procedure, and is directed chiefly towards the business and professional classes of our society. These crimes are usually violations of trust, either "duplicities" or "misrepresentations", placed in the person by virtue of his occupational norms and high position in society. Of course, these violations of trust, must also be violations of law, and not merely unethical practices or non-criminal deviations from informal conduct norms within a business or profession. The legal status of such violations has arisen a theoretical conflict that continues to the present day. Are such trust violations really crimes? Whether criminal theories are revised to include these law-breakers? If these questions are answered

19. *Ibid.*
20. August Bequai; *op. cit.*, pp. 8-9.

affirmatively, indeed the science of criminology must revise its postulates and reformulate many of its theories.[21]

Most of the laws relating to white-collar crimes differ from conventional criminal laws in many ways. In the first place, most white-collar laws are created by legislative bodies in contrast to the conventional criminal code, which is viewed as merely a legislative expression of natural crimes. Secondly, most white-collar laws treat their violations as misdemeanors rather than more serious felonies of penal law. Further, intent which is an essential ingredient in the criminal law, is irrelevant to conviction under many white-collar (regulatory) laws, although intentional violations, if proved, may increase the punishment. In these respects, white-collar violations are legally much more like traffic laws than statutes of the criminal code. Another important distinction of white-collar legislation is seen in enforcement and procedural variations from those of the conventional criminal cases. Most of the regulatory legislations are not dealt with the procedure adopted in criminal cases, but by specially created investigatory and enforcement bodies. In most of the white-collar legislation, the same agency or commission, which directs investigation, also conducts hearings of cases and administers numerous punishments or sanctions short of prison terms or the other conventional penal sanctions. In a strict legal sense, these hearings are not trials, as adopted in criminal cases. Since most of the white-collar laws are remedial in nature, they are liberally constructed, so that the aim remains prevention or correction rather than the punishment of violators. In this respect, various sanctions other than the criminal punishments of imprisonment, probation and fines are used by the enforcing agencies. Violators of such laws may be subjected to warnings, injunctions, seizure and destruction of products, civil suits of damages, licence revocation and similar informal or civil processes. This difference in the two categories of crimes is because of many factors including the high social status of many violators and the lack of consensus about the criminal nature of their behaviour. Since the main aim of enforcement agencies is to correct economic wrongs, prevent public injury, and the like, cases are more likely settled or wrongs prevented from continuing in contrast to the eye-for-eye philosophy implicit in criminal actions. Further, criminal law is based on the theory of individual responsibility and guilt, the *mens-rea* nature of intent that is inconsistent with and difficult to apply in many white-collar cases. Quite often, white-collar violators are corporations, co-operatives, or labour unions and while legal responsibility may fix to these as it does to a person, the use of the criminal sanctions of imprisonment is virtually impossible in such cases.[22]

---

21. Gilbert Gies and Robert F. Meher, *op. cit.*, pp. 52-53.
22. *Ibid.*,, pp. 53-54.

Thus, the difference in enforcement and procedure is yet another important cause of increase in white-collar criminality.

GREED OF MONEY, POWER, RESPECT AND STATUS

It is true, that in the world of today money has acquired a great importance in earning social respect, power and status. So man is mad after money. Economic life has become fundamental for every individual. In early societies when economic resources were limited, struggle for existence and survival of the fittest was the law of nature. But with the advancement of the society the means of production also developed and gradually money became important for human life to the extent as it determined the status of the individual in the society. With this change in the social values, man started committing crimes not merely for the sake of meeting necessities of life but for acquiring superfluous things. Thus, the acquisitive nature of people, their greed for acquiring surplus wealth and materialistic tendency, instigate them to commit criminal act if they cannot get them through legitimate means. Taft has rightly commented on this point that "crime has been a mere phenomenon of prosperity rather than adversity."[23]

So, with the advancement of the time, a new type of the crime, i.e. white-collar crimes could be associated with the persons who are ingenious, clever, shrewd, rich but greedy and who have developed social and political clout. The selfish and acquisitive nature of man is the root cause of such crimes in society. A man under the grip of selfish interest does not hesitate to commit any type of the crime. To earn huge money within a short span of time and without hard labour is the philosophy behind these crimes. Adulteration in food articles, duplicate medicines, false and misleading advertisements, slander of title and slander of trade-marks, etc. are the examples of such crimes committed by the traders and businessmen out of selfish nature, without caring for the loss caused to the society. It is not only businessmen, but politicians, bureaucrats, professionals and other upper class persons of the society who are busy in committing such type of crimes. Lust of money, power, respect and status has made a man mad to earn them by any means. The advancement of technology and scientific development has made the problem more acute and serious. These white-collar and economic crimes are dangerous, not only because financial losses are higher but also because they cause irreparable damage to public morals.

It has rightly been commented that "we must be realistic enough to see in these new developments that despite rich spiritual heritage and even while the life and teaching of Mahatma Gandhi are still afresh in

23. Taft; Criminology, 4th edution, p. 125.

our minds, a new materialistic philosophy has gripped nation. The philosophy of white-collar crime is that success and material advancement are the only important things that matter in life, and in achieving them one need not hesitate to adopt unethical conduct. It encourages an attitude of contempt for those who live with a semblance of idealism, who deserve failure, which is normally their lot in this competitive world."[24]

Among the various explanations given for crimes of the rich and the influential there is one given by Aristotle. He is of the view that "men may desire superfluities in order to enjoy pleasure unaccompanied by pain and, therefore, they commit crimes. The greatest crimes are caused by excess and not by necessity."[25] Thus, Aristotle also favours the view that human greed is the root cause of increase in white-collar criminality. The days have gone when one thought of crimes as the outcome to fulfil the basic needs. Today there is hardly anyone who dies of hunger but because of excessive eating causing indigestion and food poisoning.

The rise of industrial capitalism in the eighteenth century onwards opened a new chapter in the history of white-collar crimes. In capitalistic system material economic resources, means of production and money get accumulated in the hands of few landed proprietors and capitalists, while the majority of the people remain without any property. According to William Bonger capitalism was one of the potent causes of criminality because the system created an atmosphere for promoting selfish tendencies in man. Capitalism brought a radical change in thoughts, values and attitudes of people. Now, extorting money by any means became the sale aim of this newly emerged capitalist class because they thought that money meant power, respect and status. This greed to earn power, respect and status started a race of earning money by hook or crook without giving any serious thought to its impact on the society.

The industrial capitalism gave birth to an acquisitive society in which man becomes the centre of money, power and status. He, instead of looking into social good, pursues his own interest. The system provides an opportunity to acquire power and traces advantage for his own self-development and to pursue his own self-interest; it offers unlimited scope to acquire more and more money and power. The society hardly imposes any moral or social restrictions on acquiring more and more wealth and gives a free hand to an individual to pursue his own instincts.

---

24. S. Venugopal Rao; Facets of crime in India, Second revised edition 1967; p. 137.
25. Aristotle; Politics, Macmillan, London Book II, Chapter 7, p. 656.

Tawney has expressed his views on this situation. He says:

"It assures men that there are not ends other than their ends, no law other than their desires, no limit other than that which they think advisable. Thus, it makes an individual the centre of his own universe, and dissolves moral principles into a choice of expediencies. And it immensely simplifies the problems of social life in complex communities, for it relieves them of the necessity of discriminating between different types of economic activity and different sources of wealth, between enterprise and avarice, energy and unscrupulous greed, property which is legitimate and property which is theft, the just enjoyment of the fruits of labour and the idle parasitism of birth or fortune, because it treats all economic activities as standing upon the same level and suggests that excess or defect, waste or superfluity require no conscious effort of social will to avert them, but are corrected almost automatically by the mechanical play of economic forces."[26]

Another peculiar feature of capitalistic economy is the competitive tendency among entrepreneurs. The problem of white-collar crime is rooted in this competitive attitude of business world to oust their rival competitors. Though efficiency, less cost with better quality of products are some of the appreciable results of this competitive economy but when one fails to meet the competition, unlawful devices like those of infringement of trade marks, copyright, patents, etc. are adopted by the business community.

So, modern age is the age of changed values, attitudes and outlook of the society. Man is running after money, power, respect and status. He has become acquisitive in nature. New techniques of production, change in information technology, new means of transport and communication, new era of globalization of world trade making the world as one family for the purpose of trade and many more methods of modern trade have again aggravated the complex problem of white-collar criminality.

Thus, the economic and industrial progress throughout the world has been the potential cause of rise in white-collar crimes because it has made man greedy of money, power and status. The changing socio-economic structure of society coupled with increase in wealth and prosperity has furnished opportunities for such crimes. Commenting on the growing incidences of white-collar crimes in India, the Law Commission has observed that modern scientific and technological

26. R.H. Tawney; The Acquisitive Society, Sussex 1982, pp. 32-33.

developments and monopolistic trends in business world have led to enormous increase in white-collar crimes.[27]

It has also been experienced that economic and industrial growth in most of the countries all over the world and white-collar criminality goes side by side with each other. In fact, white-collar crimes are directly or indirectly connected with the economic development. The industrial revolution brought great social change in social values regarding economic and structure of property. This development caused concentration of economic and political power in the hands of few people. This super concentration of economic resources and power in the hands of few had initiated great social change of far-reaching consequences, as a result of which various factors responsible for rapid growth of white-collar crimes emerged in the society.[28]

From the above discussion it can be easily concluded that man's greed for earning money, power and status in today's world is the root cause of increase in white-collar criminality. Recent series of scams in India like Fodder Scam of Bihar, Jain Hawala Scam, Telecom Scandal, Harshad Mehta Stock Exchange Case, Urea Scam and many more such scams are the burning examples of man's greed which has caused great loss to the society and its morale.

REPORT OF VARIOUS COMMITTEES

The problem of white-collar crimes is a matter of grate concern for the present Government in India. The business community is at the top among white-collar criminals. The effective solution to handle these problems lies in evolution of effective enforcement agencies and not in persuasion. The appeals and warnings from Government to save the collapse of economic structure of the nation bring no favourable response from business community. They rather accelerate their efforts to build up a strong lobby in the corridors of power, to turn every effort of the government to use any law against them. These elements in the society exploit every opportunity to feather their own nets."[29]

Consequently corruption and kickbacks are invading the political and economic sectors in India and has become a way of life. They are not confined to individuals but have polluted. the entire social texture and are posing a threat to public welfare activities. "White-collar criminality would never have reached such epidemic proportions but for the cooperative non-enforcement of the laws by the enforcers. It may

27. Law Commission of India; 29th report (1966).
28. Friedman, Law in a Changing Society (1951), p. 186.
29. President of India's message to the Nation on 30th Independence Day, *The Tribune*, August 15, 1977.

not be out of place to state that over 225 major committees and commissions of inquiry have been instituted by various State and Union Governments in cases of misuse of power or corruption and many reports have been drafted and many recommendations have been given by them but till date not a single major fish has ever been caught or imprisoned."[30] It is generally alleged that commissions and committees are time-buying exercises and are set-up merely to side track the real issue and to create a memory lapse in the public opinion. The mechanism adopted in these commissions of inquiry are not for digging up of the truth but the digging in of it and its strangulation.[31] These commissions and committees have searched into various deep-rooted causes of white-collar crimes and gave their recommendations on various aspects. Some of them are discussed here.

Like other developed countries of the world, the problem of white-collar crimes goes on increasing with the advancement of science and technology in India. When India got freedom, the main task before Indian Government was to control and regulate the production and distribution of essential commodities for the benefit of common man in the country. This actually provided opportunity to the opportunists, self-centred people, to exploit the situation for their own selfish benefits. With the advancement of time the situation has further deteriorated to an alarming extent. The Law Commission of India also expressed its grave concern on this situation. The Commission was of the view that with the advancement of scientific and technological development, a new class, with a large rank and file and less control, emerged in the society. This development brought a radical change in social structure to which society was unable to appreciate in full, resulting into rapid growth of white-collar and economic crimes.[32]

Thus, the problem of white-collar crimes in India became quite acute in terms of variety and extent. One of the major areas of such crimes in India is evasion of taxes. Tax laws in India are very complex in nature. Business community generally takes benefit of these weaknesses in taxation laws and escape very easily. Tax authorities are generally helpless in assessing the actual income of big businessmen, contractors, professionals, etc. Consequently, it is almost impossible to estimate the true extent of tax evasion in the country per year. Santhanam Committee in its report has made a reference that, an unofficial estimate of the Central Board of Revenue is that about Rs. 45 crore of tax is evaded annually by assesses in the higher income group,

30. *Ibid.*
31. *Ibid.*
32. Law Commission of India, Twenty-ninth Report, 1966, p. 3.

the evaded income being about Rs. 230 crore. This figure must have gone very high in present time because of the unprecedented inflation in the Indian economy during last few years.[33]

The greatest effect caused by the failure to check tax evasion is the emergence of the phenomenon of 'black money' which has seriously affected the economy of our nation. It is a matter of common experience that at present two parallel economies, black and white money, are running side by side in our country. The Vivian Bose Commission (1963) appointed to probe into the working of ten companies in the Dalmia-Jain group, found that there was a loss of an estimated 3.5 crores of rupees as a result of fraud and improper use of funds of the concerned companies by the management. The Commission found 114 fictitious persons to whom shares worth Rs. 16 lakh were fraudulently issued in order to bring the secret profit of the Dalmia-Jain group into circulation and convert this 'black-money' into 'white-money'. The Commission also observed that the group had over Rs. 4 crore of secret and undisclosed assets. The Commission also estimated the illegal gains of Rs. 1,45,19,790 made by causing loss to the exchequer of the nation by just four companies of the Dalmia-Jain group by evading or avoiding taxes. The methods used for this purpose included compensation payment for termination of selling and managing agencies, under-statement of sales, suppression of profits, fictitious losses in shares, etc.[34]

In order to unearth black money and to check the problem of tax evasion, Government of India in 1970 appointed Wanchoo Committee. This Committee highlighted the following direct effects of black money economy in the country:[35]

1. It causes great loss to the revenue of the State, which ultimately contributes to the scarcity for resources of national development.[36]
2. It results in payment of inequitable taxation; only the honest taxpayer suffers in the process.[37]
3. The black money being the unaccounted money which neither car. be declared nor invested through lawful channel; a major part of it is spent on unproductive uses resulting in waste as well as in inflation.[38]

---

33. Ahmad Siddique; Criminology, *op. cit.*, p. 395.
34. Report of the Vivian Bose Commission, quoted in N.R. Menon, White-collar crime in India (1968).
35. Ahmad Siddique; *op. cit.*, p. 395.
36. *Ibid.*, p. 396.
37. *Ibid.*
38. *Ibid.*

4. The most dangerous effect of the phenomenon of black money is, that general moral texture of the society as a whole is adversely affected.[39]

The Santhanam Committee (1964) appointed to report on the prevention of corruption in the country has reported about the misdeeds of business and industry and existing corruption in the country. The Committee was of the view that corruption can exist only when there is someone willing to corrupt and capable of corrupting and suggested that this willingness and capacity to corrupt is found in large number of industries in India.[40] The Committee found that during five-year period from 1958 to 1962, licences valued seventy million rupees were obtained or wrongfully utilised by nearly 700 firms through misrepresentation, forgery or other breaches of export, import policies.[41] The Committee also found that these persons avoid payment of taxes, accumulate large amounts of unaccounted money, knows art of getting business by under-cutting, of making good the loss by passing-off sub-standard work and so on.

The Jain Commission (1991) was appointed to probe into the deep-rooted conspiracy in the assassination of Shri Rajiv Gandhi, the then Prime Minister of India. This case is an extreme case of nexus among mafia, bureaucracy and politicians. This case also exhibits an example, how commissions and committees are time buying exercises and how society is concerned for such a sensitive issue. It is highly surprising that for complete five years this Commission was not handed over the papers by the Government on which it could start functioning. It was only in May 1996 that the Commission could get some documents. The interim report of the Commission made it clear that the Government did not co-operate with the Commission and tried to wind it up. A number of files of crucial importance were not supplied in original because they had been declared missing or could not be shown in view of their sensitive nature.[42]

The nexus among politicians, bureaucrats, businessmen and criminals in India can be seen after the end of the Nehru era and since then it has gone from strength to strength. The Vohra Committee, which was appointed to look into the causes of the series of bomb blasts in Bombay in March 1993, found that crime exists in politics and exposed the nexus between criminal world with the politicians which now poses

39. *Ibid.*
40. Report of Santhanam Committee on the Prevention of Corruption, 1964.
41. *Ibid.*, pp. 18 and 65.
42. Girish Mishra and Braj Kumar Pandey: *op. cit.* pp. 308-10.

a serious threat to the fabric of the nation. The Committee expressed its views that activities of Memon Brothers and Dawood Ibrahim could not have survived over the years without the protection of functionaries of the government departments and particularly customs, income tax, police and others. It suggested that the creation of a nodal agency to collect information regarding the activities of mafia organisations is very essential. All the existing information available with RAW, IB and CBI could be made available to this nodal agency.[43]

The Director of CBI explained the nexus. "An organised crime syndicate/mafia generally commences its activities by indulging in petty crimes at the local level, mostly relating to illicit distillation, gambling, organised Satta and prostitution in the larger towns. In port towns, their activities involve smuggling and sale of imported goods and progressively graduate to narcotics and drug trafficking. "In the bigger cities, the main source of income relates to real estate—forcibly occupying lands and buildings, procuring such properties at cheap rates by forcing out the existing occupants and tenants, etc. Over time the money power, thus, acquired is used for building up contracts with bureaucrats and politicians and expansion of activities with impurity. The money power is also used to develop a network of muscle-power which is also used by the politicians during elections."[44]

The Committee clearly made an alarm that the nexus between criminal gangs, police, bureaucracy and politicians is operating clearly in various parts of the country. It insisted upon the weaknesses and inability of existing criminal justice system to deal with economic offences and the activities of these mafia gangs. Because of advanced communication system like telephone, cellular phone, e-mail, fax, etc., the mobility and connectivity among these syndicates has become much faster and beyond the reach of intelligence agencies, consequently a complete net working of various type of mafias is working through out the country.[45]

The Committee gave the following specific examples:

- In some of the States like Bihar, Haryana and U.P. these gangs enjoy patronage of local level politicians. Some political leaders with the help of these gangs, get themselves elected to local bodies, State Assemblies and the Parliament. In this way, these elements could acquire considerable political clout, seriously jeopardizing the smooth

---

43. Government of India (Ministry of Home Affairs), Vohra Committee Report, New Delhi (1995), pp. 2-3.
44. *Ibid.*, p. 3.
45. *Ibid.*

functioning of the administration and the safety and security of life and property of common man.[46]

- The big smuggling syndicates due to their international linkages, have infected various economic and financial activities of the country. These include Hawala transactions, circulation of black money and operations of parallel economy causing serious damage to the economic structure of the country. These syndicates have acquired substantial financial and muscle power and social respectability and have successfully corrupted the government machinery at all levels and yield enough influence to make the task of investigating and prosecuting agencies extremely difficult; even the members of the judicial system have not escaped the embrace of the mafia.[47]
- Some elements of the mafia group have associated themselves with the activities of narcotics, drugs and weapon smuggling across the inter-state border, particularly in the States of J & K, Punjab, Gujarat and Maharashtra. They contribute to the election expenses of the politicians in order to seek their favour in oganising their activities successfully. This virus has spread in almost all the corners of the country.[48]
- The Bombay Bomb Blast case and communal riots in Surat and Ahmedabad have exposed beyond any doubt as to how the Indian mafia elements have been exploited by the Pakistani intelligence agency ISI and other network in UAE to cause sabotage, subversion and communal tension in various parts of the country. The investigations into the Bombay Bomb Blast cases have revealed the strong linkage of the underworld with different government agencies, political circles, business sector and film industry.[49]

From the above discussion of various reports and recommendations of different committees and commissions and otherwise also, the causes of white-collar crimes can be summarized as follows:

1. General Public Attitude

The primary cause of white-collar crimes has been the long

46. *Ibid.*
47. *Ibid.*
48. *Ibid.*
49. *Ibid.*, p. 6.

neglected attitude of the society towards these crimes. Due to white-collar crimes individual is only marginally affected so he is least bothered about these crimes. This attitude makes the society unconcerned with these crimes, with the result that these activities go on increasing without much restraint from the society. In fact, many white-collar crimes have become socially acceptable.

Money making by any means has become part of the business community. Most of the white-collar crimes in business are prevalent because the business community treats such behaviour as legitimate and even praise-worthy. "A person who declares his personal property honestly is regarded as a freak. This shows that the general public mentality has accepted a particular common level of dishonesty. People practising fraud, cheating, misrepresentation, etc. hardly attract any consciousness of the society. There is a general feeling in the society that a professional such as a lawyer cannot be successful if he is completely honest. White-collar crime is the modern manifestation of the 'something for nothing' complex. Passivity on part of the general public encourages white-collar crimes. A petty pickpocket is beaten to death but a big company or businessman commits heinous white-collar crimes with perfect immunity. People pay little attention to white-collar crimes."[50]

It is also a fact that a large section of society is not aware of the existing laws regarding their exploitation by these white-collar offenders. Due to the social status, political influence and money and muscle power of these offenders, social opposition is not organized against them. They hardly treat them as offenders, so most of the white-collar crimes remain unreported. In many cases society itself contributes to the commission of various white-collar crimes. Bribery, if illegal gratification to public servants and black marketing are some of the offences which cannot be committed without active participation and demand of the society. Thus, social immunity is the root cause of increase in white-collar crimes.

2. Acquisitive Nature of Man

The acquisitive nature or money-mindedness of human beings is the root cause of these crimes in the society. The nature to acquire more money, power and luxurious articles and to seek more and more pleasure even at the cost of social displeasure is the chief cause of rise in white-collar criminality in modern time. The unlimited desires of individuals can be fulfilled only through illegal means within limited resources. This acquisitive tendency brings them easily in the world of criminals. In fact, money is the root of all evil.

3. Industrial Growth

With the advancement of time economic and Industrial growth became another fertile cause of white-collar criminality. Due to industrial growth, production increases causing great competition in the market. To beat their rival competitors, and to establish themselves in the market, these industrialists behave in an irresponsive manner, resulting into various kinds of white-collar crimes. Some times, it is suggested that such crimes are committed merely for the sake of necessity to retain their existence. Whatever may be the reason but due to industrial growth and competitive tendency among business community, white-collar crimes are increasing day-by-day.

4. Avarice

It is not need but human greed to earn huge wealth, which is the cause of rapid growth in white-collar crimes. White-collar criminals are avaricious and selfish persons. The greed and selfish nature of man is the potent cause of these crimes. The lust of wealth earning instigates even to literate and already wealthy people to commit economic offences to acquire more riches.

5. Capitalistic Economy

Capitalism is more prone to the growth of such crimes. In capitalistic economy means of production and economic resources are centralised in the hands of few capitalists. These capitalists resort to hoarding and monopolistic traits, thus, creating artificial rise in prices. This section of the society wants to earn great wealth by hook and crook even at the cost of exploitation of others, resulting into enormous increase in white-collar crimes.

6. Lack of Adequate Punishment

Though most of the white-collar crimes are crimes in India but most of them are handled by commissions, administrative tribunals and boards. This administrative handling of white-collar offences cannot result in the conviction of the offender in the legal sense and therefore, white-collar offenders do not acquire the status of a criminal in the real sense. Thus, civil penalties awarded by these commissions and boards do not involve the stigma that attends indictment and conviction. The offenders have no fear of going to jail, consequently they commit crimes more frequently for their selfish ends of earning huge wealth and that too without any fear of stigma and loss of reputation in the society. So, the existing criminal justice system is not adequate to deal with these types of crimes.

7. Social Status of the Offender

White-collar offenders are the persons who are respectable and of the upper socio-economic class of society. They belong to the 'influential and intellectual group' of society who handle their occupation tactfully and persons affected thereby hardly know that they are victimised and even if it comes to their knowledge, they hardly come forward to make any complaint because of their money and muscle power and influence in the society.

It is also alleged that judges also belong to the upper class of society, so they are generally sympathetic towards white-collar criminals. Judicial attitude is, thus, away from the white-collar crimes. These offenders are intelligent, socially, economically and politically influential, have their loud voice in electoral battle, so they are in a position to twist and influence the legislative, judicial and administrative functions of the State for their selfish ends and people generally keep silent for their illegal activities.

8. Doctrine of Caveat Emptor

The doctrine of caveat-emptor has since long been an important factor contributing to the cause of white-collar criminality. In cases of misrepresentation, concealment, frauds, etc. the courts usually place reliance on the doctrine of caveat-emptor that is 'let the buyer-beware'. This doctrine emphasises that a buyer must enter into a deal with open eyes and guard himself against ordinary dishonesty of the seller. So, this doctrine has been the chief instrument in the hands of business community to guard themselves against all their misdeeds in business transactions. As a result of this attitude of the courts, there is enormous increase in white-collar crimes. It is due to this reason that American President Roosevelt in 1933, insisted upon the withdrawal of the doctrine of caveat-emptor from the adjudication of cases involving white-collar crimes.

WHY WHITE-COLLAR CRIMINALS ESCAPE PUNISHMENT?

Following are some of the main reasons of survival of white-collar criminals in the society or why apprehended white-collar criminals escape punishment:

- The effect of white-collar crimes are so diffused over a large number of people that an individual hardly cares to file any report of these crimes.
- Law with regard to these crimes is very complex and soft in nature. It is not strict enough to deal with such criminals properly. The civil nature of remedy under most of the laws dealing with white-collar crimes is not a proper deterrence to white-collar offenders, so businessmen feel better to pay fine rather than obeying the law.

---

50. Rohinton Mehta; *op. cit.*, pp. 235-36.

- Securing evidence for prosecution is very difficult, particularly in cases of crimes by corporation.
- The olden days maxims like doctrine of presumption of innocence, i.e. the guilt of the accused should be proved beyond all reasonable doubts and benefit of doubt should go in favour of the accused, are still helping the white-collar criminals in escaping punishment.
- The high social, political and economic status and influence of these criminals help them to make contacts with the administrative and law enforcement authorities. The white-collar criminals get themselves involved in political process of the country, through economic help to various political parties in election, so they easily get their favourable legislation by influencing the policy-making mechanism of the government.
- Under the garb of 'caveat-emptor' doctrine, minor defects in goods, misrepresentation and fraud are protected and do not bring any prosecution to these criminals. These cases are generally treated as cases of ordinary dishonesty and shrewd business tactics.
- The lack of speedy trial on priority basis in such cases, ultimately brings down the gravity of such offences.
- Most of the white-collar crimes are done in such a planned manner and with careful and expert cleverness that they are not easily detected and so frustrate the very purpose of the law.
- The codes of conduct and their enforcement regarding various professions and occupations such as lawyers, doctors, engineers, advertisers, architects, etc. are made by their own professional organisations, which represent their own parochial interests. There is, therefore, only symbolic enforcement.[51]
- The class bias of the courts also helps white-collar criminals in escaping from criminal conviction. This is not true about present day courts but also the courts in the past. So the precedents and the procedures formulated in the past were in favour of white-collar criminals as a result of which, there is differential handling of white-collar cases and ordinary crimes.[52]
- The concept of *laissez-faire* and democracy, up to a great extent, brought about a glorification of 'maximizing profit'. Strict laws are generally treated against the policy of 'free

---

51. Rohinton Mehta; Crime and Criminology; *op. cit.*, p. 243.
52. *Ibid.*, p. 243.

> market' and 'promotion of trade'. They are alleged as unnecessary governmental interference in business. It is, thus, rightly said that, 'democracy itself is the greatest enemy of democracy'. The past experience has also shown that prohibitions, bans and strict governmental control pushes underground white-collar criminality, to be controlled by mafia; leading to even greater enforcement problems. Thus, the position of the government is unenviable—strict laws and controls have not worked in the past and total *laissez-faire* is not working at present.[53]

From the above analysis it can be concluded that because of various causes, white-collar crimes are multiplying each day. A sympathetic attitude or mere persuasion cannot stop the growth of such crimes. Some hard and strict measures are now needed at each level, to deal with these crimes. These crimes are no more a social problem but have become a legal problem and a challenge to the present government. Now we cannot make any distinction between white-collar and other crimes as regard to their gravity, effect and handling is concerned. If there is some distinction, it lies in the nature of crimes, which are committed to earn a material gain with no loss of status. This distinction is because of the attitude of executive and judicial authorities who are concerned with the prevention of crime and react favourably to the upper-class society and dispose of white-collar criminals with mere censures or admonition while other criminals are subjected to severe penal sanctions under the law. The time has come to organise public opinion and raise a voice against these crimes which have eaten the whole economic fabric of the nation.

---

53. *Ibid.*

3

Classification of White-collar Crimes

There is sufficiency in the world for man's need, but not for man's greed.

—Mahatma Gandhi

The traditional theory of crime, which attributed crime to the backward socio-economic conditions, has become outdated because large scale crimes are now committed by powerful and resourceful persons who are operating in the area of business, politics and bureaucracy. The reports of various commissions of inquiries and committees, established by the government to study growing incidences of crime in India have revealed in their reports that a great variety of crimes is now committed by the people of upper socio-economic group in the course of their occupation. This type of the white-collar criminality is on the increase in view of the current rapid social and economic changes and has reached to the alarming situation in the modern society. The effect of these crimes on the society is greater than that of the traditional crimes because they adversely affect the moral, economic and social structure of the society. The white-collar crime, which is a small circle within the big circle of economic crimes, dangerously affect the health and material welfare of the society and is a great threat to the entire economic fabric of the country. These criminals, due to their social, political and economic status and power, capture the administrative machinery of the state and escape from the clutches of prosecution. They are intelligent, successful and foresighted persons belonging to the prestigious group of the society and commit crimes, which are indirect, impersonal and difficult to detect in comparison to the ordinary crimes which are direct and can easily be identified and detected.

The crime rate in India has shown an increasing trend during the last few decades. The total I.P.C. crimes in the country, which was only 6.26 lacs in 1961 rose to 16.30 lacs in 1993. While the population of the country registered an increase by 101.90% during this period, I.P.C. crimes increased by 160.30%. Crime has, thus, been rising at the rate faster than that of population growth.[1]

White-collar crimes are different than the traditional crimes in many ways in their effect and *modus-operandi*. So, before advancing further, it is necessary to understand the true nature of these crimes.

White-collar Crimes may be divided into Occupational Crime and Organizational Crime but in common parlance there exist 10 popular types of White-collar Crimes as:

- **Bank Fraud.**—To engage in an act or pattern of activity where the purpose is to defraud a bank of funds.
- **Blackmail.**—A demand for money under threat to do bodily harm, to injure property or to expose secrets.
- **Bribery.**—When money, goods, services or any information is offered with intent to influence the actions, opinions and decisions of the taker, constitutes bribery.
- **Cellular Phone Fraud.**—Unauthorized use or tampering or manipulating cellular phone services.
- **Embezzlement.**—When a person who has been entrusted with the money or property, appropriates it for his or her own purpose.
- **Counterfeiting.**—Copies or imitates an item without having been authorized to do so.
- **Forgery.**—When a person passes false or worthless instruments such as cheque or counterfeit security with intent to defraud.
- **Tax-Evasion.**—Frequently used by the middle-class to have extra-unaccounted money.
- **Adulteration.**—Adulteration of foods and drugs.
- **Professional crime.**—Crimes committed by medical practitioners, lawyers in course of their Occupation.

DIFFERENCE BETWEEN WHITE-COLLAR CRIME AND BLUE-COLLAR CRIME

The vast area or conventional crimes come within the category of blue-collar crimes or ordinary crimes, which is distinguishable from

1. M.P. Mehani; Financial Crimes and Frauds in Banking Industry, an Article published in *CBI Bulletin*, Vol. VI, No. 9, September 1998 at p. 16.

another segment of crimes, which criminologists have chosen to appropriately characterise as white-collar crimes. In recent years many criminologists have tried to distinguish between white-collar and blue-collar crimes in terms to categorise workers. Blue-collar refers to the vast labour force that keeps production ticking in our factories and do their work manually but white-collar is used for salaried or professional category persons who, ordinarily, do not have to use their hand in their calling. In the latter category, are included clerks, and various categories of employees, public servants, businessmen and industrialists and others engaged in handling public funds.[2]

From the origin point of view, crimes of slums are generally known as blue collar-crimes while the crimes committed by business and professional world in their callings are known as white-collar crimes. The effect of traditional crimes are direct and specific but white-collar crimes are indirect, devious, anonymous and impersonal.[3]

The white-collar criminals select crimes, which involve high stake but only small danger of detection and they also select crimes in which proof is difficult. In white-collar crimes like that of traditional blue-collar crimes; thief is generally persistent, but the difference is that, white-collar criminals are cunning and they never repeat same type of crime or same *modus-operandi* in committing crime. These criminals try to maintain their status among their associates and successful criminals in business field like, tax evaders, cheater, adulterers, etc. and are considered as capable businessmen.[4]

A notable difference between the two is that blue-collar criminals are afraid of the law and law-enforcing agencies, but white-collar criminals have no fear of executive, legislative and even judicial organisation of the government. The blue-collar criminal considers himself as a criminal and even the society thinks in the same line .but same is not the position in case of white-collar criminals who neither themselves nor society think them as criminal. Further, these blue-collar criminals have no desire to gain public support, but white-collar criminals attempt to justify their crime or try to prove their innocence, or to avoid the liability or to influence the machinery for gain or even attempt to threat the honest officer in order to maintain their reputation in society. White-collar criminals always wish to remain in organised form, try to control legislations and even select their favourable administrator to flourish in their dishonest trade practice.[5]

---

2. John Lobo; White-collar crime- A social Malaise, an Article published in *CBI Bulletin,* March 1982 at p. 1.
3. Sutherland, "Principles of Criminology", 6th edition, p. 46.
4. Prabhat Chandra Tripathi; The Menace of white-collar crimes and need for a new code, *op. cit.*, pp. 36-37.
5. *Ibid* at p. 37.

One of the important distinguishing features of white-collar crimes is that their effect is so widely diffused in the society that no specific person is directly victimised because these crimes are against government or society at large. Further, the consumers, shareholders and even public always remain unorganised as against the effect of these crimes. So, the real effect of these crimes are not visualised in society, though it has a future cancerie effect on the social life and on economic structure of the country. Their alarm in the society is very less and these white-collar criminals, in the garb of gentleman, remain in society like serpents under the green grass.

Despite some of the differences mentioned about it must be noted that white-collar and blue-collar crimes have much resemblance in many respect. Both have their origin in common law and are adaptation of principles of theft, fraud, etc. In fact, there is no basic difference between the two, the only peculiarity of white-collar crimes is that they are committed by the persons of relatively high status of society. The criminal content in both types of crime is more or less common. It must, however, be noted that *mens-rea* or guilty mind is an essential ingredient of every blue-collar crime but in case of white-collar crimes doctrine of constructive *mens-rea* is applied.[6]

Sutherland rightly said that no distinction in terms of social status, occupational activity, attitude or gravity of consequences could separate white-collar crimes from those of traditional crimes. The only distinguishing feature of this type of crimes is the temptation for considerable material gain with little or no loss of status. According to him, "social disorganisation on account of individualistic policies and competitive economy are the root causes for this type of criminality"[7] in the modern time.

WHITE-COLLAR CRIME *VIS-À-VIS* ECONOMIC CRIME

It is a matter of common experience that due to social and political changes in the country, new areas of economic crimes have emerged and focussed the attention of criminologists. The financial implication of these crimes are much greater than those of the traditional forms of violent crimes and crimes against property. Such crimes completely disturb the basic economic and social structure of the country and through their impact on saving, investment, and foreign exchange availability, etc. result in mal-distribution of national income.[8]

6. N.V. Paranjape; Criminology and Penology, Eleventh edition, reprinted 2002, pp. 105-06.
7. E.H. Sutherland; "Is white-collar crime a crime?" (*American Sociological Review*, April 1945), pp. 132-37
8. Report of 5th U.N. Congress on prevention of crime and treatment of offenders, Geneva, 1975, p. 10.

The welfare of the whole society is drastically affected by such criminal conducts as bribery, price fixing, smuggling and currency offences, etc. It is also a disturbing trend in the modern materialistic society that social status of man is measured by the yard stick of wealth. White-collar criminality has a very close and Ii powerful relationship with the people who control and influence the administration of justice. Daily unearthing of financial rackets of crores of rupees involving top businessmen, politician and bureaucrats corroborate this sprawling anti-social malaise in India.[9]

Following few glaring examples of scams on record in India before 1995 and in modern time are enough to support this view that economic crimes has become a great threat to the entire economic fabric of the country.

1957 : The Mundra scandal
1964 : The Kairon case
1971 : The Nagarwala episode
1982 : The Antulay case and the Churhat Lotteries case
1987: The Fair-Fax case; The Bofors deal case
1991: The Air Bus deal
1992: The security scam
1993: The A.B. Loco deal
1994: The Sugar scam

These Scams are committed in a series with a gap of a few years.[10] But after 1995, the unprecedented expansion of white-collar crimes in India bursts upon the nation's conscience and almost every alternative day new scams hit newspaper headlines. Few important scams on record after 1995 are given below which are now topics of hot discussion in our country.[11]

1. Jain Hawala racket
2. The Telecom scandal
3. The Fodder scam of Bihar
4. Jhankhand Mukti Morcha pay-off case of Rs. 3.5 crores
5. Harshad Mehta stock corruption case
6. St. Kitts $21 Million forgery case and Lakhubhai Pathak cheating case.

9. Gurpal Singh; Problems of white-collar crime in India and its control. This paper was read of UGC sponsored seminar held at GND University, Amritsar on 18th and 19th September, 1977 on 'white-collar crimes in India' and published in *Panjab University Law Journal*, 1977 at p. 51.
10. *The Times of India*, New dated 17.12.95.
11. Ajit Kumar Sahu; "Lajya" published in Oriya "Praharee", dated 21.10.96

7. Plantation scam of Rs. 12 crores
8. Tax evasion of Rs. 1,56,836 crores
9. Textile corruption of 16 crores.
10. ONGC corruption (security scam) involving Rs. 680 crores
11. Bihar police dress purchase corruption.
12. Urea purchase corruption of Rs. 133 crores.

One of the interesting and notable things about these scams in India is that even after crores of expenditure incurred by the government on their investigation and legal cases, felons remained unpunished in most of the cases or no charge sheet is even filed after years and years. A leading news magazine of India, '*India Today*', has undertaken a study of following 14 such major swindles in the fast 15 years that involve Rs. 22,376 crore, 221 cases and 149 charge-sheets but till date there have been just 10 convictions.[12]

1. Bofors Gun Deal (Rs. 64 Crore Scandal)

This is one of the major political scam held in 1987 and involving Rs. 64 crore. In this case a conspiracy was hatched among executives of Bofors, middlemen and officials of the Government of India and a commission/bribe of Rs. 64 crore (SEK 319.40 million) was paid in purchase of 410FH-77 guns for Rs. 1,437.72 crore (SEK 8410.66 million). Shri Rajiv Gandhi, the then Prime Minister of India denied the charge but the Congress, which won the biggest majority ever in 1984, lost the polls in 1989. Among the accused were S.K. Bhatnagar, W.N. Chaddha, Octavio Quattrocchi, Martin Ardbo, S.P. Hinduja, G.P. Hinduja and P.P. Hinduja. A case to this regard was filed on 22.01.1990 and charge sheet was filed on 22.10.1999. Government has probably spend more than Rs. 64 crore the total cost of the scam on investigation and legal costs but there is convictions as yet and no recovery.[13]

2. H.D.W. Submarine Deal (Rs. 32.55 Crore Sacndal)

In 1981, the government ordered four HDW Submarines from Germany at Rs. 465 crore to be delivered by 1987. In 1987 only two submarines were delivered. The then Defence Minister Shri V.P. Singh ordered a fresh negotiation.

The Germans refused, to deliver and alleged the payment of a 7 percent commission. Shri V.P. Singh ordered a probe on April 9, 1987 and resigned three days later. A case to this regard was filed on 05.03.1990 and CBI filed charge sheet. Among others, the CBI charged S.S. Sidhu, former additional Secretary, Ministry of Defence, S.K.

12. *India Today*, March 3, 2003, pp. 34-39.
13. *Ibid.*

Bhatnagar, Secretary, Ministry of Defence, G.C. Hinduja of M/S Sangam, London and Howaldtswereke Deutsche Werft (HDW) with conspiracy in signing the deal in return for a payment of DEM 101.3 million (Rs. 32.55 crore). The letters rogatory were sent to Switzerland to which Germany failed to provide any evidence. The result is that no convictions as yet and no recoveries. The CBI has now asked for permission to close the case.[14]

3. Air Bus Deal (Rs. 120 Crore Scandal)

A committee in 1984 chose Boeing 757 as the new aircraft for Indian Airlines but following Rajiv Gandhi's visit to France it was Airbus which got the order for 31 aircrafts. In 1990 one A-320 crashed in Bangalore, then questions were raised on their suitability and purchase. The V.P. Singh government ordered a probe. In FIR, the CBI charged civil aviation secretary S.S. Sidhu, K. Chadha, managing director of Indian Airlines and other top Indian Airline officials with receiving kickbacks from IAE of the US (an agency responsible for supply of engines) and Airbus Industries, France. On investigation, the file with key evidence of payoffs was found mission. This case was filed on 23.03.1990 but no charge sheet has yet been filed. Consequently no conviction and no recoveries as yet.[15]

4. Indian Bank Scandal (Rs. 762.92 Crore)

In this case the main accused M. Gopalkrishnan, chairman and managing director of Indian Bank helped the borrowers, mostly small corporate and exporters from the south, to lent huge sums of money which were not repaid. Cases and charge sheets were filed over five years from 1992 onwards. The arrest were made of Gopalkrishnan who has been named in 35 cases, seven officials, and M. Varadarajalu, the biggest borrower who was extradited from France in September 2001. In this case 27 charge sheets have been filed in 45 cases since 1992 but no conviction as yet and no recoveries. Government has pumped in Rs. 2675 crores to revive the bank.[16]

5. Stock Market Scam (The Harshad Mehta Mehta Case of Security Scam: Rs. 4100 Crore)

By the grave misuse and fraud of the government securities market, Harshad Mehta raised funds and rigged the stock market by pushing shares like ACC from Rs. 500 to Rs. 10,000. As Mehta, emerged the pied piper of Dalal Street, thousands of small investors followed him

14. *Ibid.*
15. *Ibid.*
16. *Ibid.*

and invested their money in shares. As his game came unstuck, the markets came crashing with the sensex falling from a peak of 4467 on April 22, 1992 to 3896 on April 28, 1992. Parliament was stalled. The RBI, the SEBI and a JPC probed the scam. In this game his brothers, Hiten Dalal and several other market operators were also involved with him. In this scam 72 cases were filed between 1992 to 1997. 47 charge sheets were filed. Four convictions were made in this case including Harshad Mehta and Hiten Dalal but recoveries are nil.[17]

6. Housing Scam (Rs. 65 Crore)

This case is related to the jumping of queue in the house allotment. The union ministry of urban affairs and employment under Shiela Kaul and her Junior P.K. Thungon found that those needed were willing to pay to get houses allotted at chosen localities much before their turn. So, they devised a system of out-of-turn allotments for government officials waiting for accommodation on allegedly compassionate grounds for a price. Official apparently paid between Rs. 30,000 and Rs. 80,000 depend on the size of the accommodation it required. It was then estimated that the scam which flourished between 1991 and 1994 was worth Rs. 65 crore. In this scam eleven cases has been filed in March and April 1996. Three charge sheets it have been filed and four junior officials have been convicted in two cases as yet but no recoveries are made. Waiting till date, the CBI is hopeful of getting sanctions for the prosecution of Sheila Kaul and Thungon. It is also expected to file charge sheets in nine cases any time now.[18]

7. Fodder Scam (Rs. 950 Crore)

In January 1996, the Finance Commissioner of Bihar asked District Magistrates and Deputy Commissioner to check the excess withdrawal of funds by the Animal Husbandry Department, following objections raised by the Accountant General. Raids revealed a Rs. 950 crore racket patronised by politicians. Among the accused are former chief ministers Laloo Prasad Yadav (jailed six times), Jagannath Mishra and Rabri Devi. In this matter, 64 cases have been filed since March 1996 but there is only one conviction so far and no recoveries as yet.[19]

8. Petrol Pump Allotment Scam

As union minister for petroleum Satish Sharma favoured the chosen with dealerships of Cooking Gas, Kerosene and Petrol Pumps. Following public interest litigation, the Supreme Court shot down 15

17. *Ibid.*
18. *Ibid*
19. *Ibid.*

allotments and asked a committee to scrutinise 432 files relating to allocations between 1992 and 1996. Satish Sharma was also ordered to pay a fine but the order was reversed. In November 1996, the CBI registered 15 cases, including one for possession of disproportionate assets. It has since been waiting for sanction for Sharma's prosecution. In this matter CBI filed 15 cases between November 1996 and 1997 but no charge sheet as yet filed and consequently there is no conviction and no recoveries till date.[20]

9. Urea Scam (Rs. 133 Crore)

In this case a shortage of fertilizer was created in the market. C.S. Ramakrishnan, M.D., national fertilizer limited, a group of businessmen close to the P.V. Narasimha Rao regime (M. Sambasiva Rao, Sal Impex) and Tuncay Alankus of Mis Karsan fleeced the government of Rs. 133 crore for the import of urea, which was never delivered. In this matter case was registered on 28.5.1996, charge sheet was filed on 26.12.1997 but no convictions as yet and no recoveries.[21]

10. Telecom Scam (Rs. 1200 Crore)

This scam was in relation to the allotment of telecom licences for cellular and basic telephone services in 1995. All purchases were routed through the minister's office and a favoured few were benefited by allotment. The CBI found evidence to file just one case against union communication minister Sukh Ram, DOT official Runu Ghose and businessman Paturu Rama Rao. The scam that halted parliament for weeks was believed to be worth over Rs. 1200 crore. Sukh Ram himself was caught with goods worth Rs. 5.36 crore, including Rs. 3.61 crore in cash, Rs. 2.45 crore at his Safdarjung Road residence in Delhi and at his house in Mandi, a house in Ghaziabad worth Rs. 1.2 crore, an orchard in Surath in Himachal Pradesh, jewellery worth Rs. 10.29 lacs and receipts of bank deposits worth Rs. 4.92 lacs. In this scam four cases and four charge sheets have been filed since August 1996. There is one conviction but all the accused in this case are of Rs. 5.36 crore which were seized by CBI.[22]

11. CRB Scam (Rs. 10.31 Crore)

Chain Roop Bhansali (C.R.B.) created a pyramid financial empire based on high cost financing. At its peak, his Rs. 1000 crore joint financial company comprised mutual funds, fixed deposit collection, a merchant bank and a provisional banking licence. Then his luck ran out,

20. *Ibid.*
21. *Ibid.*
22. *Ibid.*

when the bubble burst in May 1997. Over one lac depositors had lost Rs. 1031 crore. Bhansali was arrested for a few weeks and later on released on bail. In this scam a case on 20.5.1997 and charge sheet on 03.09.97 were filed. There is no conviction and no recovery till date. Mr. Bhansali has now petitioned the court for a revival package.[23]

12. Kaypee (Rs. 3218 Crore)

Like Harshad Mehta, who used banker's receipts, Ketan Parekh used pay orders to built up a large empire in stock market. He funnelled crores of rupees in the K-1 0 stocks, which saw their prices spurt. Parekh tripped finally when pay orders issued by the Madhavpura Mercantile Cooperative Bank (MMCB) bounced, leading to a default with the Bank of India. Even as the Reserve Bank of India reconciled accounts, it transpired that the bigger hole was at the MMCB, which lost Rs. 1030 crore. Three cases to this effect were filed in March and May 2001 in which two charge sheets have been filed but no conviction and no recoveries till date.[24]

13. UTI Scam (Rs. 9500 Crore Plus)

The units of UTI lost their glittering effect as early as 1992 following the attack on their credibility due to scam. Thereafter for several years the trust was used as a tool of political patronage resulting in investments in useless PSU stocks and corporates. In 1997, the government asked a committee to restructure UTI and bailed it out with Rs. 3500 crore. The UTI chief P.S. Subramanayam, remained silent spectator and corporates encashed their connections with UTI, then invested recklessly in a great hurry. Allegations of political manipulation were made, resulting into formation of a Joint Parliamentary Committee and a case against subramanayam for Rs. 32 crore investment in Lucknow-based cyberspace was filed. The case was filed in July 2001 but charge sheet could not be filed till date consequently there is no conviction and no recoveries as yet. Since then the government has sanctioned Rs. 6000 crore for its bailout.[25]

14. Home Trade (Rs. 1200 Crore)

This scam is in relation to the home trade, which managed to give the impression to the investor of being the place, which could manage your money. Unfortunately for the investors, Sanjay Agarwal had simply reinvented the wheel swindling a series of co-operative banks and using their money in the stock market. As the mischief spread, it transpired

23. *Ibid.*
24. *Ibid.*
25. *Ibid.*

that more than 17 co-operative banks in Maharashtra and Gujarat had been hit.[26]

The above list of scams and scandals is not exhaustive but illustrative. These instances represent only the tip of the iceberg. Many other such scams are also published in daily newspapers and magazines almost every alternative day. It is, thus, clear that in all these scandals a great financial deal is involved in which society has suffered a huge loss of money. Another important feature is that in all these economic crimes, persons of great skill and status are involved. They, through their skill and mechanism, manage the thing in such a way that *prima facie* their activities look proper and legal and in the interest of the general public but ultimately they are injurious to the society and causes great loss of their wealth. In these scandals, technology or mechanism adopted by the criminals, is such a wonderful use of skill that they are not easily detected and when I detected, it is too late to save the society from their effect. It is also very difficult to trace the fault of culprit easily. Another remarkable thing, to be noted, is that in such type of cases, speed of investigation and action taken are so slow that people generally forget the scam at the time of decision. It is also true that in these cases the delay is also a denial of justice and it is largely done to the advantage of scamsters.

Take, for example, the 1992 stocks scam. By the time Harshad Mehta was finally convicted the first time, 126 months after the fraud was bursted, he had been dead for a year and over a dozen big and small banks, which were involved with Mehta in this case are yet to get their money back. In the Bofors case itself, while the Hinduja brothers continue to take the battle from one courtroom to another, two of the main accused—S.K. Bhatnagar and Win Chaddha—died in 2000 and 2001. It is not only in these cases that delay is caused in the courts but in many of such cases. In many cases such as fodder scam case, 1992 stocks case, special courts are set-up but even these courts did not help.[27]

The delay in decisions is great relief to the scamsters and since public memory is short-lived, these scams get buried with the lapse of time. "P.C. Sharma, Director, CBI characterises the saga of delay as intrinsic to scams. The architect of swindles is always some one in power or a person who has bought access to power. Usually, defrauders are either politicians in power or those who generate political power using public moolah. And the very access that allows swindlers to script their scams also enables them to insure themselves from what is famously called the law taking its own course. Says Sharma, "Even when the law

26. *Ibid.*
27. *Ibid.*, p. 34.

does take its own course, scamsters work the system using a combination of illicitly created cushion of wealth and circle of influence to try and evade the consequences". The surfeit of scams proves that if a system cannot punish the guilty, it will breed more scamsters."[28]

From the above examples it is easy to conclude that financial loss to the society from white-collar crimes is enormous. This is not the situation in our country only but also in many advanced countries like USA, UK, etc. As regard to the financial loss caused by white-collar crimes in USA, the most affluent country in the world, the situation is alarming. These crimes result in serious financial loss to a single individual or to the business community or consumer public. The exact financial loss to the government caused by tax fraud is difficult to determine but is undoubted enormous. The amount of reportable income that goes unreported each year is estimated to range from $25 billion to $40 billion. It is estimated that the cost to the public annually of securities frauds, is probably in the $500 million to $1 billion range. It is also estimated that nearly $500 million is spent annually on worthless or misrepresented drugs and therapeutic devices. Fraudulent and deceptive practice in the home repair and improvement field are said to result in $500 million to $1 billion loss annually; and in the automobile repair field alone, fraudulent practices have been estimated to cost $100 million annually. Individual white-collar criminals are some time responsible for losses that are quite beyond the scale of most traditional crimes.[29]

These glittering examples of corruption clearly indicate that white-collar crimes have eaten the economic fabric of nation. The crime polluted atmosphere in India is a great threat to the existence of the society and it is rightly observed by Justice V.R. Krishna Iyer that "Economic offence often are subtle murders practised on the community or sabotage of the national economy".[30] The Supreme Court of India also sharply reacted on the increasing trend of economic crimes. Hon'able Court observed, "A murder may be committed in the heat of moment upon passion being aroused. An economic offence is committed with cool calculation and deliberate design with an eye on personal profit regardless of the consequence to the community."[31]

28. *Ibid.*
29. President's Commission on Law Enforcement and Administration of Justice, Task Force Report; Crime and its impact—an Assessment, Washington, D.C., U.S. Government Printing Office, 1967, pp. 102-09.
30. Justice V.R. Krishna Iyer's address in Seminar on current trends in criminology; Vigyan Bhavan, New Delhi, Feb. 22 to 24, 1974.
31. Supreme Court viewed in State of Gujarat *vs.* Mohanlal Titamalji Porwal; AIR 1987 SC 1321; & 1987 Cr.L.J. 1061.

It is, thus, clear that financial loss to the community is greater in case of white-collar crimes than that of the traditional crimes. At present in India, creation of artificial scarcity, producing blue films, pornographic literature, circulation of black-money, creation of false shares and debentures, bogus chit funds, bogus financial institutions, black-marketing, hoarding, producing spurious drugs and cosmetics, cheating, forgery, etc. are rampant. These crimes are more devastating than all other crimes as they shocks the bone marrow of economic structure of the nation.[32]

Thus, in all the white-collar crimes, financial implications are involved. In other words, each white-collar crime has an essential element of economic interest. So, each white-collar crime, in fact, is essentially an economic crime but reverse is not true. Analysing the nature of these crimes, "Finn and Holfman (1976) have suggested that we label this type of criminal activity "economic-crime" rather than "white-collar crime", because the term "economic-crime" more accurately reflects the objective of this type of offences-economic gain and does not imply that only the wealthy or those in executive positions perpetrate such crimes".[33] This new title to the white-collar crimes seems proper because all the white-collar crimes are actually economic crimes and they involve a greater money transactions. Actually, in all white-collar crimes, economic gain is the central point.

Despite all this, white-collar criminals are not apprehensive of losing their social reputation. These people do not accept law in its real sense because their legal adviser help them in interpreting law according to their own interest and implementation of laws become difficult. Tax evasion, mismanagement in share market and administration of companies, black marketing, hoarding, violation of economic regulations, fraudulent execution of construction and supply contracts, and corruption in various activities have been accepted as some of the white-collar crimes prevalent in the society by the Committee on Prevention of Corruption, 1962 (The Santhanam Committee) in his report.

For convenience, white-collar crimes are classified in following four categories:

3.1 Professional Crimes

Crime in professionals is not new in India. In ancient India, crime in various professions was prevalent in various forms such as fraud, cheating, misappropriation, false weight and measures, etc. and they were treated as an act of severe punishment. Corrupt practice in medical profession and business was treated as equivalent to theft.

---

32. Prabhat Chandra Tripathi, *op. cit.*, p. 36.
33. Vetter and Silverman, The Nature of Crime; *op. cit.*, pp. 233-75.

There is no profession without the problem of criminality and this problem has been increased considerably with the advancement in the nature and techniques of the various professions. The professions involving technical expertise and skill provide sufficient opportunities for white-collar crimes. Such professions, which come readily to one's mind, are medical profession, engineering, legal practice, private educational institutions and so on, where opportunities for committing white-collar crimes are abundant.

3.1.1 Medical Profession

White-collar crimes in medical profession are very common since long. In ancient period Manu Smriti[34] and Brihaspati Smriti[35] specific mention of criminality in this profession in the form of plicate drugs and wrongful conduct of physicians.

It may be that "most of the people belonging to the medical profession may not commit criminal or unethical acts in the course of their profession but still the number of those who violate the professional and legal norms is not insignificant. The most common instances are illegal abortions, false medical certificates and unnecessary prolonged treatment in many cases. Another widespread violation consists of prescribing medicines, which one is not supposed to having regard to his practice or the system of medicine permitted to be followed by him. For instance, some of the medicines of the appopathic system freely administered by many physicians practising in the Unani and Ayurvedic system without their having the faintest idea of the properties and the possible repercussions of those medicines".[36] Similarly in India many medicines, which have been banned nationally and internationally, are freely available on medical stores; even doctors prescribe them. Through this unethical and illegal service, doctors and drug mafias are earning huge amount of money at the risk of public health and safety. Many expired drugs, used disposable syringes, etc. are flooded in open sale market and uneducated poor people are using them without knowing their effects.

Another area where white-collar crimes are commonly committed by persons belonging to medical profession include secret service to criminals by giving expert opinion leading to their acquittal and selling sample drugs and medicines to patients or chemists. Causing unnecessary delay in treatment, keeping to the patient for a long time in nursing home, unwanted operation and many other such tactics are frequently

---

34. Manu IX: 284; Manu Smiriti; *op. cit.*, p. 522.
35. Brihaspati smriti: 360-68; *op. cit.*, pp. [illegible]-80.
36. Ahmad Siddique: Criminology; *op. cit.*, pp. [illegible]08-[illegible]

adopted by the doctors in their profession with a view to extracting huge sums from the patients. All these have, become an accepted norm, particularly by those who either do not have a good practice or have only marginal earning.

The fake and misleading advertising is yet another area in this profession in which the white-collar criminals operate. They make illegal and misleading claims of medical cure through advertisements in newspapers, magazines, radio and television. Similar advertisements for cosmetics and adulterated food are also widespread in practice. The innocent public is cheated and misguided by such advertisements. This type of the practice adopted by these persons is not only criminal in nature but also anti-social and injurious to public health.

3.1.2 Engineering Profession

Engineering profession is another floodgate area in which white-collar criminals are flourishing in modern India. In this profession underhand dealings with contractors and suppliers, passing of sub-standard works, use of sub-standard materials and maintenance of bogus records of work charged labour, are some of the common examples of white-collar crimes. Scandals of this kind are always reported in newspapers and magazines almost every day. Construction of buildings, roads, canals, dams and bridges with sub-standard material not only endangers public safety but also results into huge loss to public exchequer. Since this profession is based on high technical skill, defect is not very easy to detect and culprits escape easily. Engineering profession is a backbone of the country's development and so, corruption in this profession is a setback to the development plans of the government.

3.1.3 Legal Profession

One time most reputed legal profession in India is not looked with much respect these days. It is not, however, true that all lawyers are dishonest but many adopts corrupt and unethical methods just to procure clientage. Deteriorating standards or legal education in India is yet another reason of degradation of this profession. The instances of fabricating false evidences, engaging professional witnesses, violating ethical standards of legal profession, delaying litigation and use of other dilatory tactics with the help of staff of the court, are of some of the common practices which are prevalent in this profession in modern India and code of conduct for legal professionals is only an ornamental document.

Generally, the professional crooks and criminal gangs have their trusted lawyers who arrange things for them and keep themselves ready with bail bonds or other legal weapons to avoid arrest of these criminals. If they are arrested, their lawyer comes forward by ways and means to arrange their release. These lawyers arrange professional alibis, cooked witnesses in close liaison with the police for defending the gangsters and in return they extract huge money by these unethical tactics. It is, perhaps, because of the peculiar nature of this profession that the lawyers have to resort to these tactics in order to survive in the profession which is becoming Barnes and Tetters have made the following comment to this regard:

"A lawyer must do his duty in defending a person accused of crime. This applies equally to thöse from known criminal elements. There is a difference between a criminal lawyer and lawyer-criminal. So long as he handles his defence in a legal and ethical manner, he is only dispatching his duty as an attorney. It is when he carries his defence beyond the law and the ethical standards of his profession that he may be labelled a lawyer-criminal."[37] And in the present time latter category is abundant.

3.1.4 Educational Institutions

Education is yet another field where white-collar criminals operate more frequently. Illiteracy is the biggest crime against the people in India. Approximately half of Indian population is illiterate. According to Prof. J.K. Galbraith, an important requirement for economic development in any country is an educated population. It is rightly said that, "with nearly half the people and close to two-thirds of the women illiteracy, the transformation of the Indian economy is not an easy task. Even an efficient utilization of the world market requires production to specification, needs quality control and on an informed consciousness of the economic tasks involved. The success of the East Asian "tigers" and more recently of China has been based on a much higher level of literacy and basic education than India has. The persistence of endemic illiteracy in India, even in the younger age groups, is one of the basic social failures that shackle the Indian economy and society."[38]

Unfortunately, Indian States are not worried about this shameful state of affairs. According to Dharma Kumar, a distinguished Scholar of India's economic history, "public expenditure on education in India was a miserable 0.2 percent of National income in the nineteenth century and never much above 0.5 percent in the twentieth."[39]

37. Barnes, and ....
38. Jean Dreze and Amartya Kumar Sen, India: Economic development and social opportunity, A paper distributed by Dreze at a seminar in New Delhi, organized by the observer foundation in the first half of 1995.
39. Dharma Kumar (ed.), The Cambridge Economic History of India, Vol. II (UP), 1982, p. 937.

It clearly indicates that Indian States have failed in fulfilling their primary duty to educate people, which is pre-requisite of economic development of any nation. The result is that more and more private educational institutions are coming in the field. The foundation societies of these institutions manage to secure large sums through Government grants or financial aid by submitting fictitious and fake details about the institutions. The teachers and other staff, working in these institutions, are paid much less than what they actually sign for, thus, a huge amount is grabbed by the management in an illegal manner. The victimised teachers can hardly afford to make a complaint about this exploitation to high ups due to fear of being thrown out of job. They are, therefore, compelled to compromise with the situation. The fake and bogus enrolments of students, living in interior or distant places, is yet another source of illegal earning for them. They charge huge amounts by way of donations or capitation fees from these needy students. Even rackets operate in these institutions for procuring students to appear in different examinations on the basis of manipulated eligibility certificates or domicile certificates in return to huge sums. This has lowered down the standard of education in India which has made dark the future of younger generation.

Many privately run educational institutions and particularly those imparting professional education like medical, engineering, etc. enjoy the patronage of some influential politicians and education mafias and many of them are even owned by them. Many of such institutions are run only on papers and are functioning as commercial hops. Their main task is simply to arrange degrees to the students in return of huge money which is against the norms and spirit of government and U.G.C. rules.

According to one of the inspection report of the directorate of Delhi Government in 1997, of 16 private public schools, published in *Times of India* (August 20, 1997), the Schools are collecting quite a large amount of money from the students in the name of various funds such as pupil's fund, excursion fund, magazine fund and so on but the funds are used by the school authorities for other purposes. Many societies are using this fund in opening new Schools even outside Delhi. Most of the schools are collecting huge sum through selling thousands of admission forms at a high rate and their admission fee is also very high. These schools collect a large amount in the name of security or caution money which is either not refunded or if refunded it is returned very late and that too, without any interest. One of the interesting fact to be found by the inspection committee was that, schools are collecting science fees every month from all students, however, there was no separate laboratories for middle class and secondary classes. In some of the schools, a building fund is collected even though their building is complete in every respect.[40]

It is, thus, clear from the above discussion that these public schools have become educational shops and they are robbing the public. The nexus of businessmen; mafia, bureaucracy and politicians is clearly visible in the field of education. Businessmen and politicians treat opening and running schools as nothing but profit making activities. In this situation, setting up educational institutions has become a profitable business both financially and politically. According to one of the estimation more than 200 formers and present legislators and parliamentarians in Bihar are associated with colleges and universities to pursue their political and economic interests.[41] Similar is the position in other states of the country. The situation has become more critical in recent years because more and more colleges and schools are opening in the names of politicians or by the persons who are directly or indirectly connected with some politicians. This has polluted the climate of educational institutions, which have become a work-field of political activities in which more and more political interference persists at all level.

The P.B. Gajendragadkar Committee, appointed to look into the affairs of Banaras Hindu University, the most reputed university of India, wrote in its report: "The atmosphere in the university campus is surcharged with suspicion and fear, division runs through all the sections of the university community; the teachers appear to be divided." The students are divided and even the class IV employees are divided. Further it added that, "some of the causes which, in our view, have led to the recent unrest consist of incidents which partake of a criminal nature."[42]

The another area, which is to be taken care of, is that virus of casteism and regionalism plays its decisive role in all matters of educational institutions of modem time. Even in appointments, these factors are considered and academic qualifications and other qualities are sidetracked. So, education which these institutions are imparting, and the skill which they are producing is full of virus of many diseases which is supposed to be spread by them in the development process of the country. It has, therefore, rightly been commented that "In India there are more "Seminarists" than serious scholars doing teaching and research in so-called institutes and centres of excellence, whom Arthur Koestler

40. Girish Mishra, and Braj Kumar Pandey, *op. cit.*, pp. 142-43.
41. *Ibid* p. 147.
42. Report of the Banaras Hindu University, Inquiry Committee, New Delhi, July 1969, p. 13

aptly termed as "call girls". They hop from seminar to seminar and committee to committee with hardly any time for reading, writing and reflection. These people are nothing but parasites on the society and after they retire, there is nothing left behind to remind that they once existed. Since they manipulate to grab the resources belonging to the society without any *quid pro quo*, they are nothing but thieves and criminals."[43]

3.2 Business Crimes

Business community is the backbone of the economic development of a nation. This community generally controls most of the manufacturing assets of a nation. This super concentration of assets in the hands of business community and industrial corporations pose a great threat to our economic, political and social structure. In views of a British writer C.S. Lewis:

> "The greatest evil is not now done in those sordid dens of crime at Dickens loved to paint. It is not done even in concentration camps and labour camps. In those we see its final result. But it is conceived and ordered (moved, seconded, carried and minuted) in clean, carpeted, warmed and well-lighted offices, by quietmen with white-collars and cut finger nails, and smooth-shaven cheeks who do not need to raise their voices. Hence, naturally enough, my symbol for hell is something like... the offices of a thoroughly nasty business concern."[44]

White-collar crimes are rampant in business world. In most of the cases these crimes have been the result of violation of trust. Sutherland's research of white-collar crimes was also based on business, trade, commerce and industry. All the corporations, under study, were found to have been guilty of white-collar crimes and 98 percent of them were in the category of recidivist. Many were either illegal in their origin or began illegal activities immediately after their origin. The crime committed by them involved illegal contracts, combinations or conspiracies in restraint of trade, misrepresentation in advertising, infringement against copy rights and trade marks, unfair labour practices, bribing public officials and so on.[45]

---

43. Girish Mishra and Braj Kumar Pandey, *op. cit.*, p. 155.
44. C.S. Lewis, The Screw tape letters and Screw tape purpose (New York: Macmillian, 1961).
45. E.H. Sutherland: Crime of corporations, Gilbert Geis and Robert, F. Meher; *op. cit.*, pp. 79-84.

These crimes are rampant in the business world with a sole 'objective of profit-earning'. Modern age of competitive economic and life style has brought a radical change in increasing human needs and such crimes are actually the result of human greed and not of human need. These crimes are committed by top ranked executives of a corporation who deals with the planning, manufacturing, distribution, pricing and advertising. These corporations are generally engaged in many illegal actions such as- undermining the effectiveness of collective bargaining efforts by unions, conspiring with competitors to keep prices on a level with their products, drastically cutting prices in only one product area for the purpose of eliminating competition, misrepresenting products in advertising or in sales practices and so on.[46]

Dishonesty in commercial transactions is not a healthy trend for free and fair economic development of a nation. In the words of Marshal B. Clinard, problem of white-collar criminality has its root in competitive business community which tries to oust their rival competitors in order to earn huge profits. This is also not good from society point of view. In fact, competition is not always bad. Good quality, less profit of margin, honesty in dealing with consumers, free hand to choose anything from anywhere are some of the admirable results of competitive business. So, practices or arrangements that disparage honesty in commercial transactions are detrimental to our economic growth. In order to be successful, competition must be free and fair. As Kintner rightly said that:

> "Honest competitors must be protected from predators and shielded from temptation to adopt the tactics of tricksters in the battle for business survival. And consumers must be protected against commercial chicanery, because fairness requires that they receive an honest product honesty represented, and because consumers are citizen and will ultimately determine the degree of control that government will exercise over business."[47]

Thus, white-collar crimes represent the offences of businessmen who are in a position to determine the policies and activities of business.[48] Sutherland also attributed the highest degree of criminality to business world which includes traders, businessmen and industrialists and their immunity from criminal sanctions in the following words:

---

46. C.H. Mc Caghy: Deviant Behaviour, New York, The Macmillian Co. 1964, p. 204.
47. E. Kintner; An Anti trust primer; New York, The Macmillan Co. 1964, p. 14.
48. Walter Reckless: The Crime problem; p. 345.

> "The most powerful group in medieval society secured relative immunity from punishment by 'benefit of clerg' and now the present most powerful group secures relative immunity by benefit of business."[49] He concluded from his research that the ideal businessman and the large corporations are very much like the professional thief. Firstly, because their violations of law are frequent and continued, secondly, the illegal behaviour by the corporations is much more prevalent than what the prosecutions indicate, thirdly, the businessmen who violate laws regulating business does not loose status among his business associates and fourthly, businessmen feel and express contempt for legislators, bureaucrats and other government officials and for the law.[50]

What has been discussed above for the American society is equally true for Indian business community. During the last century, economic and political system in India has changed considerably and business community played a powerful role in this change. The Primary concern of businessman is to earn a huge profit, may it be at the cost of sacrificing the general principles of free and fair competition.

Due to this materialistic tendency of business community and unfair competition tactics "there are striking pressures that promote white-collar crime in business. The decline of the *laissez-faire* ethics has imposed contradictory conditions on business operation. On the other hand, there is an espousal of the doctrine of fierce competition, while on the other hand they search for security—for protection against market uncertainty."[51]

So, the problem of white-collar criminality in business world is very acute, both in terms of variety and extent, in India, as is evident from the conclusion of the Santhanam Committee, appointed to report on the corruption in India. The committee commented on the corrupt behaviour of businessmen and industrialists in the following words:

> "To these, corruption is not only an easy method to secure large unearned profits, but also the necessary means to enable them to be in a position to pursue their vocations or retain their position among their own competitor. It is these persons who indulge in evasion and avoidance of taxes, accumulate large amounts of unaccounted money by various methods such as obtaining

---

49. Sutherland; White-collar crime (1961), p. 47.
50. E.H. Sutherland; Crime of Corporations; *op. cit.*, pp. 83-84.
51. Michael Conaut; Antitrust in the Motion Picture Industry (Berkeley: University of California Press, 1972), p. 1.

licences in the name of bogus firms and individuals, trafficking in licences, suppressing profits by manipulation of accounts to avoid taxes... and under-valuation of transactions in immovable property. It is they who have control over large funds and are in a position to spend considerable sums of money on entertainment. It is they who maintain an army of liaison and contact men, some of whom live, spend and entertain ostentatiously. We are unable to believe that so much money is being spent only for the purpose of getting things done quickly.... Contractors and suppliers who are perfect in the art of getting business by under-cutting, of making good the loss by passing-off sub-standard works and goods generally spare no pain or expenditure in creating a favourable atmosphere. Possession of large amounts of unaccounted money by various persons including those belonging to the industrial and commercial classes is a major impediment in the purification of public life. If anti-corruption activities are to be successful, it must be recognised that it is an important to fight these unscrupulous agencies of corruption as to eliminate corruption in the public services. In fact, they go together."[52]

Commenting on the extremely dishonest behaviour of Indian business community, it has been observed:

> "Business community in India of large and small merchants are basically a dishonest bunch of crooks... while it is true that the object of businessmen is to make profit, there are degrees and degrees of making profit, and no where in the world do businessmen get rich so quickly as they do in India..."[53]

It is, thus, clear that white-collar criminality in Indian business community is also of a high degree like other developed countries of the world. Following are some of the main white-collar crimes committed by Indian traders. The list is not exhaustive but illustrative only.

3.2.1 Hoarding, Black Marketing and Adulteration

The white-collar crimes commonly committed by the Indian trade and business community are hoarding, profiteering and black-marketing. The report of the Monopolies Inquiry Commission expressed great

52. Report of Santhanam Committee on the prevention of corruption 1964, pp. 18 and 65.
53. Winifred Bose, The Trader in 'opinion', quoted by N.R.M. Menon in his unpublished thesis, a Socio legal study of white-collar crime in India, 1968.

concern about the chronic problem of hoarding, profiteering and black-marketing of essential commodities by traders in India. In times of shortage and scarcity of consumer commodities, the traders withdraw the stock and subsequently dispose it at exorbitant prices. Commenting upon the inquiry commission expressed its grave concern as follows:

> "There is hardly anybody in India who has not been a victim of the practice of hoarding, cornering and profiteering. Whenever there is a slight shortage even temporary- in any consumer goods for which the demand is urgent and inelastic, almost every trader—it is perhaps unnecessary to use the qualification 'almost'—conceals his stock and blandly tells the customers that he has not got the commodity in stock, often putting the blame on producers for keeping him in short supply. After some time when the customer can no longer do without the goods, he proceeds to dispose of his stock at exorbitant prices... Wheat, rice, sugar, edible oils, drugs, baby food, each of these commodities and many others have had their share of hoarding and cornering practice... They have been called wicked, anti-social, and criminal but still these make their appearance every time, there is any apprehension of even a slight shortage of such commodities."[54]

Adulteration in food items, drinks and spurious drugs are yet another criminal activities that are frequently committed by businessmen. These activities are not only injurious to public health but sometime causes death of customers. In our country, the problem is so widespread that from 25 percent to 70 percent of most of the foodstuffs consumed are adulterated or contaminated.[55] The problem is more acute in present time than ever before. Fruits and Green vegetables, which were once treated as most safe and hygenic to the health, are no more safer. Recently a study is made by U.K. Department for International Development, in Partnership with the Indian Agricultural Research Institute, Delhi University and Banaras Hindu University about the vegetables grown and sold in Delhi and Varanasi. They tested heavy metal contents in Okra (Bhindi), Cauliflower and Spinach. According to their just released findings about Spinach, as much as 72 percent of the Spinach tested had lead concentrations higher than the prevention of food adulteration permissible limit of 2.5 mg/kg. What was most disconcerting was the fact that prevention of food adulteration standards

54. Report of Monopolies Inquory Commission of India.
55. *Swasth Hind*, Ministry of Health, Government of India, March 1963, Quoted by Menon.

were much higher than the international limit of 0.3 mg/kg set by the international food standards, set by the Codex Alimentarius Commission. So, "if we had gone by the international standards, none of the spinach samples would have been within safe limits," says Dr. Dolfte Lintelo, one of the authors of the study.[56]

The same is true for sale and production of spurious drugs in our country. According to the Pharmaceutical Inquiry Committee, Government of India, "the spurious drugs trade flourish in India to a colossal extent. This is due to the greed of the manufacturers, ignorance of the poor consumers who go in for cheap medicines from unauthorised dealers and the shortage of genuine goods."[57]

These crimes are actually the outcome of desire of businessmen to minimize their cost of production and increase their profit. Adulterated and substandard products are thrust on customers in order to increase profits but they are dangerous to them and sometimes lead to deaths. For example, substandard cooking stoves, pressure cookers, LPG gas cylinder with defective regulators, substandard electric goods and so on, cost many lives. These deaths could have avoided, but they are not avoided intentionally because business community has scant regard for human beings as compared to the profit deity.[58]

Our society is afraid of these adulterated food, drugs and articles and they are vigilant enough to save themselves from bad effects of these adulterated goods. In West Bengal several citizen signed and submitted to the law commission, suggested that persons guilty of adulteration of medicines and food should be punished with death and life imprisonment respectively, their property should be confiscated and publicity be given to their misdeeds through the mass media.[59] Law Commission, however, did not consider the suggestion because of some other reasons but this is clear, that gradually public opinion is organising against these crimes.

Thus, the answer to the question, why Businessmen violate the law, is their greed for earning wealth by shortcut methods and very fast. It is rightly commented that "most businessmen, run afoul of the law of economic reasons—they want to make a fast buck."[60]

---

56. *Sunday Hindustan Times*, New Delhi, Late city edition dated March 30, 2003, p. 15.
57. Pharmaceutical Inquiry Committee, Ministry of Commerce and Industry, 1954, pp. 146-47.
58. Girish Mishra and Braj Kumar Pandey, *op. cit.*, p. 54.
59. Twenty-ninth Report of Law Commission of India (1966), p. 71.
60. Robert E. Lane, Why Business Violate the Law, Published in Gilbert Geis and Robert, F. Meher, *op. cit.*, p. 103.

3.2.2 Tax Evasion and Problem of Black Money

Tax evasion is not confined to businessmen alone, nevertheless it is one of the most important offences, which is frequently committed by business community in India. Income tax, wealth tax, estate duty and sales tax are some of areas where tax evasion is very frequent. The loss resulting from these violations to the state exchequer in tremendous. Apart from the financial implications of the problem, there are other dimensions of this evil such as, the use of the tainted black-money on corrupting governmental machinery and public servant, degradation of the moral and ethical values of the society by the impact of such money, disrespect, contempt and cynicism towards law in general and so on.[61]

There is, however, a distinction between tax evasion and tax avoidance. While for the society point of view, there is hardly any real distinction between the two, but in law, the former is a crime and the latter is regarded as legitimate. So, in the areas of income tax, wealth tax, estate duty and sales tax the offender generally does not evade but avoids paying taxes.[62] The Bombay High Court recognized the distinction between the two and observed as follows:

> "A citizen is perfectly entitled to exercise his ingenuity so as to arrange his affairs as may make it possible for him legally and lawfully not to pay tax, and if his ingenuity succeeds, however reluctant the court may be to acknowledge the cleverness of the assessee, the court must give effect to the letter of the taxation law rather than stain that letter against the assessee.[63]

The approach reflected in the judgment is in line with the fundamental principle of criminal law that an act cannot be a crime till it is fixed in the express words of the law. Nevertheless, the fact remains that such an interpretation of tax statutes gives a long rope to those who have scant respect for taxation laws.[64]

The main reason of the problem of tax evasion is the complicated nature of tax laws in our country due to which they cannot be administered smoothly. This complexity of tax laws in India has provided sufficient scope for the taxpayers to evade taxes. Tax evader generally takes benefit of these loopholes in laws and manages to manipulate their affairs accordingly. Tax authorities are generally helpless in estimating the real and exact income of the businessmen and

---

61. Ahmad Siddique, Criminology *op. cit.*, p. 394.
62. *Ibid.*, p. 396.
63. Provident Investment Company *vs.* I.T.C., AIR 1954, Bombay, 95.
64. Ahmad Siddique, *op. cit.*, p. 396.

professionals. It is often alleged that the actual tax paid by them is only a fraction of their income and rest of the money goes into circulation as "black-money". Due to complex nature of the tax laws the menace of tax evasion and 'black-money' continues unabated and it is causing great loss to the government exchequer.

Thus, black money economy is flourishing in India unabated its dangerous effects are spreading day-by-day. However, government has been trying its best to handle this evil and adopted, various measures from time to time, but all failed in their required results. Indian judiciary has also expressed its grave concern over the spreading virus of this black money. In a majority decision in *R.K. Garg* vs. *Union of India*, Supreme Court upholding the validity of special Bearer Bonds (Immunities and Exemption) Act, 1981, observed that the Act was not intended to encourage tax evasion in future and condone such evasion committed in past, but the real object of the Act was to launch a nation-wide search to unearth undisclosed wealth by encouraging small incentive to those who declare their undisclosed cash. The main intention was to unearth black-money so as to prevent further loss of government revenue.

This view of our Supreme Court actually encourages and upholds the various initiative measures adopted by the government to unearth the black money through the method of mobilising public opinion instead of adopting coercive methods. This, I think, is the best way in the present environment to bring black money and black money holders in the mainstream of economic development of the nation.

3.2.3 Fraud, Cheating, Misrepresentation and Violation of Export, Import Regulation, etc.

Other white-collar crimes which are quite prevalent in business world are fraud, cheating, misrepresentation and violation of the Foreign Exchange Act and Imports and Exports Act. According to the report of Santhanam Committee, secret hoards of foreign exchange are built up abroad by Indian businessmen through under-invoicing of exports and over-invoicing of imports.[65] The committee also found that many firms are involved in cheating, forgery, misrepresentation and other breaches of export and import regulations.[66]

Fraud, cheating and misrepresentation in advertising are very common in Indian business community. It is a matter of common experience that most of the advertisement in periodicals, radio and television, exaggerate the value of the product and quality. Many

65. Santhanam Committee Report, p. 253.
66. *Ibid.*, pp. 18 and 65.

advertisements are designed to sell products, which are physically dangerous with the dangers, denied, minimised or unmentioned. Most of these advertisements belong to the drugs and cosmetics business. There are corporations or companies, set-up with the sole purpose of pursuing criminal activities like smuggling, defrauding and cheating people and government. In India many non-banking financial companies are mushrooming and deliberately defrauding innocent investors who are tempted through attractive plan and higher rates of interest. They collect a great sum of money from innocent subscribers and run away with it without leaving any symbol of their existence. We can name many such companies as Bagrian Shoes, Gangappa Paper, Rama Fibres, Mayur Syntex, Padma Paper, Multitech international and more recently J.V.G. Pvt. Ltd. and so on. They freely roam about and carryon their activities with the connivance of the stock exchange and public sector banks. Consequently, Government of India realised it and bring in SEBI (Securities and Exchange Board of India) in order to curb the activities of these white-collar pickpockets, but even now these operations are not completely curbed.[67] How they cheat to the innocent investors may be illustrated by the following well-known scam in India:

3.2.4 Harshad Mehta Stock Market Scam

This scam had once shaked the confidence of innocent investors in Indian stock market. It is alleged that this scam of which Harshad Mehta was the key hero, was the result of nexus between politicians, public sector banks and Harshad Mehta. "In 1992 Harshad Mehta made the share prices skyrocketting instigating the innocent investors to buy shares and get rich overnight. In this process, quite a substantial number of them went to their ruin when the bubble burst after fictitious trading rings came to light and the banks found themselves cheated of $ 1.4 billion."[68]

Soon after the scam came to light, the Reserve Bank of India set-up the Jankiraman Committee and a Joint Parliamentary Committee was also set-up, for some time.

On the basis of various reports of the Jankiraman Committee, K.N. Kabra in a pamphlet presented his analysis that "through share market operations financed by means of illegal transfer of bank's funds via deceitful deals in securities represented by bogus BRs and other devices, the brokers would have by means of the sale of the public sector undertaking (PSUs) shares booked enough profits to be able to square up their accounts with the banks and organisations like NHB, that such

67. Girish Mishra and Braj Kumar Pandey, *op. cit.*, pp. 47-48.
68. *Ibid.*, p. 50.

stock exchange deals were financed by banks funds would have remained buried in the account books of the banks. It may be noted that the banks had an interest in rising share prices. The banks and the mutual funds floated by them were to off-load the cheaply obtained PSUs shares. Thus, the funding of brokers by them seems related to the manner in which PSUs disinvestments took place."[69]

Unfortunately, stock market crashed and a situation of crisis was created. Many innocent investors, especially small ones, lost most of their savings and some sank deeper in indebtedness. Most of this belonged to banks and public sector financial institutions.

There are many other such scams of this nature in which public is cheated or rather looted by the connivance of business sectors. Unlike common crimes these crimes are generally non-violent in nature. This kind of robbery is committed not by weapons but by cunningness and deceptive methods of the business community. It is, thus, clear that white-collar crimes are rampant in business sectors and perhaps there is no business without the problem of white-collar criminality.

3.3 Political Crimes

Misuse of public position by public servants and politicians have reached at a saturation point in Indian society nowadays. Bribery and corruption is one of the most talked about subjects today in India. They have penetrated deeply almost in every department of government, central or state, public or private enterprises and so on. There is a general feeling that it is very difficult to get things done without bribing to the present bureaucracy and political machinery, which leads to unnecessary delay in the disposal of files. Instances are not wanting of the improper use of the authority by the politicians in power, leaders of government, both at the centre and the states and people in public and private life. For example, the central bureau of investigation, while inquiring the conduct of public affairs in the State of Orissa under Mr. Biju Patnaik and Mr. Biren Mitra as successive chief ministers of the State after the mid-term election of 1961 has made the following observation:

> "There was gross evasion, by the administration under Mr. Patnaik and Mr. Mitra's tenure of office as the then chief ministers of the State of Orissa, of all the normal rules of procedure in the purchasing of the Orissa Government to the direct benefit of companies in which the two ministers or their families had substantial financial interests."[70]

---

69. Kamal Nayan Kabra, Financial Sector Scam; Fruits of Liberalization, New Delhi, 1992, p. 3.
70. *The Hindustan Times*, Feb. 1965; Quoted by K.D. Gaur; Criminal Law and Criminology (2002) at p. 287.

Mr. C. Subramaniam, the then minister of Steel and Heavy Industries, Government of India was charged by the public accounts committee for protecting a group of black listed commercial firms from taking action against such firms.[71]

Corruption[72] in various forms has always existed, not only in India but almost in all the societies, despite that they are politically more advanced. What distinguishes India from other societies is the variety, degree and frequency of corruption affecting our society. To quote James Cameron an eminent journalist of Fleet Street:

---

71. *The Hindustan Times*, August 6, 1966; quoted by *ibid.*
72. The Commission on the prevention of corruption has defined 'corruption':
 (i) Corruption includes improper or selfish exercise of power and influence attached to a public office or to the special position occupied in public life.
 (ii) The Prevention of Corruption Act, 1988 in section 13(1) (a), (b), (c), (d) and (e) defines the offence of criminal misconduct by a public servant as follows:
 a. if he habitually accepts or obtains or agrees to accept or attempts to obtain from any person for himself or for any other person any gratification other than legal remuneration as a motive or reward such as is mentioned in section 7; or
 b. if he habitually accepts or obtains or agrees to accept or attempts to obtain for himself or for any other person, any valuable thing without consideration or for a consideration which he knows to be inadequate from any person whom he knows to have been, or to be, or to be likely to be concerned in any proceeding or business transacted or about to be transacted by him, or having any connection with the official functions of himself or of any public servant to whom he is subordinate, or from any person whom he knows to be interested in or related to the person so concerned; or
 c. if he dishonestly or fraudulently misappropriates or otherwise converts for his own use any property entrusted to him or under his control as a public servant to allows any other person to do so; or
 d. if he—
 (i) by corrupt or illegal means, obtains for himself or for any other person any valuable thing or pecuniary advantage; or
 (ii) by abusing his position as a public servant, obtains for himself or for any other person any valuable thing or pecuniary advantage; or
 (iii) while holding office as a public servant, obtains or any person, any valuable thing or pecuniary advantage without any public interest; or
 e. if he or any person on his behalf, is in possession or has, at any time during the period of his office, been in possession for which the public servant cannot satisfactorily account, of pecuniary resources or property disproportionate to his known sources of income.

Explanation: For the purposes of this section "known sources of income" means income received from any lawful source and such receipt has been intimated in accordance with the provisions of any law, rules or orders for the time being applicable to a public servant.

"In India, corruption, public or private venality, is sanctified by the oldest traditions, it is denied by nobody, indeed, the totality and pervasiveness of Indian corruption is almost a matter of national pride. Just as India's droughts are the driest, her famines the most cruel, the over-population the most uncontrollable, so are all aspects of India's corruption and bribery the most wholly widespread and spectacular."[73]

Thus, corruption in its wider sense includes all forms of dishonest gains in cash, kind or position by persons in government and those associated with public and political affairs. Corruption in political persons is a matter of serious concern because they are the persons who lead the country and to shape its future through their position and capacity. They are the law-makers, policy-makers and people have faith in them. It is, therefore, rightly said that:

"Corruption among ministers and other political personages is more dangerous than corruption in the bureaucracy or in governmental machinery in terms of the enormity of the stakes involved in public life. Corruption and indecency in political life informs all the sections of society since violations are committed by those very persons who are expected to set the norms of social and political conduct. It is common knowledge that many politicians in power and their kith and kin have reaped a good harvest in terms of money and good positions through the abuse of government machinery at their disposal."[74]

Unfortunately, there is no effective mechanism to check the misdeeds of politicians. The Santhanam Committee noted that while there were elaborate rules to ensure probity among officials, there were none for ministers, legislators and political parties.[75]

3.3.1 The Nexus among Criminals, Bureaucrats, Businessmen and Politicians

The most common forms of political corruption in India are in the forms of organised crimes such as political grafts, violation of election laws, and abuse of official and political machinery to maintain nexus with big business. White-collar crime being a king of organised crime, so all these are the result of nexus of criminals and politicians.

73. Ahmad Siddique, Criminology, *op. cit.*, p. 397.
74. *Ibid.*, p. 398.
75. Santhanam Committee Report, pp. 101-02.

One of such nexus commonly operates at the time of elections to the Parliament, State Assemblies and local bodies. In order to capture political power and their party's victory at polls, the politicians generally take support of criminal elements and utilize them for illegal practices, such as booth capturing and rigging, to accomplish their political ends. Black money and muscles power is frequently used in these elections, which results in to poll violence, vote buying and even mass causalities. The recent election of few State Assemblies including Bihar is a glaring example of such nexus. This has resulted into criminalisation of India's politics. Though corruption in public life has been witnessed ever since the beginning of human civilization, it has assumed a widespread global phenomenon only in recent years. It is not limited to the boundaries of a state or nation only but in many cases it may have its connections across local limits. Bofors case, Harshad Mehta bank scam, sugar scandal, Jain Hawala case, Jharkhand Mukti Morcha M.P.'s bribery case, urea scam, Lakhubhai cheating case, Bihar fodder scam, out of term government accommodation allotment scam, allotment of gas and petrol pumps are some of the examples in which corruption is not confined to the four corners of one nation. With economic globalization, problem of corruption in public life has become more and more complex.

Many instances can be cited where well known criminals and members of mafia group contesting and even winning elections. A senior police officer has cited the following facts and figures to show the extent of criminality in politics:

> "...in the panchayat elections held in 1984, out of 75,000 Gram Panchayats more than 50 percent of the candidates were reported to have had a criminal history. In one Gram Panchayat, according to a police officer, the prospective candidate announced on the eve of the election that anyone contesting against him would not be found alive. The message went home and he was elected unanimously. Elected Gram Panchayats appointed 8,905 Block Pramukhs, more than 30 percent of whom had a criminal history, according to police sources. There have been a number of people with criminal background who have contested and won the state assembly elections".[76]

Similarly in recent panchayat election held in 2005 in M.P., many candidates of criminal background, not only contested but won the election due to money and muscle power and through terrorising people of grave consequences. In few villages and blocks, there was a fear of a

76. P.R. Rajgopal, Violence and Response, p. 134.

local notorious dacoit gang due to which people did not come out for poll and their relatives and near and dear won the election without any hard labour. Several such instances can be cited to show the close association between politicians and criminals.

Once politicians take help of criminals for their political benefits, they become bound to oblige them on reaching to the power. Consequently, these criminals are helped by the politicians in their criminal activities like smuggling, kidnapping, manufacturing and vending of illicit liquor, forcibly taking possession of land and house properties of others and so on. In return to their help, politicians oblige these criminals by granting permits for bus and truck, dealership of cement, iron and steel, fair price shops and so on. Thus, a nexus has been developed between politicians and criminals.

These criminals operate in the various parts of the country in encroachment upon public land, forest resources and mineral wealth, illegal mining and pilferage of minerals. They operate all these illegal activities fearlessly because of protective umbrella provided by politicians. Government of India has shown its serious concern about this deadly nexus and adopted various precautionary measures to curb this dangerous trend.

3.3.1.1 The Vohra Committee Report

The Government of India appointed a five-men committee under the chairmanship of Shri N.N. Vohra on 9.7.1993 to probe into the nexus among politicians, government high officials and industrialists with the mafia gangs. This was apparently done after a series of bomb blasts in Bombay, occurring shortly after the demolition of the Babri Mosque in Ayodhya for which the hand of under world don, operating within and outside India, was suspected. It was suspected that this could not have happened without these elements having been protected by the functionaries of the concerned government departments, especially customs, income tax, police and others. It was, therefore, necessary to identify the linkages and also to determine how such information could be timely collected and acted upon in future.[77]

The committee examined the reports and material provided by the secretary, Research and Analysis Wing (RAW), Director of the Central Bureau of Investigation (CBI) and the Intelligence Bureau (IB) regarding the present state of affairs and various suggestions and measures to curb the criminal nexus among mafia, politician and bureaucrats and presented its report which was tabled before the house of the parliament on 3rd August, 1995.

---

77. Government of India (Ministry of Home Affairs), Vohra Committee Report, New Delhi, 1955, p. 2.

The committee acknowledged the existence of such a nexus and reported that "All over India syndicates have become a law unto themselves. Even in the smaller towns and rural areas, muscle-men have become the order of the day. Hired assassins have become a part of these organisations. The nexus between the criminal gangs, police, bureaucracy and politician has come out clearly in various parts of the country. The existing criminal justice system, which was essentially designed to deal with individual offences and crimes, is unable to deal with the activities of the mafia; the provisions of law in regard to economic offences are weak; there are insurmountable legal difficulties in attaching/confiscation of the property acquired through mafia activities".[78]

It has been alleged in the report that criminal gangs enjoy patronage of politicians. The report mentioned the name of Iqbal Mirchi of Bombay, one of the main accused in the Bombay blast case of January, 1993, as an example to show, how a ordinary person rose to a gangstor.

The director of Intelligence Bureau told the Vohra Committee that "There has been a rapid spread and growth of criminal gangs, armed senas, drug mafias, smuggling gangs, drug-peddlers and economic lobbies in the country which have, over the years developed an extensive network of contracts with the bureaucrats and government functionaries at the local levels, politicians, media persons and strategically located individuals in the non-State sector. Some of these syndicates also have international linkages, including the foreign intelligence agencies."[79]

Thus, Vohra Committee concluded that criminalisation of Indian politics is a dangerous threat to the Indian society in general and to the Indian democracy in particular. In this present scenario; the observation seems right that "when democracy becomes corrupt, the best gravitates to the bottom, the worst floats to the top and the vile is replaces by more vile".[80]

The Vohra Committee has recommended various measures to curb this nexus but the nexus among politicians, Government officials and criminals continues unabated as is evident from tehelka dotcom episode in which hero of this episode, Mr. Tarun Tejpal has exposed a nexus among many top politicians, military officials, government functionaries and criminals. Many other scams in India like Bofors, Urea, Sugar imports, Sukhram affair and Hawala deals are the glittering examples of such a nexus.

78. *Ibid.*, p. 3.
79. *Ibid.*, p. 4
80. Published in *Hindustan Times,* dt. 17.8.95

Due to these white-collar economic crimes which are the outcome of such a deadly nexus, India is facing a danger of economic imbalance. Economic crimes are now a universal truth and they have been prevalent in almost all the time but in our country, since the last general elections held in September/October 1999, there is an enormous increase in these scams. Corruption and scams have become rampant in this period, with the result, a large number of industries are showing losses. Never did the country face so many scandals and scams before. In this series of scams, some of them are discussed here to show the nexus among politicians, criminals, bureaucrats and big business houses.

3.3.1.2 The UTI Scam

In the early Nineties, US-64, a scheme of UTI, became a popular scheme for the middle class to park its savings. After P.S. Subramanyam took charge as the chairman in 1998, UTI equity investments became arbitrary and funds were deliberately invested for certain considerations in equities of companies that were worthless. Suddenly in July 2001, UTI announced that sale and repurchase of US-64 were being suspended for six months. Most corporate investors, who had the information that US-64 was likely to collapse, had redeemed their units before this announcement. But approximately Rs. 12,000 Crore of the innocent middle class was blocked in US-64. The UTI later admitted that reserves of US-64 have been wiped out. What would be more scandalous than this?

The Ketan Parekh Scam was unearthed around March 2001. He used the Bank of India's discounting facility and pay orders from the Madhavpura Bank. This scam was exposed when the Madhavpura Bank was burst.

3.3.1.3 The Tehelka Episode

Tehelka expose was one of the most alarming scam of recent time that shook the whole country. It has stalled the working of Indian Parliament many times. This scam is a drastic example of corruption in high places involving bureaucrats, military officials and politicians. Bangaru Laxman, the then BJP president was caught on film accepting a new years party donation of Rs. 1 lakh and asking for further payment in US dollars. Jaya Jaitly, Samata Party leader, was also involved in the tehelka revelations. Many army officers were seen pocketing handsome amounts. Call girls were used to seduce and, expose the army officers. Here we may not agree with the manner in which the whole episode was conducted. It may also be regarded that tactics used in tehelka expose were highly objectionable. I also agree with the view that this was totally a fake dealing done in an artificial manner. We all believe in rightful means to achieve any end. But all the same, tehelka outcome came as a great shock to the public and it has damaged the public image of our country, nationally and internationally. May it be conducted artificially, but it has exposed the true extent of corruption and criminal nexus in high places and particularly in politics.[81]

Soon after this episode was depicted on T.V. and other media, its mastermind Tarun Tejpal tried to justify it in the public interest. He explained their methods to the media and tried to convince that whatever may have been the methods and manner in which his team conducted the whole episode but the nexus, he has exposed was a true piece of facts whether may have been the methods and manner in which his team conducted the whole episode but the nexus, he has exposed was true piece of facts.

Any way, after that, government appointed a inquiry commission with justice K. Venkataswami as the head of tehelka probe commission. As the tehelka probe came to its last stage a controversy was raised by opposition parties in the Parliament on Justice Venkataswami's appointment as chairman of authority of advance ruling on customs and excise even before he had completed the probe into the alleged irregularities in defence deals. It was alleged by opposition members that Justice Venkataswami's integrity had been sought to be compromised for his new appointment, which has violated constitutional norms. Though it was made clear by the government that he was chosen by the Chief Justice, way back at the beginning of the year, in response to the centre's request to the Chief Justice to name a retired Supreme Court Judge for the position but opposition was not in mood to change its stand, with the result, he proposed to resign from the position as well as from the tehelka probe. This is an example as to how a reputed person like justice Venkataswami became victim of shoddy politics in India.[82]

An edited extract from a letter sent to journalists and MPs in this tehelka matter has been published in *Hindustan Times* with the heading "Prison note book/Kumar Badal, Emergency—2002", showing as to how the persons who exposed this tehelka episode, were apprehended, tortured and harassed later on. It is written and I quote here, "Implicated in a false case by the CBI just because I am a journalist working for tehelka. I was sent to two jails and subjected to sub-human conditions. I helplessly watch CBI sleuths connive with the jail authorities to leave no stone unturned to put me under all sorts of mental and physical pressure. On the first day in the prison, they stripped me naked in front

81. Source of information: An extract from an article; Midway to elections written by K. K. Birla, published in *The Hindustan Times*; Late city (New Delhi) edition dated 7/8/2002, p. 8.

82. *The Hindustan Times*, Late city edition, (New Delhi), dated 22.11.2004, p. 1.

of the jailors office, with ten staff members laughing and a crowd of prisoners watching. Their reason for stripping me in front of the crowd: he is a tehelka journalist. Let's see what he is hiding? This was done after they had kept me in custody for 27 hours, and frisked me many times. Even as tears rolled down my face, they laughed. The CBI officials did this after physically torturing me, and threatening me."[83]

He further stated that, "the only reason I am suffering is because I am a journalist from tehelka, which exposed corruption in high places. The government's invisible hand is present in all this. The arrest of Shankar Sharma and Aniruddha Behal is testimony to the fact. The CBI should be asked if they have arrested a single poacher of hundreds of elephants? Did they investigate a single case of Gujarat carnage in which 2000 human beings lost their lives? Will they investigate the petrol pump scam? How long will they curtail my freedom? Am I such a danger to the society that I can't even get bail?"[84] This is an example how politics is conducted in India for such a sensitive issue.

In recent development, three years after tehelka operation, the CBI filed bribery cases against former BJP President Bangaru Laxman and former Samata Party President Smt. Jaya Jaitly, Mr. Laxman booked with ›of his personal staff members, Uma Maheshwari Raju and Satyamurthy, under section 120-B of IPC and sections 7 and 9 of Prevention of Corruption Act and Jaya Jaitly has been booked along with Former Major General S.P. Murgai, Surendra Surekha, a Kanpur-based industrialist and Gopal Pajiwal, Rajasthan based Samata Party Leader, under section 120-B IPC and section 9 of the Prevention of Corruption Act. The cases has been filed before the court after the prosecution division of the CBI had weighed all the evidence, including the tapes of tehelka which purportedly showed politicians accepting bribe and other gratification.[85]

3.3.1.4 Petrol Pump Allocation Scam-II (during BJP regime)

Recent petrol pump allocation scam is yet another example of political corruption of the present time on which last BJP central government had to cut a sorry figure. It was alleged that since the party came in power, all the allotments of petrol pumps dealership, LPG gas agencies and kerosene agencies have been influenced by government and in most of the cases BJP leaders and their nears and dears have been the beneficiaries of such a allotment. In first instance the then petroleum minister Mr. Ram Naik contradicted the allegation made by the

83. *The Hindustan Times*: Late city edition, (New Delhi), dated 13.8.02 at p. 10.
84. *Ibid.*
85. *The Times of India*, Late city edition (New Delhi); dated 07 December, 2004.

opposition parties in the Parliament but when he faced with the facts—which clearly showed that those close to the BJP were indeed favoured—he amazingly stated that he was not involved in the allotment process. This is not so important that he himself was involved or not but as a minister of the department he was definitely accountable for the mess.[86]

When this scam was exposed, BJP leaders came out with counter-attack on Congress leaders by alleging that several Congress leaders and their relatives, who are now crying over the alleged irregularities in the allotments of petrol pumps and LPG agencies, had been among the major beneficiaries of such allotments in Madhya Pradesh under the 'Jubilee Retail Outlet' and 'Company Owned and Company-Operated' (COCO) schemes during Congress regime. Oil company's sources said that over 80 percent petrol pumps under these schemes were allotted to either the Congress leaders or their relatives. They released a list of names of many Congress leaders and their relatives from Madhya Pradesh and 36 beneficiaries from Congress-ruled Karnataka, including brother of chief minister S.M. Krishna so they demanded cancellation of all allotments since Congress regime. This attack and counter-attack hampered the normal working of the Parliament many times and ultimately Prime Minister Atal Bihari Vajpayee on 5.8.2002 ordered the cancellation of allotment of 1144 petrol pumps dealerships, 1788 LPG outlets and 236 kerosene agencies made by public sector oil companies since January 2000. It was concluded that though allotment had been made on the recommendation of dealership selection boards, public perception was not favourable to the government and BJP.[87]

So, it is clear from the above discussion that, how political parties are behaving in India? They serve their own interest and innocent public is being cheated. By allegation and counter-allegations in this case is a simple saying that if Congress and other opposition parties can petition the government, why not us? If Mr. Satish Sharma of congress and the then petroleum minister, can have out of turn allotments, why not us? The problem with pursuing this line of logic is that corruption in politics has become an obvious fact.

Apart from these scams of recent time there are others also in the series, which shows the criminalisation of politics:

3.3.1.5 Bofors Gun Deal

Bofors Gun deal symbolised, perhaps India's first major political scandal held in 1987. Rs. 1437 crore were paid to buy 410 Bofors guns, it was alleged that Rs. 64 crore were paid as bribes to middlemen by the

86. *The Hindustan Times*, Late city edition (New Delhi); dated 9.8.2002, p. 8.
87. Source of information and Dated: Published in *Hindustan Times*, Late city edition (New Delhi), dated 6 August, 2002, on Front page.

then Prime Minister Rajiv Gandhi's government under a conspiracy hatched among executives of Bofors, middlemen and officials of the government of India. It was also alleged that commissions were paid in India to people close to Shri Rajiv Gandhi. Shri Rajiv Gandhi refuted the charge and said that "neither I nor any one from my family had taken any money in the deal". A case to this regard was filed on 22.01.1990 against the main accused S.K. Bhatnagar, W.N. Chaddha, Octavio Quattrocchi, Martin Ardbo, S.P. Hinduja, G.P. Hinduja and P.P. Hinduja. After a decade of investigations, charge-sheets and letters rogatory, no body has been convicted as yet. Recently CBI has admitted that there is no concrete evidence so far to suggest that any public servant received money. This was revealed by additional solicitor general Mukul Rohatagi on a specific query from Justice J.D. Kapoor of Delhi High Court. Whether any public servant got money from the deal signed with the Swedish arms manufacturer.[88] Consequently after more than 17 years since this scam rocked the country, the Delhi High Court gave clean chit to former Prime Minister Mr. Rajiv Gandhi in February 2004 due to lack of evidence.[89] Whatever may be the result but this scam has come to symbolise corruption in politics. Here we are not concerned as to who paid the bribe, who were the middlemen to whom commission were paid, where bribe's money has gone, who were the beneficiaries, but it is a fact on record that Bofors came to be regarded as a synonym of corruption in high places. In a sense, Bofors, the shoot-and-scoot gun, has also come to symbolise the scam-and-scoot culture, highlighting the failure of the criminal justice system in India.[90]

3.3.1.6 Fodder Scam of Bihar

Out of the biggest political scam of post-independence India, the fodder or animal husbandry scam of Bihar is one of them that has rocked the country. This scam is a perfect example of criminal nexus among politicians, bureaucrats and businessmen. Among main politicians and other involved in this scam were two former chief ministers of Bihar, Laloo Prasad Yadav and Jagannath Mishra, three former ministers, Mr. Bhola Ram Toofani, Mr. Vidyasagar Nishad and Mr. Chandradev Prasad Verma, a number of IAS officers, one commissioner of income-tax, three MLAs, a number of serving and retired officers of the State Animal Husbandry Department and businessmen.

Though the scam was continue since long back in Bihar, it was made open to the public view from 1995 onwards. The scam involves

---

88. *The Times of India*, Late city edition (New Delhi) September 15, 2003, p. 4.
89. Source of information, competition success Review, *General Knowledge Today*, special, January 2005 issue, p. 82.
90. *India Today*, Magazine (English Edition), August 18, 2003 at p. 69.

unauthorized and excess withdrawls of money from the government treasury and its account in the State Bank of India for payment of false bills of the purchase of the cattle feed and certain kinds of animals and poultry and of their transportation. The money, thus, taken out of the government was allegedly shared by scamsters and they used it in building their estate in various important cities of the country.[91]

It was found that many of the firms supplying cattle-feed, animals and poultry were owned, in the fictitious names by the officials involved in the scam. The CBI, detected seven such fake firms in the name of key person of the scam, Shyam Bihari Sinha and his relations in Calcutta. It also detected three financial companies, namely, Narang distributors, Raman commercial and toy mark consultancy through which Sinha made huge investment in the share market. These companies also provided loans to private firms as well as individuals. Sinha's wife, Rama Sinha, was a director of all these three companies. It was alleged that many top politicians of the State have made investments in the share market in the name of their wards through these three companies. Thus, a huge loss to the state exchequer has been created through this scam and many other scams in Bihar during Laloo Yadav's regime.[92]

The important thing to anybody's surprise, was that Mr. Laloo Yadav, according to the CBI report, was fully aware from 1993 onwards about various facets of the scam. In spite of excess withdrawals from the government treasury, he did not bother to initiate any action against guilty persons. It was alleged that this was going on with the implied consent of Mr. Laloo Yadav in return to various considerations and facilities provided by such scamsters to him and his family members from time to time.[93]

The power of scamsters can be assessed with the fact that they were provided all the modern facilities and comforts in Beur Central Jail, including mobile phones with which they keep themselves in touch with the outer world. They frequently ask their family members to pick them in car from the jail gate in order to bring them out and return back before the locking time. In fact, they used the jail as if it was a rest house for them. What can be more surprising than this? A raid was conducted which recovered six mobile phones, foreign liquor, expensive cigarettes and even blue films from the possession of three jailed legislators. Beside all this, a cash of Rs. 2 lakh were also recovered from one of the legislator, Mr. Dhruv Bhagat.[94]

---

91. Source of information: *The Hindustan Times* (Patna Edition), February 6, 1996.
92. *The Hindustan Times*, October 29, 1996.
93. Girish Mishra and Braj Kumar Pandey; *op. cit.*, p. 307.
94. The Source of information, Prabhat Khabar, June 30, 1997.

3.3.1.7 Hawala Scam

Hawala scam is one of the important scam showing political involvement in corruption at high places. CBl had recovered a diary from Jain brothers, which contained the names and initials of a number of important political leaders of various political parties, top bureaucrats and public sector functionaries. The diary indicated that the names and initials written in it were the beneficiaries of the dirty Hawala money. Here I am not concerned with the fact, whether these persons actually received the money or not, neither I am concerned with the fact that the diary containing names and initials, is admissible as a piece of evidence; or not, I am only referring this case to show the nexus among politicians, bureaucrats, businessmen and criminals. It was alleged that from April 1988 to March 1991, vast sums received from sources abroad were distributed by Hawala racketeers to Kashmiri terrorists, politicians, bureaucrats and criminals.

3.3.1.8 Harshad Mehta Payoffs Scam

The nexus between politicians and criminals was again caught fire in the head lines of news papers when Mr. Harshad Mehta, the one time big bull of the stock market scam released a statement in June 1993 that he had paid one crore rupees packed in a suitcase to Shri P.V. Narasimha Rao, the then Prime Minister of India. According to Mr. Mehta, his meeting with Sh. P.V. Narasimha Rao was arranged by one businessman Mr. Sunil Mittal whose father Satpal Mittal was a nominated member of Rajya Sabha. Mr. Mehta released a tape-recording evidence in support of his statement in which there was a telephonic conversation with Mr. Mittal. This conversation had a reference of the meeting and payment of money. Mr. Mehta, through his statement, tried to convince that a part of money which he had earned through fraudulent means, was used in political payoffs and that politicians were aware to what he was doing. Though Mr. Rao denied such a payment but he did not dare to take any legal action against Mehta. Here again, it does not matter, whether Mr. Rao had received payment or not. The only thing is that in this scam also, there was much on record to believe the possible involvement of influential politicians, which proves a nexus of politicians with scamsters.[95]

3.3.1.9 Coffins Purchase Scam

Political corruption in India has entered in almost all fields including matters which are very sensitive and of national interest, like defence deals. One of such example is the purchase of defence materials

---

95. Girish Mishra and Braj Kumar Pandey; *op. cit.*, pp. 285-86.

and coffins during Kargil War. The report of Controller and Auditor General (CAG), regarding defence purchase during Kargil War was placed in Rajya Sabha on 11 December 2001. It was alleged in the report that out of 123 defence purchases for Rs. 2163.09 crore, 35 purchases were wrong, in which rules and procedure were violated and for them government paid Rs. 44.21 crore extra. The report exposed that the order of Rs. 260.55 crore was placed for the goods, which were not of prescribe standard. The purchased defence explosives for Rs. 91.86 crore were of expiry date, Rs. 107.97 crore purchases were unnecessary, Rs. 342.37 crore defence explosives were purchased, though the same quality explosives were available in our own country. This report exposed the corruption in defence, purchases and opposition parties demanded the resignation of the then defence minister George Fernandez.[96]

The above list of political scams is not exhaustive but illustrative. There are many more which are published frequently in news papers and periodicals. It is, thus, clear from the above discussion and from few examples of recent political scams, that corruption in politics is at its climax. It has become evident phenomenon in day-to-day life of the politicians. The interesting thing is that neither people nor politicians take it seriously; rather they do not treat it as a crime or wrongful act. Politicians continuously exploit peoples' sympathy and faith and even then remain their ideals.

After independence, the main cause of corruption in politics, reaching to the climax, in an idealist and high moralist country like India, is the growing dependence of politicians and political parties on black money and its operators. Money plays a great role in politics. Politicians gather power by climbing the ladder of expensive elections. In India, in the name of democracy, any kind of election is conducted almost every alternative day. For these elections, political parties need money. From where this huge amount of money will come? This makes politicians dependent on the big business houses and industries. Apart from elections a high standard of living of politicians and their family, their greed for acquiring immovables, ornaments, wealth and luxuries, make their life dependent on black money. This is clear from day-to-day income tax raids that crores of unaccounted money and immovables are always recovered from the houses and lockers of these reputed persons of the society. Due to this need for money, politicians and political parties came forward to accept the help extended them by opportunist big business houses and industrialists. This was actually the start of corruption in politics in post-independence period.

96. *Nav Bharat*, Gwalior (Hindi) Edition dated 12 Dec. 2001.

In order to have their involvement in political decision-making I process and getting licences, permits and government facilities at concessional rates, if they come to power, these business houses came forward to help political parties. They not only help to the political parties in power but to opposition parties also, to keep them silent from raising their voice against them. These businessmen and industrialists arrange their affairs in such a way, that some of their trusted men get entry in important political parties. Thus, there developed a close nexus between the moneybags and political parties and people in power. Both needed each other. The days of simple and dedicated leaders have gone. The new class of leaders have emerged who hate to live a simple life. Their lifestyle is very costly. They prefer to travel by air conditioned coaches or aeroplanes. They need air-conditioned cars to travel to their constituencies. Election campaign has become costlier and costlier. Electoral lies and electoral bribes came to be used frequently by political parties without thinking of their effect on cultural and moral values of the society. Election manifesto has become ornamental to them. They make many promise of social development during election but forget them when election is over. This shows the national character of political parties.

So, now we have come to an era when political parties are no more to fight for clean and corruption free politics. They only play a dirty game of politics to capture power by any means. What has happened in Gujarat, Tamil Nadu, Bihar, Uttar Pradesh and more recently in Jharkhand are the glaring examples of valueless politics.

3.3.1.10 The Godhra Carnage and Best Bakery Episode

The Godhra Carnage and Best Bakery episode has put the name of Gujarat on the world map in the black worlds for its communal-based politics. On Feb. 27, 2002 Sabarmati express was attacked by a mob and one of its bogie was put to fire by spreading petrol on the railway track at Godhra station. It was alleged that at least 58 Hindus were massacred by a mob of over 1000 Muslims on that fateful morning. Mr. Narendra Modi, the then Chief Minister of Gujarat has a high stake in ensuring that his image of being the iron man of the Hindutva brigade is not dented. So his government took the investigation of this massacre on the priority basis. 81 of total 126 accused were arrested and charged under POTA. It was alleged that muslim families had hatched a conspiracy to kill Ramsevaks on the night of February, 26 when they were returning from Ayodhya. This was really a crime against humanity to which every person of conscience must discard.[97]

97. Source of information: *India Today*, Magazine (English); July 21, 2003, p. 34.

Following this carnage, communal riots broke down throughout the State in which thousands of men, women and children were brutally murdered, property were looted, women were raped and burnt alive. Among all these, the disaster that followed the tragedy, was the incident of Best Bakery. On March 1, 2002 an armed mob attacked Best Bakery at 9 PM. There were at least 20 people in the Bakery, including its owner Sehrunissa's family at the time of attack. The mob set ground floor on fire. Sehrunissa escaped to terrace with daughter Zaheera, three sons and her mother. Others trapped on first floor. Mob started killing the people. Two people were dragged out and burnt alive. Others, including two children were killed inside the Bakery. Sehrunissa; her children and mother spent the night hiding on terrace. The next day police found 12 dead bodies in Bakery and two more found outside. A FIR was filed on March 2, 2002 on Zaheera's version in which she described the attack and named the assailants. She openly took an oath that she will not marry until all the guilty are punished. The charge sheet charged all the 21 named by Zaheera. However, after that, the true story of dirty political game through pressure tactics started. The three statements taken from Zaheera and others between March 9 and April 1 had several contradictions. When the trial started, 39 of the 73 witnesses in the case turned hostile including Zaheera, her mother Sehrunissa and her brothers Nafitulla and Nasibullah. Zaheera retracted her statement made to the police on May 17, 2003 in the court and went into hiding. In her retracted statement she changed track and said that "It was dark and smoky on that fateful day, so I could not figure out clearly from the terrace who the attackers were. My earlier statement was taken by the police in the hospital while I was undergoing treatment".[98]

Consequently, on June 27, 2003 the judge A.D. Mahida of the fast track court announced its judgment in which he acquitted all the 21 accused. The court said that though the reports of the violence were true, there was not enough evidence to convict the accused persons. It further said that evidence had been fabricated against the accused and the police got them signed from the injured. The court, however, commented that Massacre was a blot on the cultural city of Vadodara and took the police to task for sloppy investigation.[99]

Following the verdict there raised a voice of protests from I human rights activists, who accused the government of a conspiracy to bailout the killers. National Human Rights Commission Chairman Justice A.S. Anand called it "miscarriage of justice" and urged the Gujarat government to appeal in the High Court against the verdict.[100]

98. *Ibid*, pp. 28-35.

99. *Ibid*.

100. *Ibid*.

Later on, disappeared Zaheera appeared in Mumbai and said that she and her family was constantly threatened by many political persons, including the BJP MLA Madhu Srivastava and Madhu's cousin Congress councel lor Chandrakant Srivastava, with dire consequences if they testified against the accused. Zaheera said that she had only two options; get justice for slain family members or save those who were living. She said that no body, even from my own community, came forward to help me. She also demanded a retrial of the case outside Gujarat. Zaheera, spoke with extraordinary courage on national television, which shaked the country's collective conscience.

In this case there are many troubling questions emanated as to how sincere the prosecutors, who represented the State government, were in bringing the preparations of the carnage to justice? Why police did not build a strong case to indict the accused? What was the prosecution and government doing while the key witnesses were being threatened and getting hostile? Why didn't the court direct the state to protect the witnesses? Fair trial being an integral part of the constitutional mechanism, is it functioning in Gujarat particularly in this case? The answer to these questions, if any, will certainly be disturbing for the nation.[101]

The investigation conducted in this case also raised many doubts. The investigation officer in-charge Mr. P.P. Kanani seemed to rely on eye witnesses only without making any serious effort to search for supportive evidence, that would indict accused. In his judgment, Justice Mahida observed, "There was not even an iota of trustworthy evidence in the crime of the accused presented before the court." He described it as a case of producing a dead horse for the prosecutor to flog. Even the role of public prosecutor, Raghuvir Pandya does not seem fair. Zaheera charged Pandya with not even meeting her before she stepped into the witness box. When key witnesses turned hostile, Pandya did not exercise his right to cross-examine them. As witness after witness turned hostile, the public prosecutor didn't find it necessary to seek adjournment and use the extra time to strengthen his case, or even appeal to the court to take cognizance of these developments. The defence, on the other side, was able to hold its key witnesses together. It seems true that if the Best Bakery was a test case, the legal system of the state appears to have failed miserably. Zaheera's surrender under pressure in the court and her subsequent confession before the media in Mumbai, has thrown up a larger public issue that of protecting the rule of law from political interference.[102]

101. *Ibid.*
102. *Ibid.*

The demand of Zaheera and Human rights organisations for retrial outside Gujarat had sparked off a debate in legal circles. The opinion of legal experts in the country was sharply divided on the issue of retrial in the case. One of the opinion was that retrial is impossible under the existing law and only an appeal can be made on the available material. On the other hand, some of the experts including, Mr. Shanti Bhushan were of the view that a retrial is possible in an appellate court which sets aside the acquittal on the ground that the trial at the fast-track court was unfair. Judicial opinion in the country was also divided on the feasibility of reopening of this case because the constitution and the criminal procedure code prohibit a person once acquitted from being trial again for the same offence. Besides all this, Zaheera will remain the key witness, even if the case reopened some how, the statement of Zaheera will be seriously doubted and will create many legal problems, if she again changes her story, saying on a second oath, that she had lied on oath earlier will that not be confession of pejury?[103]

Any way, subsequently a petition was filed by Human Rights Commission and Zaheera Sheikh in the Supreme Court for seeking reinvestigation and retrial of the Best Bakery case outside Gujarat. The Supreme Court on 13 September 2003, in its unprecedented move, said that the "government should quit if it cannot punish the rioters and protect the innocent people in the State". Chief Justice U.N. Khare said that "I have no faith left in the prosecution and the Gujarat government. I am not saying article 356 (president's rule) be imposed. You have to protect people and punish the guilty. What else is Raj-Dharma? You quit if you cannot prosecute the guilty." He further commented that "Democracy does not mean that you will not prosecute anyone". The Commission also termed as "eyewash" the State government's appeal before the High Court in this case and doubted the government's intention on punishing the guilty. Supreme Court summoned the Chief Secretary and Director General of Police and asked, "who has drafted such an appeal?, Is this an appeal? Even counsel with one year's experience will not draft such an appeal. It is just an eyewash and nothing else."[104] What can be more shameful and dirty game of politics than this?

Finally, Supreme Court on 12 April, 2004 in an unprecedented move, ordered transfer of this case from Gujarat to Mumbai in Maharashtra.[105] As the case proceeded, the eye witnesses and brave workers of the Bakery gave their eye witnesses account in the court and identified a considerable number of accused. But the wishes of those

103. *Ibid.*

104. *The Times of India*, Late City edition dated 13 September 2003 at p. 1.

105. *Dainik Bhaskar* (Gwalior Edition) (Hindi) dated 23rd December 2004, p. 1.

who, on the transfer of the case outside Gujarat; thought victory of justice, got sudden shock when the star witness of the case Zaheera Sheikh changed her testimony yet again to say that she couldn't identified the accused of the Best Bakery case and that she did so under pressure of social activist Teesta Setalvad to implicate persons in the case. Zaheera on January 3, 2005 also told the Supreme Court that no affidavit sworn by her was filed in the apex court, based on which the trial was shifted from Gujarat to Mumbai and acquittal of the 21 accused was quashed. She also said that what she testified in fast-track court of the Vadodara, was the true piece of her evidence. Consequently, Supreme Court on 10.01.05 ordered a high level inquiry by its Registrar General to find out as to who was telling the truth—Zaheera or Teesta Satalvad.[106]

Ultimately, money surfaced in this case to bring a turn to the present scenario. It is alleged in this case that a sum of Rs. 18 lakh has been paid to Zaheera for his change testimony. Once again tehelka team conducted an intensive operation to capture in film to the controversial BJP MLA Madhu Shrivastava purportedly saying that Zaheera Sheikh was paid Rs. 18 lakh to turn hostile. The tehelka editor-in-chief Mr. Tarun Tejpal showed a 10 minute video tape recording containing conversation on the alleged bribe deal at a press conference in New Delhi. Madhu Shrivastava's cousin and Congress councillor Chandrakant Batthoo was shown as saying that the Gujarat government had given 100 percent money to Zaheera to change hes testimony in Mazagaon special court in Mumbai. Zaheera, however, denied the payment or such money and said that it was a conspiracy hatched by social activist Teesta Setalvad and Chandrakant Shrivastava, Congress Corporator from Vadodara to defame her.[107] It is, however, to be noted that there are facts on record that Zaheera Sheikh and her family members, according to a T.V. Channel, have been regularly receiving money from unknown sources in two bank accounts in Bhayander.[108]

Whatever may be the truth but once again shoddy politics and flaws in prosecution process, resurfaced in this case. This is all done by politicians to create or save their vote banks. From the very beginning the indifference of law-enforcing agencies to record FIRs, collection of evidence and protection of witnesses is visible in this case. Delivery of justice is not the only concern of Judiciary and NGOs all the time, but it is an essential duty of any government. And in this case it is totally lacking. It is a fact that to prosecute a case, we need a prosecution. The

---

106. *The Times of India*, Late city edition, New Delhi, January 11, 2005, p. 6.
107. *The Times of India*, Late city edition, New Delhi, December 23, 2004 on front page.
108. *The Times of India*, Late city edition, New Delhi, January 12, 2005, p. 1.

prosecution in such cases, is the State government and its various agencies. Then question is how do you prosecute when the prosecution seems keen to sabotage the case? If the State itself is the criminal, who is to initiate action against State?

3.3.1.11 The Tamil Nadu Episode

Tamil Nadu is yet another example of dirty and revengeful politics in our country. On June 30, 2001 former Tamil Nadu Chief Minister M. Karunanidhi was arrested in the night under a criminal complaint filed just a few hours before his arrest. His arrest was result of Tamil Nadu Chief Minister J. Jayalalitha's revengeful attitude. In 1996, DMK Chief and then Chief Minister, Karunanidhi, had arrested and jailed Jayalalitha in a case of assets disproportionate to her known sources of income. For around 20 days, she remained in jail. Since then, she appears to have had just one thought in her mind: revenge. She slept revenge, ate revenge and spoke revenge at every public meeting she addressed. Revenge for putting her in jail, in a dirty cell infested with insects and for serving her food in a crumpled aluminium plate—the ones used by every jailed criminal.[109]

Due to this arrest Jayalalitha suffered a severe blow to her image. She looked antidemocratic, vicious and revengeful. All the democratically elected State governments and Central government condemned the arrest in such a way. Even the court expressed dismay and anger at the conduct of the State government. The High Court: went a step ahead and wondered how the Jayalalitha government could undertake such arrests as her position is in the nature of a "caretaker". She has yet to contest and win herself a place in State Assembly before she can become a full-fledged Chief Minister. Jayalalitha had clearly taken a calculated risk-preferring revenge to whatever it might do to her image. People, in India, have a short memory and will forget every thing within no time.[110]

If we look to the historical background of Jayalalitha, then it is clear that she always has been in limelight for one reason or the other from 2001, first when she became Chief Minister of Tamil Nadu. A controversy was raised for State Governor's wisdom in appointing her as the head of the government when she had been convicted in corruption case. Ms. Jayalalitha and her friend Ms. Sasikala had been found guilty of irregularities in the purchase of land and buildings by the State owned Tamil Nadu Small Industries Corporation (TANSI) by Jaya publications and Sasi enterprises, firms owned by them. In the pleasant stay hotel case, Ms. Jayalalitha was convicted for using her official position to

109. *The Hindustan Times*, Late city edition; July 8, 2001 p. 10.
110. *Ibid.*

benefit the promoters of the hotel and awarded a year's rigorous imprisonment. She was also debarred from contesting the May 2001 assembly election. Once again Ms. Jayalalitha was back on the centre stage, when she won a legal battle on Dec. 4, 2001. Madras High Court acquitted her of corruption charges in the TANSI land deal and pleasant stay hotel case due to failure of prosecution to establish charges against her. Consequently she was appointed as Chief Minister again.[111]

Bihar is yet another example of anarchy and Jungle Rajya. When Laloo Prasad Yadav was in Pakistan in August, 2003 one of RJD strongman. Mr. Shahabuddin, a don, surrendered before the court in Siwan. He was alleged to establish a reign of terror in Bihar by conducting a series of kidnappings of children for ransom. Among the victims was Sidhant, the nephew of powerful-cabinet minister Raghvendra Pratap Singh. The surrender of Mr. Shahabuddin was also very dramatic as that of Laloo Yadav in connection with fodder scandal six years ago. His supporters organised a caravan of 400 cars and as many motorbikes that reached the court. People gathered in bulk in the streets to greet and cheer the "hero". All his supporters wore black badges and chanted slogans like "BJP-DGP Murdabad, Shahabuddin Zindabad." Mr. Shahabuddin, clad in a striped maroon coloured shirt and blue jeans and sporting trendy sunglasses, arrived in his white Scorpio car from his native village Pratappur.[112]

Nonetheless, Mr. D.P. Ojha, DGP Bihar, despite political pressure, was determined to hunt down the don. He said that "A criminal is a criminal irrespective of the political garb or his position." Mr. Ojha sent a 15-page note to State Home Secretary V.K. Haldar that the RJD M.P. had openly been challenging the rule of law and criminal justice system. "If his activities are not contained now, the entire system will be shattered in the State and in its place the rule of Shahabuddin will be established". Of the 36 criminal cases pending against him, Shahabuddin had been exonerated in 14. The DGP asked the Home Department to approach the higher court to review these cases and start a re-trial because "witnesses did not turn due to reign of terror unleashed by the don's men. Had Siwan been Kingdom, Shahabuddin would have been its Shahenshah", the DGP says. According to police sources Shahabuddin has created an underworld network of 500 criminals and has built an arsenal that included over 100 AK 47s. The police also believe that he has built-up an illegal empire worth Rs. 100 crores.[113]

111. *Competition Success Review*, Special, January 2002, issue; p. 30.
112. *India Today*, Magazine, August 25, 2003, pp. 37-38.
113. *Ibid.*

3.3.1.12 The Taj Heritage Scandal

Uttar Pradesh is another burning hot ball of corrupt politics. The rivalary between Chief Minister Mulayam Singh Yadav and BSP Chief and Ex-Chief Minister Mayawati is well known in the country. Both have gone to the extent of taking revenge with each other. After the expose of Rs. 175 crores Taj Heritage corridor project scandal, Mayavati decided to quit as chief minister of the State. She has been charged of having her hand in Taj scandal and collecting lakhs of rupees from MPs and MLAs as shown in "bribery tapes" produced by Mulayam Singh Yadav's Samajwadi Party. During her chief ministership, Mayawati registered 140 criminal cases against Mulayam Singh Yadav in a clear case of political vendetta. After losing her chief ministership, Mayawati faces as much as 131 charges but this time, it is the Supreme Court that has asked the CBI to lodge FIR against Mayawati, her former excise minister Nasimuddin Siddiqui and six other officials for alleged irregularities and malpractices with regard to the controversial Taj Heritage corridor. Also in line are cases on possessing assets disproportionate to income. The cases relate to acquiring and transfer of property by Mayawati and her relatives between 1995, when she "first became chief minister and now." Most transactions happened during the 15 months of her third chief ministerial term that ended in August 26, 2003. Preliminary investigations suggest that the amount involved runs in to hundreds of crores of rupees. The property transfers are mostly in Bulandshahar, Lucknow, Noida and Ghaziabad in UP as well as in Delhi.[114]

India Today has collected documentary evidence in several of these cases. They include the following:

(a) On August 5, 2003 just three weeks before Mayawati's resignation, 18900 Sq ft. of commercial property at Lal Bahadur Shastri Marg, Lucknow was arbitrarily auctioned and transferred to her for Rs. 45.75 lakh only when the actual market value is estimated Rs. 1.75 crores. About 2900 Sq. ft. of adjoining Government land worth Rs. 25 lakh was charged to freehold and confiscated.[115]

(b) On August 18 M/s Bahujan Foundation (through its trustee Kanshi Ram) sold three industrial plots in Noida to M/s Ashian Needles Pvt. Ltd. for Rs. 5.91 crores.[116]

(c) On August 19, the bungalow of Yunus Delhvi, at Delhi's posh area, 11, Sardar Patel Marg was purchased in the name

114. *India Today*, Magazine, October 6, 2003, pp. 32-36.

115. *Ibid.*

116. *Ibid.*

of the BSP for Rs. 7 crore. The market value of the property is reported to be Rs. 35 crore.[117]

(d) On August 29 (the day Mulayam Singh Yadav was sworn in as Chief Minister), Maya Ashok, wife of Dharam Veer Ashok, a protege of Mayawati, transferred 2.5 hectares of farmland in Mauzpur, Bulandshahar, to Tej Singh, Mayawati's cousin for Rs. 9 lakh. This land was transferred on January, 27 by Mayawati's father Prabhudayal to Maya Ashok for Rs. 7.2 lakh.[118]

(e) In October 2002, Mayawati's brother Anand Kumar bought a 450 sq.m. plot at Sector 44, Noida for Rs. 16 lakh when its market value was just Rs. 1 crore.[119]

Apart from these properties, the others to which CBI has made a special concern are Mayawati's 7 acre farmhouse at Gyaspur, Bulandshahar- Aligarh road, and at least eight other cases of property transfers in Gyaspur, where the recipient was Nirmala Rai, wife of Mayawati's brother Rajkumar. There are nine other cases of land purchases tnade by Mayawati from her father and nine other similar cases of land transfers against two of her brothers, Ashok Kumar and Subhash Kumar and their wives, Hemlata and Rachna Devi. According to agency sources, most of the portion of the construction contracts in Noida was given to the National Project Construction Corporation, the firm involved in the Taj Heritage Corridor scam. The chairman of Greater Noida has ordered an inquiry into these "illegal cases of subcontracting".[120]

Moreover, Mayawati's brother Anand was allotted a plot, B-182, in Sector-44 Noida. He later purchased this plot worth Rs. 1 crore for just 16 lakh. Mayawati's brother-in-law also acquired two other plots in Noida.[121]

A major source of information for the CBI is the blind dealings of the controversial Taj Heritage Corridor. Taj Heritage deal is a classic case of politician- bureaucrat nexus, mainly involving two ministers and the four senior bureaucrats, her principal secretary P.L. Punia, chief secretary, D.S. Bagga, principal secretary (environment), R.K. Verma and secretary (environment), V.K. Gupta. CBI raided various properties and houses of Mayawati and these bureaucrats. It is alleged that the pre-poll

117. *Ibid.*
118. *Ibid.*
119. *Ibid.*
120. *Ibid.*
121. *Ibid.*

offensive raids against Mayawati raises doubts on whether the country's premier probe agency is being used as political tool. Mayawati alleged that CBI is no longer independent. It is now a political agency.[122]

Whatever may be the outcome, but this case is a classic example of corruption resulted from the nexus between politicians and bureaucrats. The named four bureaucrats of Mayawati's government, were actually "the brain behind her government". Ironically it was this gang of four, which in the ultimate analysis did Mayawati the most harm by their manipulation of official files.[123]

Thus, the year 2003 is described as the year of scams. Many financial and political scams has hit the headlines of news papers throughout the year. End of the year witnessed yet another scams like Telgi's stamp scam of Maharashtra and Judev-logi scam of Chhattisgarh just before Assembly elections in Chhattisgarh and exactly 32 months after Tehelka. The dreaded spy camera caught the BJP minister once again. The union minister of state for environment Dilip Singh Judev, shown downing whisky and then accepting a newspaper-wrapped bundle of what was described as money in 500 rupee notes. The happening stirred the BJP and consequently Dilip Singh Judev was forced to resign. The Judev expose was carried by the Indian Express newspaper on November 16, 2003 which claimed that it had received a VCD from reliable sources and published the story after verifying the authenticity of its contents. The film, shot with a hidden camera in a room at Delhi's Taj Mahal Hotel, showed Judev accepting money from someone who claimed to represent as Australian company that was seeking mining rights in Chhattisgarh, among other places.[124]

The interesting thing about the whole episode was that Chhattisgarh Chief Minister Ajit Jogi claimed soon after the newspaper scoop that the filming was done at the Taj Mahal Hotel. How Jogi came to know the venue of the secret filming when even the newspaper had not mentioned it, is mysterious. It suspected the hand of Jogi and his son in this episode who tried to take benefit of this episode in regaining the power of the state in Dec. 1 assembly elections. Whatever may be the truth, CBI has registered a case of inquiry in this expose.[125]

In recent development the Hyderabad based forensic science laboratory has certified as "genuine" the videotape purportedly showing Dilip Singh Judev accepting a bribe in a hotel room. In its report to the CBI, the laboratory said the video sequence of tape has not been

122. *Ibid.*
123. *Ibid.*
124. *gdfg.*
125. *Ibid.*

tampered with and "there is continuity in the tape and lip synchronisation (of all characters in the tape) is also perfect." The report further says that, no picture has been super imposed and those shown on the tape are "genuine".[126] However, the case is in process and time will tell the truth.

3.3.1.13 Telgi's Stamp Scam

Telgi's Stamp scam of Maharashtra is recent in series, which tells the story of how one man used politicians and police officers to set-up the largest ever stamp paper racket. The scandal involving at least 4800 crore scam now threatens to engulf governments of many States. Telgi, a commerce graduate, used to sell fruits at local railway station in Belgaum in early 1980s. Later on he shifted to Mumbai and worked in a hotel and ran a travel and recruitment racket to the Gulf. In the early 1990s he began selling fake stamps. Tempted by huge profit margins, he acquired 12 Machines from the India Security Press and recruited several people to run the press. Gradually he spread his operation across the country and started investing in, immovables and movies. In reaching to this hight, he took help of many influential political leaders and officers of police and government functionaries. He acquired a licence in March 1994 for vending stamp papers by using his contacts with Anil Gote, an influential MYA of Maharashtm, who pitched his case to Vilasrao Deshmukh, the then revenue minister in Sharad Pawar government. Telgi set-up his own parallel security press and recruited people with connections and skills, like Madhav Tikaram Kulthey, a former employee at the Indian Security Press (ISP), Nasik, who was acquainted with the tactics of printing, size of rolls, and the suppliers. By using Kulthey's links he met Ramchandra Reddy, a clerk in the perforating machine and dyes department and Shivraj Sharma, chief of purchase in Indian Security Press Kulthey, Reddy and Sharma conspired to get machines deelared obsolete which Telgi bought to set-up his press at Mint Road, Mumbai. He recruited young men across the country luring them with higher commissions for selling fake stamps in the different parts of the country. Thus, his business reached to hundreds of crores of rupees in a short span of time. Telgi's fraud and decent network grew to Rs. 4800 crore empires in just 10 years. According to one, Sri Kumar, the scam figure could be anything between Rs. 10000 crore to 25000 crore. A diary seized from his accountant lists payoffs to several politicians, IPS and IAS officers.[127]

The biggest scam of the year, has so far taken under its grip many senior police officials and political leaders including Maharashtra Deputy

---

126. *The Times of India*, Late city edition, New Delhi, Dec. 31, 2003 Front page.
127. *India Today*, Magazine, Nov., 24, 2003 pp. 66-68.

Chief Minister Chhagan Bhujbal, who resigned from his post though he assigned a different reason to his resignation, and two MLAs, besides threatening the stability of the State Government of Karnataka and Maharashtra. Telgi's network was spread across an astonishing 22 states. What is shocking here is not the size of the scam but the impunity with which Telgi operated.

3.4 Other Crimes

Despite various categories discussed above, there are some other areas in which white-collar crimes are very rampant. With the advancement of science and technology the nature of white-collar crimes has also taken a considerable change, new kinds of these crimes the emergence in the modern time. Some of them are discussed here.

3.4.1 Computer-related Crimes or Cyber Crimes

During 1990's the development in information technology and electronic media have given rise to a new variety of computer-related 'White-collar crimes which are commonly called as cyber-crimes. The various crimes which are committed by computers include fraud, theft, larceny, embezzlement, bribery, burglary, sabotage, espionage, conspiracy, extortion and so on. Generally, the agencies which are associated with the administration of criminal justice have limited knowledge of computer technology and they think that such type of white-collar crimes occur inside computers. Another view is that it is the use of computer as an instrument of business crime. The media have further added a confusion through sensational, distorted and often incorrect reporting of such crimes through their various sources, who do not understand computer technology properly. This narrow definition of cyber crimes has been broadened in recent times due to frequent use of computers in most of the day-to-day activities. However, a consensus does not exist on the definition of computer crimes.

In fact, computer-related crimes are not well understood in the criminal justice system and in business communities in our country, because these crimes are of recent origin and are based on perfect use of technical skill. Here the term 'crime' is used for convenience to mean 'alleged crime', because no harmful act can be crime till it is a violation of some law. So, computer crime is a common term used for illegal computer abuse, however, computers are directly used in committing many kind of crimes in the present changed scenario. Criminal law recognises the element of *mens-rea,* thus, criminal law relating to computer crime must distinguish between accidental misuse and intended misuse of computer system. In this area, criminal justice system is deficient in many respect and there is an urgent need to handle these crimes at the priority basis.

Due to advance in computer technology, the problem in the area of white-collar crimes, i.e. crime by computer technology, are growing very fast. With the help of this new technology, white-collar criminals have vast opportunities of computer crimes in the field of financial or economic sector. Economic fraud, fictitious assets and earning equity funding, creation of bogus insurance policies, etc. are the crimes which can be committed by simple manipulation of computer system. These crimes can be classified in the following categories.

3.4.1.1 Computer Manipulations

The large scale computer crimes through computer manipulations are generally seen in invoice manipulations regarding payment of bills and salaries of industries, manipulation of account balances and balance sheets in banks and financial institutions. In recent time, various misuse of ATM cards and other similar means of payment have further added to these crimes. Apart from ATM cards other magnetic cards such as phone cards are also manipulated through computer technology.

Since PIN-code is necessary for the use of cards, offenders generally get them with the help of phone call trick by preparing a false keyboard. The manipulation in the use of telephone network has also become a grave problem in the present time. Offenders generally misuse telephone network in avoiding their own phone expenditure and even financial manipulations in the form of transfer of money are also made possible through insufficiently protected telephone network by mobile and telephone companies.[128]

In this background of misuse of telephone network, a new wave of manipulations has started all over the world. "Sex telephones" and "Party Lines" in many countries are very frequent in recent time which shows a large scale misuse or manipulation of telephone network. The recent raids in Agra, Indore and Gwalior on various cyber-cafe shops in which many youngsters and school boys were caught red handed in misusing cellular and computer network for sex purposes are the glaring example of such crimes in India. The crimes of child pornography are also very common these days. In this crime, images of children are shown in varying stages of dress and performing a variety of sexual acts. So, computer manipulation is very common in this world of advance technology.

3.4.1.2 Computer Sabotage or Vandalism

One of the most common computer crime in recent time is computer sabotage or vandalism. This crime involves some damage to

128. Dr. U. Sieber, Computer Crime and Criminal Information Law, pp. 77-78.

the computer system itself or its components, caused by virus programme or worn programme. These programmes are spread through illegally copied software or in networks. The object of this crime is to destroy the system or to make it inoperative or to cause extra expenditure and delay to the user. This crime is essentially the outcome of competition in business in which competitors generally sabotage a computer system to undermine the financial stability of a firm.[129]

Computer viruses are programmes which spread in other programmes of a computer system to cause its damage. Quite a large number of such viruses are in circulation in recent years. Some times, it is also observed that the original software issued by the producing company was already infected by such virus. There is a difference in the use of term 'virus programme' and 'worm programme'. While viruses are spread locally, the worm programmes attack foreign computer systems, so it is popularly known as "Internet Worm". The cases of computer sabotage is a serious problem of the present time because, the economy, the companies and trade or business, the administration and even individual working depend, up to a high degree, on the use of modern computer technology and communication system. This dependency of the society on computer system makes computer extortion a dangerous form of attack. The victim is threatened with the destruction or the sabotage of his computer systems and data stocks.[130]

3.4.1.3 Computer Hacking

The term 'hacking' legally mean "an act of unauthorised access to programmes or data held on a computer system".[131] This act is not done with the object of manipulation or sabotage but for the sake of pleasure of overcoming the technical security measures. This type of the crimes are abundant in the modern society which are generally committed to threaten to the attacked computer user. One of the interesting case of hacking, which is cited here as an example, is done by German teenagers. They had managed to get access to various American computer systems and then sold the knowledge obtained in their data-journeys to the former Soviet Secret Service KGB....... The case was of a particular interest because information on new techniques of computer manipulation was revealed in the course of this proceeding.[132]

---

129. August Bequi; White-collar Crime, *op. cit.*, p. 106.
130. Dr. U. Sieber; *op. cit.*, p. 80.
131. R.K. Suri and T.N. Chhabra, Cyber Crime, reprint 2003, p. 365.
132. Dr. U. Sieber; *op. cit.*, p. 81.

3.4.1.4 Computer Espionage

Espionage means the process of collecting or receiving data by clandestine means.[133] Through this illegal act, offenders gain intelligence data. This type of data can be illegally gained from the web Industrial corporations like to spy on their competitors or enemies. They, through network system, illegally get information about product development and marketing strategies without leaving behind any evidence of such a theft.

Computer espionage is a great danger of computer technology in the modern time. In computer system, a large number of data can be stored in a narrow space and these data can be copied easily with the help of computer trick. Under this offence, data of research, defence, commercial transactions and addresses of clients can be collected through secret methods. This technology can also be used in telephone tapping which is very common these days. In telephone tapping, the criminals penetrate in telephone exchanges and telephone communications of targetted telephone numbers can automatically be recorded. This technology is frequently used by political parties in tapping talks of their opponent politicians.[134]

3.4.1.5 Software Piracy

Software Piracy is a crime relating to illegal or unauthorised copying of a computer software. The offenders generally use this technology in copying of standard software for their personal use or to sell them to others. They sell these copies for significantly less money in comparison to its original and thus, illegally earn a huge amount of money. Piracy is very easy and existing law is also not very harsh for these criminals, so these crimes are showing signs of rapid increase day-by-day.

The Problem is so grave and wide-spread that, "In Europe, on an average 0.5 computer programme are sold per personal computer in use. The Industrial organisation "Business Software Alliance" estimates the market share or illegally copied software at, 40% in USA, 76% in Germany, 81% in Japan and 98% in Thailand. Therefore, the total damage of software piracy is with a rising tendency very high."[135]

Despite these categories of computer crimes, there are other cases also which involve computer technology in committing traditional crimes for the purpose of pecuniary benefits and even to attack human life. The manipulation of a flight control system or of a hospital computer are the examples in which great loss to human life is involved. Computer is also used in the field of organised crimes.

---

133. R.K. Suri and T.N. Chhabra, *op. cit.*, p. 343.
134. Dr. U. Sieber; *op. cit.*, p. 82.
135. *Ibid.*

Computer technology has entered in almost all areas of human life so new crimes may also come up in the field. Our defence system, nuclear technology, traffic control system, trade and business, security and other control systems are all dependent on computer technology. Due to more and more dependency on computer and telecommunication technology, computer misuse has become a global threat and therefore, the need of security of computer system is a prime concern of the present society.[136]

In the modern computer system a large number of storage capacity is available. It can process millions of instructions per second and a large number of data and computer files can be stored and manipulated in any desired manner. Today, quite a large number of computer offences, with high financial losses, are done in the industrialized countries all over the world. USA is one of the country having world's largest computer network and is largest Internet user. According to an estimation of US Justice Department, computer crime losses are as much as 10 billion dollars per year. In UK, according to British Banking Association estimation, the losses due to computer crime are 8 billion dollar per year. Similar condition is in other European Countries.[137]

It is, thus, clear that the problem is serious and increasing rapidly. It has become more acute because security measures, to secure computer, are not enough. This is also a matter of great concern that, "the existing law and enforcement and prosecutorial machinery has been slow to adopt to this new form of crime. Our legal system in fact, has fallen behind our technology."[138]

So, computer crimes, which are the outcome of modern technological development, have posed a great threat all over the world in recent time. The computer-related crimes in India are comparatively less due to less use of computer in service sector but gradually they are showing a increasing trend. Keeping in view the urgent need to check these crimes, our Parliament has passed Information Technology Act, 2000 and amended various existing laws. This Act has made various activities regarding tampering with computer source documents, as punishable offences but due to lack of awareness regarding computer technology, this Act is not so effective. It is, therefore, a need of the day to make effective legislation to deal with this growing threat of today and tomorrow.

---

136. *Ibid.*, p. 84.
137. Gulshan Rai, R.K. Dubash, A.K. Chakravarti; Computer-related Crimes Government of India, Department of Electronics, New Delhi, p. 7.
138. August Bequi; *op. cit.*, p. 109.

3.4.2 Environmental Offences

Bhopal gas tragedy in which Methyle Isocynide gas was escaped from an American-based Union Carbide Corporation and in which thousands of men, women and children were dead or sustained dangerous diseases and many flee their homes. The cases of other such gas escapes, food and vegetables that had been treated with pesticides and many more are the examples of environmental hazardous which are the great concern of public and government both. It is also a matter of great concern that quite a large number of chemical and other industries are discharging their chemical wastes in rivers. Dumping of industrial and cities wastes in water is a big problem of the present time. This type of environmental offences are the new and expanding area of white-collar crimes for which public is charged with a heavy cost.

According to an estimation, the extent of environmental pollution is very astonishing. "In metropolitan cities around 800 to 1000 tons of poisonous gases are being released every day in the atmosphere in which 50% is contributed by motor vehicles, 20% by housing fuels and the rest by industries. In big cities, noise pollution has reached up to 90 decibels against the human tolerance of 20-40 decibels. This may cause high blood pressure, cardiac diseases and deafness. In Delhi, dust and ashes in the atmosphere has reached up to 600 micrograin per cubic metre, whereas in the cities of western countries it is around 150 micrograin per cubic meter. In India, around 6 lakh metric tons fertile soil is being washed every year in flood and land erosion, which indirectly costs around 700 crores per annum".[139]

The present environmental crisis is the result of developmental process in which man has become more materialistic and money minded. The industrial, economic, scientific and technological development of present century has caused serious environmental problems like pollution and exploitation of natural resources.

Forests are "life line" of a nation because environmental and ecological balance largely depend on them. It is a matter of great concern that due to greed of money, man has destroyed forests so rapidly that forest areas has decreased considerably, nationally and at global level. Due to this ecological imbalance, the life and existence of common man is in danger.

Industrial development is a parameter of economic prosperity of a nation but it has caused many environmental problems. "Rapid rate of industrialization resulted in to rapid rate of exploitation of natural resources and increased industrial output. Both these components of industrial development have created a large scale environmental

139. Dr. G.S. Karkara, Environmental Law, Ist Edition 1999, pp. 1-2.

problems and ecological imbalance at global, regional and local levels in a variety of ways. Besides desired production, there are numerous undesired outputs from the factories such as industrial wastes, polluted water, toxic gases, chemical precipitates, aerosol ashes and smokes, etc., which pollute air, water, land soil, etc., and thus, degrade the environment and have brought the human society on the brink of its destruction."[140]

Unfortunately, this environmental damage was not taken up seriously till the United Nations conference on the Human Environment held in Stockholm in June, 1972 which focussed world-wide attention on this global problem of ecology and environment. It was soon realised that the main source of environmental pollution are industrialization and population growth. For the prosperity of society, an important obligation on us is to keep clean air, clean water, greenery and open land. With the growth of industries and population, man started polluting these natural resources due to competition in business, living, and in other areas of present materialistic world.

The Earth Summit in June, 1992 organised by United Nations was in continuation of earlier Stockholm conference on Human Environment. This was the largest international conference attended by 178 nations which adopted 27 fundamental principles for protection of environment. It was accepted in the conference that "to achieve sustainable development, environmental protection, shall constitute an integral part of the development process and can not be considered in isolation from it."[141]

As regard to India, the Indian constitution in Part IV, Directive Principles of State Policy, has provided for a welfare society. If this constitutional obligation is not discharged by state in protecting environment, the future generation will not forgive us for this grave act of human tragedy. It is rightly said that, "If the administrators shows indifference to the principle of accountability, law will become a dead-letter on the statute book and public interest will be the casualty. Entitlement to a clean environment in one of the recognised basic human right which can not be permitted to be thwarted by status quoism on the basis of unfounded apprehensions."[142]

As a result of UN Conference and increasing problem of pollution, our parliament enacted, The Water (Prevention and Control of Pollution) Act, 1974 to prevent water pollution. The second legislation enacted by parliament was, The Air (Prevention and Control of Pollution) Act, 1981 for prevention and control of Air pollution. The

140. Dr. I.A. Khan; Environmental Law, Ist Edition 2000, pp. 12-13.
141. *Ibid.*, p. 18.
142. P.M. Bakshi; Public Interest Litigations; Edition 1998 (Oct.), p. 220.

third legislation in the series was, The Environmental (Protection) Act, 1986. All these three legislations deals with maintaining of quality of environment along with various developmental activities in India.

Despite various legislations which shows grave concern of our legislature, the judiciary has also maintained in various decisions that pollution free water, air and land are the basic human right of every individual included in the 'right to life' under Art 21 of the constitution.[143] In *Vellore Citizen's Welfare Forum* vs. *Union of India*,[144] the Supreme Court observed that:

> "...Such industries though are of vital importance to the country's development but they cannot be allowed to destroy the ecology, degrade the environment and pose a health hazard and can not be permitted to continue their operation unless they set-up pollution control devices".

The environment concern and consequently the environmental laws are the outcome of our diminishing natural resources: water, air and land which are limited resources of human survival and ecological balance. The laws made by our parliament is only a beginning of environmental protection, many other such steps are yet to be taken in this direction. The problem lies in complete dedication and lack of commitment on the part of administrative and bureaucratic machinery. It has rightly said that:

> "For the last century, we have abused and polluted our environment as no other society before us. The water, land and air that we use daily, has been poisoned and contaminated and, perhaps in some cases, lost for centuries. The cost has been enormous, not only financially but also in terms of ill health and even death. Criminologists have long neglected to study or include within their scope of interest offences against the environment. For too long, we have studied only the interaction between individuals and have neglected that between the individual and his environment. In the last analysis. it is this wider scope of activity that may determine, if our civilisation survives or falls. Crimes against the environment merit d 145 concern an study".[145]

---

143. Subhash Kumar *vs.* State of Bihar, AIR 1991 SC 420; M.C. Mehta *vs.* Union of India (1986) 2 SCC 176 and M.C. Mehta *vs.* Union of India (1996) 4 SCC, 750.
144. (1996) 5 SCC 281.
145. August Bequi, *op. cit.*, p. 119.

3.4.3 Consumer-related Crimes

Consumer related white-collar crimes is a serious problem of recent time which is, unfortunately, on an increase. The loss to the innocent consumers are very large. The vast categories of consumer frauds in various forms are prevalent in almost every commercial dealing. Due to these crimes an atmosphere of disbelief has been built in our economic system, which has caused a great loss to the society as a whole.

Consumers have been exploited and defrauded since the very beginning due to caprice of business community. "Consumer fraud may be defined as an intentional act to cause another to surrender money or property over which he has a right. It is a false or misleading representation of a material fact, whether by words or conduct, that causes a consumer to be deceived. At times, it may take the form of the concealment of a material fact. The objective of consumer fraud is to deceive the consumer into acting to his legal detriment. Consumer frauds are essentially confidence games, usually contrived to appeal to the greed of the victim".[146]

The false and misleading advertising is a common problem of consumer deception. Innocent public is generally cheated by misleading information regarding product or service. It is a matter of common experience that the qualities, effect and use of the product is generally exaggerated with no reality at all. Many times, some incentive is the form of bonus, gift or more quality and better quality are also offered at a low price. It is told that the product or scheme is available for a limited time and thereby consumers are attracted to buy soon. Once the consumer enters the shop, the salesman induce him to buy the product what they intended to sell. When they buy the product, it comes to their knowledge that they have been cheated, as the product had no such quality as was described to them and that the advertisement was merely a bait.

The fraud in land scheme by land Mafias is a white-collar crime which is growing very fast and causing loss of billions of rupees to the innocent consumers. The big builders or colonizers project that there is an excellent opportunity to invest in the real estate with all the facilities and without any risk to the consumers. They adopt various tactics of selling their plots, without telling to the consumers that the land is not developed and that they have no plan to provide even the basic requirements such as roads, sewer line or water facilities, etc. They simply lure the customers and once they enters in dealing, they feel that they have been cheated and suffered a huge loss. Many such consumers are exploited in such real estate fraud schemes every day. Many times it has been experienced that plots are sold on maps, though such a land or

146. *Ibid.*, p. 51.

colony is not in existence or if it is in existence, it is a agricultural land without having or if it is in existence, it is a agricultural land without having any diversion or it is a Governmental land to be used for public purposes. Under such a scheme deserts or useless land is usually sold for a high price and consumer is always a casualty.

Energy-related consumer frauds are also very common these days. Many energy saving, fuel saving, electricity saving devices have been projected as if these are for the consumer benefits. But in fact most of such claims are false and misleading. In many cases such devices are even harmful to the vehicles or the system. Similarly, vehicle repair frauds, the professional schools fraud in education field, fraud in false visa and passport and many more such frauds are prevalent in almost every day-to-day dealing. As the public are lured to earn more, new consumer crimes are growing very fast. The invent of new technology and changing economic environment have victimized the consumers to a billions rupees loss every year.

To check this epidemic, consumer-related laws have been enacted in almost all the countries and it is claimed that it is a consumer market now-a-days. Consumer Protection Act, 1986 in India is such a legislation in this direction which has been enacted to control the exploitation of the innocent and uneducated consumers. Much of the awareness has come in recent time but much more is required. The real consumer movement is yet to come in India. It is generally alleged that due to failure of prosecutors, judges, administrators and legislators to act with dedication, is the main cause of failure of consumerism in India.

3.4.4 Insurance Crimes

Insurance crimes are prevalent in the society in the form of various frauds, popular among them are false insurance claims and misrepresentation of material facts. These frauds runs into millions of rupees annually. The insurance companies are not the only losers but some times policyholders also suffers a great loss.

The modern insurance industry has expanded rapidly in the last century. In early times the scope of insurance was very limited. Life insurance and fire insurance were popular since long but in present time many new areas have been covered such as medical, health, domestic goods, vehicle, business, accident, and even farmers' crop, etc. The insurance in present is a powerful industry. Due to increase in scope, insurance frauds are also on increase.

Among various categories of insurance crimes, the category of false claim against insurer stands first. "The policyholder may be an individual or another corporation; an insider may also be involved, who assists and arranges to have the false claims honoured. The fraud could involve a well-organised national gang, which stages phony accidents and injuries and then files false claims with the unsuspecting insurer."[147] Similarly, false claims for vehicle accidents, fire accidents and even death claims are very rampant for which insurance companies are charged millions and millions per year. In such swindles many reputed persons of the society such as doctors, lawyers, investigating agencies and even policemen are included who help them in return to their own share in such false claims.

The fraud by insured is not always the case, but many times cases of fraud by insurers against the assured are also seen. With the advancement of time many new companies are coming in insurance field. The cases are not wanting when many such companies misrepresent their assets in order to induce the people to take their insurance policies in order to earn huge amount of money. These companies influence people through various attractive schemes and more return of their premium. Once people enters into agreement with these companies, they latter on come to know that it was a fake company run on papers by some criminal elements. These criminal companies make unnecessary delay in payment of legitimate claims of the people and finally disappear, leaving behind a number of victims. People loses millions by these schemes.[148] It is, therefore, necessary to review the entire insurance industry and to make effective legal and regulatory framework, in order to curtail the wide-scale frauds.

147. *Ibid.*, p. 79.
148. *Ibid.*, p. 80.

4

Prevention and Control of White-collar Crimes

In keeping silent about evil, in burying it so deep within us that no sign of it appears on the surface, we are implementing it, and it will rise up a thousand fold in the future. When we neither punish nor reproach evil doers—we are ripping the foundations of justice from beneath new generations.

—Anon

Statistics indicate that white-collar crimes are progressively increasing day-by-day and this trend will continue till adventurers find new areas for exploitation and the problem of effective control mechanism remains unsolved. We have never realised the unique nature of these crimes. Some years ago, "Reader's Digest" conducted an exercise in USA and found that 63% of Auto garages overcharged in their bills or opened up the vehicle replacing unnecessary spares. Same was the experience with watch repair shops. In almost 50% cases, the shops charged for cleaning work not undertaken or for parts that were neither needed nor inserted. Same will be the experience in India if we conduct a similar exercise in our cities with tradesmen, selling essential commodities or with undertakings that offer repair services, after-sales maintenance services for T.V. sets, electronic or domestic goods, etc.[1]

1. John Lobo; White-Collar Crime-A Social Malaise; *CBI Bulletin*, March 1982, pp. 1-2.

Following examples show the nature and extent of these crimes[2]

(i) The false and misleading advertisements by various business enterprises, showing unwanted exaggeration of quality and result of their products, that do not follow.

(ii) Putting a patient to a series of unwanted laboratory tests as part of a racket for earning easy money.

(iii) Unethical and immoral practices by professionals such as Lawyers, Doctors, Contractors and modern nursing homes.

(iv) The issue of false cheques by a company for various purchases in the name of fictitious or non-existent parties in order to misappropriate funds.

(v) Adulteration in foods, drinks, vegetables and various other eatables and, thus, creating danger to human life.

(vi) The sale of essential commodities by traders at non-statutory prices by creating artificial scarcity or by hoarding.

(vii) Tax evasion by traders, professionals and businessmen through false income-tax returns and by suppression of real wealth.

(viii) The mass scale violations of import and export regulations and building foreign exchange reserves abroad.

(ix) Supply of sub-standard material and other governmental supply by contractors.

(x) The public servants, who accept bribe and illegal gratification in showing favour or to certify sub-standard public works.

The list is not exhaustive but could be extended ad-infinitum. Despite financial implications of these crimes, the greatest hazard is the damage it causes to our social structure, since it engenders distrust, lower morale and produces dis-organisation on a wide scale. It is, therefore, necessary to prevent and control the growing trend of these crimes which is definitely a big challenge for the modem society.

There are certain problems of great relevance, which hamper the measures adopted for prevention and control of these crimes. So, I before discussing preventive measures, it is necessary to discuss these problems, whose solution is necessary for effective control: mechanism of white-collar crimes.

4.1 THE PROBLEMS OF ASCERTAINING QUANTUM OF WHITE-COLLAR CRIMES

Despite the wide-ranging effects of white-collar crimes, it is not easy to assess the true extent of these crimes. One of the reasons is that

2. *Ibid.*

the usual sources of crime statistics do not provide adequate information about the extent of white-collar crimes, since they confine their interest to the cases tried in ordinary criminal courts, and many white-collar crimes are dealt by tribunals, administrative boards and commissions of inquiry. Secondly, social attitude in case of white-collar crimes is unorganised, so, most of such cases remain unreported. Thirdly, many white-collar crimes are of recent origin. In India, the crime statistics given in 'Crime in India,' complied by National Crime Records Bureau, Ministry of Home Affairs, Government of India, provide hardly any information, regarding the extent of white-collar criminality in the country. The only possible sources, therefore, are the reports of the Government of India and findings of the various tribunals and commissions dealing with white-collar crimes. Such information, as is available with these sources, indicate that white-collar crimes are pervasive, in almost all the professions and occupations in our society.[3]

So one of the big problems is to ascertain true quantum and effect of these white-collar crimes. Since white-collar crimes cause indirect effect to the individual, unlike blue collar crimes which have direct effect, an organised agitation of society could not be initiated against these crimes. Consequently, these crimes are increasing rapidly without any resistance of the society.

It is rightly said that "The precise statement regarding the extent of white-collar crimes is impossible. Such crimes go undetected, un-prosecuted or unpunished, therefore, the statistical figures, available regarding white-collar crimes and consequent convictions, represent a picture far from the truth. Gross forms of fraud may be easily detected but it is difficult to deal with the subtler forms of fraud which flourish in many areas of business and profession. It is not possible at present to compile quantitative data regarding white-collar crimes rate and, therefore, it is not possible to make accurate comparisons of the total criminal behaviour of the classes."[4]

"Walter Reckless after conducting research, in the United States in mid-1950s, found that crime among the social classes is bi-modal, with a high peak for the members of the lower classes, a low valley for the members of the middle class, and a very high peak for the members of the upper class. This very high peak in the upper-class is due to white-collar crimes."[5]

3. Ahmad Siddique; Criminology, *op. cit.*, p. 388.
4. Rohinton Mehata; *op. cit.*, p. 240.
5. *Ibid.*, p. 241.

4.2 THE PROBLEMS OF INVESTIGATORS

White-collar crimes are the product of planned effort and lack the spontaneity that generally accompanies conventional crimes. These crimes are not easily traceable, due to their complex nature. They are not only dangerous to the individual but also to the society at large. Unlike others, white-collar offenders are enjoying a variety of social and economic advantages. They are well educated, trained and better equipped to earn their livelihood through skilled and other means. "The traditional crimes may be expanded of its *modus-operandi* or *mens-rea* or the intention behind it, regarding existence or bringing up in a society of feeble mindedness, poverty stricken or emotional instability but white-collar crimes can not be expanded in that way. Their expansion can be said, although not fully but partly, depending on growing moral degradation, individualistic selfishness and high aspirations towards reaching of infinite and limitless, so-called earthly happiness and total bankruptcy of moral ethos and ethics and forgetfulness and shutting eyes towards the traditional and legendary values of life, not only of a community but of the country as a whole."[6]

Because of complicated nature or white-collar crimes, investigation in such cases is a big problem which the investigators face. These crimes, being committed by the higher and more affluent members of the society, therefore, investigation is done through step-by-step enquiries, well-planned exertions, skilled application and analytical approach. The whole operation is needed to be done in a secret manner and adequate precautions are necessary to be adopted. However, the course of investigation does not always run smooth, depending on the financial affluence and political clout of the accused party. Many times investigations are frustrated by inter-locutory petitions in courts, contested through a legal counsel. What then are the requisites of an officer and teams, investigating such crimes? What precautions and mechanism are to be adopted, in investigations of such crimes? These are some of the questions of great importance which are to be taken care of by the investigators of such crimes.

Following are some observations or essentials for investigation in such cases to combat these crimes:[7]

1. A close study of the law and its ingredients is necessary before investigation. The Inquiry officer must satisfy

---

6. Justice Prasun Kumar Deb, High Court, Patna, "White-Collar Crimes", Crime committed by a person of respectability and High Social status, in course of his occupation published in Cr.I.J., 2000, pp. 60-61.
7. John Lobo; *op. cit.*, p. 3.

himself that he is competent to take cognizance suo-motu or after obtaining sanction.

2. A close study of the procedure, regulations, and mode of working of the undertakings is essential.
3. There must be a full proof plan for investigation and, the I.O. must reduce to writing how he will proceed, to collect material evidence, in order to frame a full proof scheme of offence.
4. Careful and intelligent scrutiny of documents and record is necessary. These crimes are generally built-up, on documents and records and, therefore, there is a need for an analytical and studious approach in order to conduct a fact-finding inquiry in depth.
5. Selection of the right personnel, for the investigation of such crimes, is needed, otherwise, it will give a wrong direction to investigation and will cause unnecessary delay which will ultimately frustrate the cause or gravity of these crimes.
6. A background knowledge of commercial accounts and its procedure is essential to catch the crime. A capacity for enquiry with patience and clarity of thinking are essential as the I.O. has to go through complex accounts and records to unravel the fraud.
7. In order to save the destruction of evidence, all the necessary precautions must be taken at the time of search of the documents. It is also necessary that search should be undertaken, after obtaining a search warrant from the court. If searches are to be undertaken simultaneously at several places, it is essential that each team is adequately briefed, as to how to proceed with.
8. Some legal and technical experts must also be associated with the team in order to avoid impediments in search of difficult accounts or legal matters.
9. Expert opinion must be undertaken from technical and forensic scientists on handwriting, finger-prints, secret writings, forgeries, etc. or on other means such as, metals, wood, building materials and other suspected material.[8]

A big hurdle in free and fair investigation is the social and economic status of white-collar offenders and their political links. White-collar offenders belong to the upper class of the society, so they easily

8. *Ibid.*

influence the political leaders to come forward for their help. Secondly, due to technical nature of these crimes, most of the members of the investigation team do not find themselves suitable and trained to handle these complicated cases, so, they generally try to escape from investigation in such cases. In an American case which is cited here as an example, "A Prince Georges County, Maryland, Grand Jury indicated the Sheriff and his assistant in an alleged scheme, to misappropriate county funds. The grand jury also charged that the Sheriffs office had cheated and misused jail trustees for personal gain and had lied. In addition, the grand jury found that the Sheriffs deputies were undereducated and untrained. In a separate investigation, involving one of the nation's largest urban police force, it was reported that, detectives refused to handle difficult cases. It appears that, the detective bureau was concerned that its failure to make arrests would hurt its performance record. Detectives sent back more than 30 percent of all cases sent to them by other divisions."[9]

The main role of investigators is to collect relevant evidences for a particular offence and bring the cases to the prosecutors for a successful prosecution. Without this investigatory apparatus, the prosecutorial machinery would cease to function. It is, however, a matter of common experience that the investigators are ill-trained and poorly equipped to combat the task of complex white-collar crimes. Many of investigation agencies are further handicapped by corruption and political interference in their every day operations. Such an apparatus has, and will continue to have, difficulty in meeting the challenges of white-collar criminals till they are not well equipped and set free from any interference.[10]

It is accepted principle of criminology that prevention of crime is best achieved through prompt cognizance, effective investigation and speedy punishment and this is more required in complicated cases, such as white-collar crimes. It is possible only when investigation machinery is competent, trained and prompt in detecting and initiating action. Generally, in our country, whenever a big economic scam involving crores of rupees by any business house, bureaucrats or politicians, becomes a public issue or a question is raised in Assembly or Parliament, an inquiry commission is appointed to look into the matter.[11] "This is the only workable excuse to side-track the issue for the time being. The commission, generally takes a long time for giving its findings because himself. On the basis of the findings of the commission, criminal case

9. August Bequai; White-Collar Crimes, *op. cit.*, p. 137.
10. *Ibid.*
11. Section 190 Cr.P.C.

is registered with the local police station, where t he offence is alleged to have been committed. Generally in such cases, either by political pressure or by money force, the investigating agency concludes that there is no *prima-facie* case exist against the accused for want of evidence. Therefore, it recommends the case to the court for cancellation. Thus, the findings of a legal luminary, who is generally a judge either of High Court or of Supreme Court, based on evidence adduced before him and further substantiated by his own logical reasoning; meet a tragic death in the unscrupulous hands of investigation police officer."[12]

It is, therefore, suggested that such a big scam either be handed over to the CBI for investigation or complaint be made to the magistrate under Section 190 of Code of Criminal Procedure, 1973. The magistrate must inquire the case himself and shall not direct the investigation by police officer under section 202 of Criminal Procedure Code. The practice of appointing Inquiry Commission in such cases should be avoided and investigation by CBI or by a special Judge or by a special investigation agency, made for that purpose, must be promoted.[13]

There is a vigilance wing in almost all the states in our country to deal with the cases of corruption. Due to political interference, its working can not achieve desired objects. Its efficacy may be estimated from the interview of S.P. (Vigilance) Punjab, published in *The Tribune* on 10th July 1977. He said, "His stint in the department gave him an opportunity to see corruption from close quarters. It had spread its tentacles to grab ministers as well as officers. He saw how graft not only went unchecked but also flourished under political patronage". The efficiency of this department depends upon the quality of its staff and its immunity from undue government or political interference in day-to-day working. Therefore, it is suggested that vigilance wings of states must be separated from police department and made an independent department with less interference of the state governments. The recommendations of the commission must be made binding on the Government. The cases of corrupt public officers, politicians, big businessmen and other high ranking persons, who may influence politicians or other government functionaries, must be referred to CBI. To make CBI more effective and efficient wheel of investigation, its staff must be strengthened with expertise personnel. The state must be restricted to exercise its prerogative to withdraw proceedings against white-collar criminals.[14]

12. Gurpal Singh; Problems of White-Collar Crimes in India and its Control, Published in *Panjab University Law Journal*, 1977, p. 55.
13. *Ibid.*
14. *Ibid.*, p. 56.

This is not only the position in states but at central level too. The recent revelation of Shri U.S. Mishra, Director CBI, also supports this contention that how country's premier investigating agency CBI, works under pressure from those wielding power and influence. He described CBI autonomy as a myth and admitted that the agency at times comes under political pressure and pulls from important quarters. He said that the moment a case is registered by CBI and reported by media, phones of influential people start ringing, exerting pressure in the form of 'requests'.[15]

The CBI Chief also highlighted the weaknesses in our existing law and procedure. He said that, "Our job is to strike at the roots of corruption, but the laws and codes, guiding the functioning of the agency, are constantly pulling us back". He pointed out that although the anti-corruption drive tops his agenda but inadequacies of power hinder the agency's work. According to Mr. Mishra, the biggest hindrance in the efficiency and working of the agency is the provision in the Central Vigilance Commission Act, regarding prior sanctions for investigating senior officials.[16] This provision has proved a big impediment for free

15. *The Times of India*, Late City Edition (Delhi), dated 16.04.05, p. 1.
16. In pursuance of the recommendations of the committee on prevention of corruption (The Santhanam Committee), the erstwhile Central Vigilance Commission was set-up. Initially it was attached to the Ministry of Home Affairs. Our Supreme Court vide its order dated 18th December 1997 in Vineet Narain and other *vs.* Union of India and other (Jain Hawala Case) struct down the provision known as 'single directive' and directed that statutory status should be conferred upon the Central Vigilance Commission which is responsible for the efficient functioning of the CBI. In pursuance of the directions of Supreme Court, the Government moved Central Vigilance Commission Bill, 1999 in Lok Sabha who passed it but in the mean time Lok Sabha was dissolved in 1999 and so Bill was lapsed. To continue the Commission the Government issued a resolution dated 4th April 1999. The Central Vigilance Commission is presently continuing on the basis of this resolution as a non-statutory body attached to the Ministry of Personnel, Public Grievances and Pension (Department of Personnel and Training).
Subsequently, Central Vigilance Commission Bill was passed by Parliament and after taking assent of the President the present Act, known as "The Central Vigilance Commission Act, 2003", came into existence. In this Act, the Government reintroduced the provision regarding 'single directive'. Section 6A of the Act provides:
Approval of central government to conduct inquiry or investigation.
The Delhi Special Police Establishment shall not conduct any inquiry or investigation in to any offence alleged to have been committed under the Prevention of Corruption Act, 1988 except with the previous approval of the central government where such allegation relates to (a) the employees of the Central Government of the level of Joint Secretary and above; and (b) such officers as are appointed by the Central Government in Corporations established by or under any Central Act Government Companies, Societies ancl Local authorities owned or controlled by that government.

and fair investigation. Some time it results in delays, at times it means compromising secrecy and very often meet with refusal, said Mr. Mishra. He cited example of a recent case involving Delhi Development Authority and a former High Court judge, in which agency had to wait more than seven months to get prosecution sanction. He was at pains to reveal that a former Petroleum Minister against whom CBI conducted a probe and found sufficient evidences to press for prosecution but agency filed for closure last year since it was denied sanction.[17]

In reply to a question, asked during an interview conducted by '*The Times of India*' Newspaper, why do some cases virtually go into hybernation after an initial splash by the agency. Mr. Mishra said, "Investigation is a quiet business. The expectations are high from the agency but what one has to understand is that, CBI is not the total criminal justice system of the society".[18]

From this free and frank admission of facts of CBI Chief, it can be concluded safely that CBI, which is required to be an independent body, is subject to rampant political interference in India. It is, therefore, suggested that CBI needs autonomy, freedom from political interference and an independent statutory status. Its officers should be selected from different pool, instead of being taken from Indian Police Service. The CBI Chief should not be answerable to the home ministry or any other ministry, including the Prime Minister's Office.

His appointment should be made through a process supervised by the Supreme Court.[19]

In our country, it is needless to say that, "The CBI is a crucial institution, because it has to act as a buffer against possible perfidies of the political and administrative machinery in specific situations. Civil society institutions, in search of justice, tend to demand a CBI probe to redress their grievances. The organisation, in the popular perception, has a quasi-judicial aura about it. Hence, it is vital that, in a conflict-ridden democracy, such as ours, the CBI comes across as credible influence. It should, at the least, act as a leash on erring officers. Sadly, politicians and bureaucrats use the CBI to settle personal scores. At present, senior bureaucrats enjoy extraordinary immunity, their prosecution often require ministerial sanction. A reformed CBI could help clean up our system considerably."[20]

Investigation process is also hampered by the issue of writs, prohibiting the taking into possession of documents or continuance of some steps, necessary for completion of the investigation. In most of the

17. *Ibid.*
18. *Ibid.*
19. *Ibid.*
20. *Ibid.*

cases, the main object behind the prayer for writ is to stall or delay the investigation process. It is, therefore, submitted that while exercising writ jurisdiction in cases of white-collar criminals, the courts should not ignore the paramount need for speedy and unhampered investigation of these offences which has paralysed the economic system of the country and hence, a threat to the democracy. Similarly, this must also be taken into consideration, while dealing with the grant of anticipatory bail to white-collar criminals.[21]

With the rapid advancement of technology, white-collar crimes have achieved greater international dimensions. This has further made the work of investigation agencies more difficult and challenging. In India, most of the investigation work is undertaken by police, so it requires the police to make more efforts to improve their effectiveness, through various training programmes, in the fields such as commerce, accounting, computer science, security frauds, etc. Their success, to cope with these problems also require international co-operation. It is, therefore, necessary to take steps to improve international co-ordination among police and intelligence agencies, so that there must be free flow in exchange of information.

4.3 THE PROBLEM OF ENFORCEMENT

White-collar crimes have become a matter of grave concern for the present government. The real solution of this problem lies in evolving effective enforcement agencies. Persuasion and warning by government, to save the collapse of economic structure of the country, brought no favourable response from business community. Consequently, these crimes are invading the political and economic sectors of our nation and have posed a great danger to the entire social texture and a threat to public welfare activities.

Despite their wide ranging effects, these crimes are not easily detected, due to their advanced technique, planned operation, complicated and well-executed affairs. These crimes, being a kind of organised crime, involve some form of organisation for economic gain, having formal arrangements between the various persons committing illegal acts. They involve the misuse of the legitimate technique of business, profession or high position and the persons involved in such crimes have high social and political power. Such crimes involve best available brains in the country to manipulate their activities and to find out the loopholes in the law to run their activities safely. Consequently, detection of these crimes become very difficult which ultimately make the enforcement of law almost impossible.

---

21. *Ibid.*

For example, Maintaining of Internal Security Act (M.I.S.A.), against economic offenders and Foreign Exchange and Prevention of Smuggling Activities Act, against hoarders and black-marketers for the protection of common man, has been thrown into a dustbin. This is the outcome of resentment of strong lobby, built by business community which has strong political clout. Due to this lobby, government is forced to give up its legitimate functions and allow the administrative machinery to be subverted. Many strong measures adopted by government, to control the alarming situation of economic exploitation, has been put off, by this strong class of society. The economic power, political influence and social status of white-collar offenders largely provide protection to them from prosecution and punishment. Consequently, these crimes go undetected, if not so, then unpunished despite the existence of various regulatory legislations which modify the traditional rules or criminal jurisprudence, to the disadvantaged of the white-collar criminals, by dispensing with the requirement of *mens-rea*[22] which is a necessary clement for criminal liability. Moreover, to make the enforcement of these social legislations more effective, the ordinary rules of Criminal Procedure Code and Evidence Act have been modified to the effect that the court shall presume the truth of the contents of document or statement or other matter produced by the prosecution which otherwise requires to be proved by the prosecution.[23] Similarly, benefit of probation laws has been denied to the white-collar criminals by making suitable amendments in pursuance of 47th report of the Law Commission of India.[24] The problem of punishing companies, for the commission of white-collar crimes, has also been overcome by making the manager, general secretary, or the person responsible for the conduct of business, at the time of the commission of the offence.[25]

In spite of all these efforts, to overcome the weaknesses of public welfare legislations, big businessmen, top politicians or bureaucrats escape from the claws and teeth of these absolute liability legislations. Commenting on this state of affairs, Mr. Justice P.N. Bhagwati, in his keynote address at the third All-India Congress on consumer protection,

---

22. *Ibid.*
23. For example, Section 39 of Foreign Exchange Management Act, 1999; Section 36A of Central Excise and Salt Act, 1994, Section 123 and 139 of customs Act, 1962; Section 14 of the Essential Commodities Act, 1955, etc.
24. E.g., Section 292A of Income Tax Act, 1961; Section 98D of Gold Control Act, 1968; Section 9E of Central Excise and Salt Act, 1944; etc. bars the application of Section 360 of the Criminal Procedure Act, 1973 and the probation of offenders Act, 1958; to the persons convicted for violation of these laws.
25. E.g., Section 10 or Essential Commodities Act, 1955; Section 17 of prevention of Food Adulteration Act, 1954.

held at Surat, on November 7, 1976 observed that, "During the course of his judicial experience, he had found that most of the cases which were brought to the courts, by the enforcement agency were cases involving small tradesmen, such as milk-vendors and grocers. It was rarely that he had cases where big dealers were involved, such as, wholesale dealers or semi-wholesale dealers. Somehow or the other, real culprits, who adulterate food are not caught. The enforcement agency directs inquiries and investigations against small traders or retailers whereas the evil lies with the stockiest, manufacturers and wholesale dealers."[26] So, the real problem in handling and disposal of white-collar crimes, lies with the enforcement agencies, who are not serious enough to perform their social obligations honestly. No serious efforts have yet been made, by enforcement agencies, to enforce laws relating to white-collar crimes properly in the modern developing economy of our nation.

Due to peculiar nature of these crimes, there is a practical difficulty in the enforcement of laws relating to white-collar crimes. It is extremely difficult to discover the existence of white-collar crimes. Similarly, it is also not very easy task to secure the evidence of criminal guilt of these criminals. Many times these crimes involve acts of omission rather than commission which can not be noticed easily. Most of these crimes are often committed under the privacy of business and hence not visible to nascent public eye. The victims of these crimes may not be aware at the time of offences that they have been victimised and so, they do not make any complaint to the law enforcing agencies. Since these crimes are generally committed in the course of ordinary business activities and thus, they are not easily distinguishable from non-criminal business conduct. There are also some serious practical problems in imposing sanctions upon the corporate employees. The top executives do not ordinarily carry out the criminal act themselves, rather it is done by lower or the middle functionaries, in the official hierarchy, who are generally associated with such crimes. Under the traditional doctrine, to hold superior responsible, it is required to be participated by him in his subordinate's criminal activities by an act of encouraging or aiding in its performance. In most of the cases it is very difficult to obtain evidence of such participation and so, they escape prosecution.[27]

One of the major problems in this field is the difference in the implementation of the criminal law in two types of classes, i.e. lower and Upper classes. The respect in which the crimes or the two classes differ are the incidentals rather than the essentials or criminality. The crimes of the lower class are handled by policemen, prosecutors and judges

26. Gurpal Singh; *op. cit.*, pp. 54-55.
27. Hon'ble Mr. Justice Prasun Kumar Deb, High Court, Patna, *op. cit.*, p. 63.

according to regular penal sanctions in the form of fines, imprisonment and death, while the crimes of the upper class, either result in no official act at all or result in suits for damages in civil courts or are handled by inspectors and by administrative boards or commissions, with penal sanctions: in the form of warnings, orders to cease and desist, occasionally the loss of a licence, and only in extreme cases by fines or person sentences. Thus, the white-collar criminals are segregated administratively from other criminals and as a consequence of this, are not regarded as real criminals by themselves, the general public, or the criminologists. The difference in the implementation of the criminal law is due to the difference in the social position of the two types of offenders. Because of their social status, they have a loud voice in determining, what goes in to the statutes and how the criminal law, as it affects themselves, is implemented and administered.[28]

It is also felt that traditional law enforcement process is by and large designed for the control of individuals and not for the control of organisations. So, the main task is to apply criminal sanction against white-collar crimes which are generally the result of some organisational behaviour. What is required, therefore, is to enact adequate and appropriate laws and their efficient implementation. As regards the existing law in our country regarding white-collar crimes, they could not achieve their targets very effectively because of political interference and corruption in enforcement officials. So, the real task is to take steps to keep enforcement agencies free from political influence as far as possible.

It is, therefore, necessary that a central enforcement agency must be created which must include persons, trained in various economic laws and their implementation. White-collar organisations operate not only intra-state but inter-state also, in such a situation centre can not investigate such crimes without consent of the concern states. Even CBI has no such power *suo-mottu*. It is, therefore, desirable to create a central task force to have all-India jurisdiction in cases of white-collar crimes.

4.4 THE PROBLEMS OF PROSECUTORS

One of the major problems of criminal justice system with regard to white-collar crimes, not only in our country, but worldwide is the nature of prosecutorial system. Cases are not wanting to illustrate the highly political nature of our prosecutorial system. In criminal cases, state is the prosecutor, so it is represented by public prosecutor. Public prosecutors for every high court are appointed by centre government or

28. E.H. Sutherland; White Collar Criminality, Geis, *op. cit.*, pp. 38-49.

state governments to conduct any prosecution, appeal or proceeding on behalf of the Central Government or State Governments. Similarly, Public Prosecutor and Additional Public Prosecutor for every district is appointed by the State Governments. It is, thus, clear that appointing authority of the whole prosecutorial system is government, so political interference is always there. In India, Attorney-General is appointed by President to perform duties of legal character assigned to him by the President. Similarly, Advocate-General for the state is appointed by the Governor. In England, the office of the Attorney-General is regarded as a political office in the sense that he is a member of the ministry and comes in and goes out with it. In India, the Attorney-General and Advocate-General are not the members of Council of Ministers but there is a practice that they also resign on the resignation of the Council of Ministers.[29]

It is the duty of Attorney-General to give advice to the Government of India upon legal matters and perform such other duties of legal character as may be assigned to him by the President. He has to appear on behalf of the Government of India in all cases. He has to represent the Government of India in any reference made by the President to the Supreme Court under Article 143. He may be required to appear in High Court also on behalf of the Government of India. The Attorney-General is the head of the Indian Bar and as such is entitled to precedence in all courts. In the United States of America, the Attorney-General is the chief federal prosecutor and belongs to the Department of Justice. He has to give opinions on legal matters referred to him either by the President or the departments. The prosecutorial system of United States, from the very beginning, was a political creature, responsive to the needs and whims of political powers.[30] In India, though the appointment of the Attorney-General is not purely political but it must be admitted that only a person who agrees with the policy of the political party in power would be able to discharge the functions of this office satisfactorily.[31]

Similar is the position of Advocate-General in the states. It is his duty to give advice to the government of the state upon all legal matters and to perform such other duties of legal character as may from time to time be referred to or assigned to him by the Governor and discharge the function conferred on him, under the constitution or any other law for the time being in force. He holds the office during the pleasure of the

29. Mahendra P. Singh, V.N. Shukla's Constitution of India; 8th edition (Reprinted) 1992, p. 279.
30. August Bequai; *op. cit.*, p. 149.
31. T.K. Tope, Constitutional Law of India; IInd edition, 1992, pp. 451-52.

Governor like Attorney-General who holds the office during the pleasure of the President. So it is understood that, though the appointment of Attorney-General and Advocate-General in India are not political in legal sense but nevertheless their office is a political office in the sense that a person who is appointed Attorney-General or Advocate-General must agree with the broad policy of the government.[32]

Like England, in India also, an attempt was made in 1962, by the then Law Minister, A.K. Sen, to merge the office of Attorney-General and the Law Minister and to make the latter the Attorney-General. This proposal sparked-off a controversy, between government of India and Bar Association of India. As the public reaction to the proposed merger was intense and against the proposal was dropped.[33] Thus, a move to make their office a political office was stopped.

It is, thus, clear from the above discussion that, like other countries, our prosecutorial system also suffers a set-back because of political interference. "It has been observed on investigation that U.S. Marshals and their deputies, in several major cities, were involved in many offences, such as, mob pay offs, extortion and narcotics trafficking, etc. Many of them were forced to resign. When a key official of the Marshal's service was asked why there has been no prosecutions, he noted that this was up to the U.S. Justice Department. In a large eastern city, a well known U.S. Attorney resigned under White-House pressure. This official held an excellent record in the area of white-collar crime prosecutions. Not to be outdone, prosecutors in a large southern city charged that the local U.S. Attorney had dropped a criminal investigation involving a friend of the President of the United States in order to stay in office another year, and not to jeopardize his government pension."[34]

These examples show the highly political nature of U.S. prosecutorial system. White-collar criminals have easy access to large sums of money and could influence powerful political officials. The prosecutors generally sustain the political process that produced them. The office of the prosecutor suffers from heavy political interference in its working and policies in the area of white-collar crimes. Many prosecutors, lack the requisite training, skill and resources to meet the great challenge of these crimes of recent origin. Whether the present apparatus will meet the future challenge of white-collar crimes is a question mark.[35]

---

32. *Ibid.*, p. 683.
33. M. Hidayatullah; Constitutional Law of India, Volume-I, First Published-1984, p. 786.
34. August Bequai; *op. cit.*, p. 147.
35. *Ibid.*

In India, our prosecutorial machinery is divided in two categories, namely: (a) central, and (b) state. Public prosecutors, in every High Court, are appointed by central or state governments after consultation with the High Court, to conduct prosecution on behalf of the central or state governments as the case may be. Similarly, public prosecutor for every district is appointed by the state government. A person may be appointed as Public Prosecutor if he has been in practice as an advocate for not less than seven years and his name appears on the panel of names prepared by the District Magistrate in consultation with the session judge. Additional Public Prosecutors for district may also be appointed by the state government. The central or the state government may appoint for the purpose of any case or class of cases an advocate as special public prosecutor provided he has been in practice for not less than ten years. For conducting the prosecutions in the courts of magistrates, the Assistant Public Prosecutors are appointed by the State Government in every district.[36] The Public Prosecutors appointed under section 24 of Criminal Procedure Code represent the state in all trials before the court of session and it is only he who is entitled to conduct prosecutions in a court of session.[37]

So, it is evident that all the prosecutors are appointed officials of Central or State Governments, so, they remain responsive to the political pressures of their environments. It is also a matter of common experience that our Attorneys and Prosecutors suffer from outdated practice, lack of funds and poor training. Prosecutors generally rely on the local police departments to investigate and bring cases to their office for prosecution. The strongness or success of their case depends upon the effectiveness of the investigation team who brings the case to their office from the grass-root of the case. Unfortunately, our law enforcement agencies lack such skill and special training and also lack of necessary funds to conduct extensive and complex investigations, such as those involving white-collar crimes. Since the cases of white-collar crimes are of complicated nature and usually quite difficult to investigate, so, they are poorly investigated and prepared, with the result that criminals of these offences can not be prosecuted. There is neither money nor the manpower to pursue such cases. So, to handle these crimes, a special skillful prosecutorial machinery must be developed with full manpower, funds and trained officials.

It has been experienced that the prosecutorial machinery at the local level is too small in number, ill-equipped and politicized to act decisively against major white-collar crime scandals. It is, therefore, suggested that a special training programme, funding and a sense of

36. Sections 24, 25 of "The Code of Criminal Procedure, 1973".
37. Section 225 of "The Code of Criminal Procedure, 1973".

professionalism are urgently needed, to bring this machinery in line with the tune of time.

Our prosecutorial system is as old as the republic itself, and from the very beginning, prosecutors have been political creatures, responsive to the need and whims of political powers. In this regard, one U.S. Attorney has noted that, "Loyalty to the political interest of the administration often required disloyalty to the goal of impartial justice..... It is not enough to change the label on the department of justice. What must be done is to change the functions of the Attorney General up and down the line."[38] So, what is needed, is to bring a change in the functioning of the prosecutorial machinery as regard to white-collar criminality. Our prosecutorial machinery has no specialised unit to handle white-collar crime cases and if some economic offence investigation bureau has been created recently, they are too small to handle the bulk of white-collar crimes and also lack of resources and manpower. It is, thus, easily concluded that the white-collar crime prosecutions are hampered by bureaucratic red tape, absence of firm commitment and the publicised nature of the prosecutorial system. The entire prosecutorial apparatus is, thus, in need of review and revision and what is needed to handle these crimes, is a strong will and strategy that must apply to them.

The above discussed problems, and many other such problems, have hampered the progress in the field of prevention and control of white-collar crimes. The basic principles of criminology, i.e. prompt cognizance, efficient investigation and speedy punishment are, unfortunately, missing in case of white-collar crimes. Consequently, these crimes are increasing very fast. The available data regarding white-collar crimes show an increasing trend with a fall in conviction rate.[39] This shows that more and more people are committing crime and getting away with it. Cases are settled alter a long time. Justice is being delayed and denied. Obviously, criminal justice system has failed in achieving its objectives in this field. Then question is, how has our government responded to the controlling of crime. Incidentally so far, we have not evolved a coherent well-knit national policy to deal with white-collar crimes and criminals. The working of our government in this field has been narrow, fragmented and *adhoc*.

Since independence, our government has adopted various measures and has made a huge expenditure on the various social welfare schemes but has failed to control the white-collar activities of corrupt officials, businessmen, traders and contractors. No doubt, the country has made some progress but still we have a long way to go to control these crimes.

---

38. August Bequai; *op. cit.*, p. 149.
39. M.P. Mehani, Financial Crimes and Frauds in Banking Industry; *CBI Bulletin*, Vol. VI, No. 9, September 1988, p. 16.

4.5 DEFICIENCIES IN EXISTING LAW AND LEGAL SYSTEM, TO COMBAT WHITE-COLLAR CRIME AND NEED FOR A NEW CODE

From the foregoing discussion, it is clear that our existing legal system is deficient in many ways and is inadequate to tackle the spreading dimensions of white-collar crimes. The investigating agencies are showing their incapability to cope with the challenge, prosecution is helpless, enforcement machinery is handicapped and society is worst sufferer. Corruption is rampant, fraud is visible in most of the transactions, public or private, atmosphere of chaos is all around and the show of money and muscle power is going on and has posed a great danger to the economic stability of the nation. In addition, imposition of fine on white-collar criminals is inadequate for a number of reasons. Penalty of fine can not be construed as adequate deterrent in cases of white-collar crimes. Most of the white-collar crimes are not specifically defined in the conventional criminal codes. The existing criminal law, through its different legislations, is not appropriate measure to deal with every type of white-collar misconduct.

The Indian Penal Code, the main substantive criminal law in India was first enacted in 1860 by Lord McCauley, the then President of Indian Law Commission. Similarly, Criminal Procedure Code, the main procedural criminal law in India was first came into effect in 1862. Both these criminal codes are old enactments but still deals with many white-collar crimes. With the advancement of time, these codes could not be changed in order to handle these newly grown crimes with Iron hands. In fact, our criminal law is favourable to the accused in many ways. Indian Penal Code does not prohibit people from committing offences, rather it encourages criminal minded persons to commit any offence, taking care that their act does not fall within the given definition of any offence. In other words, it educates criminals to escape prosecution charge, when caught, in spite of their intelligent execution of crime. So, there is a need, due to change of time, to redefine the offences. The penal code defines offence and prescribes punishment. Courts have been interpreting that if an alleged act fulfils all the essential conditions given in the definition, then only accused can be held guilty otherwise not. White-collar criminals are more educated and clever, so, they manage to commit an act in such a way as not to come within the defined comers of the offence.[40]

40. Prof. N. Narayana Swamy, Redefining Offences in Pental Code—An urgent necessity; Cri. L.J. 2002, p. 93.

Though Indian Penal Code deals with many white-collar crimes but considering the seriousness and gravity of these crimes, no proper punishments are provided in the code. The existing code provides penal sections for bribery and corruption by public servants in sections 161 to 165; for misuse of position by public servants in sections 168, 169, 207, 222 and 225; for counterfeiting of coins and government stamps in sections 230 to 263-A; for offence of weight and measures in sections 264 to 267; for adulteration of food stuffs and drugs in sections 272 to 276; for crimes of theft, misappropriation of public property, extortion, criminal breach of trust in sections 379, 380, 181, 405, 407, 408 and 409; for cheating and dishonestly inducing delivery of property in sections 415 to 420; for forgery and offence relating to documents in section 463 to 489 respectively. In support of the inadequacy of the punishment, few examples of the existing laws can be cited here according to which, when a person risks the lives of hundreds of persons by disobeying quarantine rule, is liable under section 271 I.P.C, for selling adulterated food and drink affecting thousands of people are liable under sections 272 to 273 I.P.C., and for default in selling of life protecting drugs is liable under sections 274 to 276 I.P.C. But in all these crimes, the code provides that the offence committed is a non-cognizable silly offence.[41]

In this reference it is said that, "In the paradox of existing legal system, stealing a bread by a poor hungry person and looting to government exchequer by person in authority, fraud or misappropriation of few rupees and big scams are considered as same offence and are dealt with on one legal platform. Corruption of few rupees by a government servant for his need and corruption of crores of rupees by powerful persons due to their greed are defined as same crimes in the Penal Code."[42]

In the present time, banking industry is facing lots of problems such as frauds, forgeries, manipulation of cheques and drafts, etc., computer crimes or cyber crimes are at the increase in the form of unauthorised attempt to access, alter, add, delete or hide date and change or alteration of the defined systems, etc., environmental crimes have made the public life miserable, consumer frauds have become talk of the day, almost every alternative day, there is a new economic scam published on the front page of the newspaper. Fraud in capital on stock market, tax fraud, insurance frauds, fraud in government contracts are very common these days but due to lack of effective provisions in our existing penal law, these crimes have become a great social risk.

---

41. Prabhat Chandra Tripathy; "The Menace of White-collar Crimes and need for a new Code", Cr.L.J./3-III, 1997, pp. 37-38.
42. *Ibid.*

White-collar crimes are rampant in other countries also but their government and judiciary are now handling the situation with the iron hands. They are enacting new laws to tackle this problem and judiciary too, is contributing to the national cause. "But, unfortunately, in our country still all types of big and small crimes are treated on an equal footing. No doubt, many special statutes have been enacted in India to control white-collar crimes but many of these acts are non-cognizable and police have no power to investigate these crimes. The present system to seek sanction of government to file charge-sheet in certain white-collar crimes and its power to withdraw the white-collar crimes, seems like corruption itself in legal system inserted to the advantage of the criminals. Though we have many laws on almost every aspect of public life but they are not properly enforced. Mark Twin has commented on this situation that, there is no end to the laws and no beginning to the execution of them."[43]

On the procedural side, our investigating officers are not well trained, well equipped and have no such skill and sound knowledge to fight with professional giants. The investigating officer with traditional qualification is not expected to investigate technical crimes like, computer crimes, bank frauds, share scam and consumer frauds, etc., effectively. With the advancement of science and technology, many advanced white-collar crimes are done through manipulation of records and documents which are diverse and complex in nature and are not easily accessible. Investigation, verification, expert's opinion and other scientific texts of such documents, take a lot of time. "Limited legal knowledge of investigators, common court trial in existing judicatory system, delay in delivery of justice, prevalence of accused favouring judicial system and rampant prosecution failures, now turn into a blessing for white-collar criminals. In the existing criminal justice system and particularly in white-collar economic crimes, involving crores of rupees, punishment till the rising of the day or punishment of fine seems totally unjustified, when a simple pickpocket stealing even a small sum of money would be sent to jail at least for six months."[44]

Hence, a new criminal jurisprudence is urgently needed to deal with the white-collar criminals. The existing criminal justice system is out modeled and so, in view of rapid rise in the magnitude of white-collar crimes, it is now an urgent need to draft a full proof code and to introduce a new justice system to prevent and control white-collar crimes in larger interest of the society. The Indian Penal Code does not provide appropriate punishment for white-collar crimes and so, is outdated. The

43. *Ibid.*, p. 39.
44. *Ibid.*

new code, is suggested to have new form of penal treatment, like public censure, canceling of licences, forfeiture of property, application of probation laws in deserving cases only and mandatory minimum imprisonment and fines. The burden of proof should lie on the accused, the presumption of innocence should not be stretched too far. The proof of *mens-rea* element should not be applied in cases of white-collar crimes. White-collar criminals should be treated like other criminals of lower class and no leniency is needed to be shown to them. The trial of these cases must be made speedy and if necessary, special courts to try these cases must be established.[45]

Therefore, to achieve the desired result in order to prevent and control the white-collar crimes, it has become necessary to review not only the existing legislative provisions but also the scheme relating to their cognizance, investigation, trial and punishment. What is needed, is an altogether new legislative, administrative and judicial rethinking to protect the economic interest of the society. The law must be effectively enforced and complied with. It is also needed to have specialised agencies with trained and skilled persons for investigation of these crimes and our courts should be trained to deal with these offences. It is, therefore, necessary for law-makers, lawyers, judges and people in general to think afresh on the subject and to make a full-fledged comprehensive penal code as required for today and tomorrow.

45. T.N. Ashok, White-collar crime, "Lawyer" 1983, Vol. XV, p. 105.

5

Judicial Trend against White-collar Criminality

Laws rule the poor, rich men rule the law.

—Oliver Goldsmith, "The Traveler"

It has already been noted that white-collar criminals are more dangerous than blue-collar criminals, as regard to the economic stability of the country, but even then in most of the cases they remained unpunished. One of the reasons, as explained by Sutherland himself, is the difference in implementation of the criminal law by the courts in white-collar crime cases. He has observed that:

> "The difference in the implementation of the Criminal Law is due principally to the difference in the social position of the two types of offenders. Because of their social status, implementation of the criminal law in relation to white-collar criminals becomes difficult. They are more powerful than the traditional criminals. Consumers, investors and stock-holders are unorganised, lack of technical knowledge and cannot protect them. White-collar crimes goes undetected because it transcends the visibility of ordinary cheating practices of small merchants."[1]

Another factor responsible for failure to punish the white-collar

---

1. Ahmad Siddiqui; *op. cit.*, p. 382.

offenders is that, the judges of the Courts Ordinarily belong to the upper section of the society and this factor may determine their attitude towards the white-collar offenders, who also come from the same social group.

The difference in the implementation of the criminal law and a soft attitude of the judiciary, since long back in cases of white-collar criminals, has been a great contributing factor to the increase of white-collar criminality. Courts generally have been giving light or even token punishments to white-collar criminals, not only in India, but all over the world. This can be illustrated from the following examples of the American society:

> "John B. Swainson, former Governor of Michigan and a judge of that state's Supreme Court, was convicted in 1975 of three perjury charges. He could have been sentenced to 15 years imprison; instead, he received a sentence of 60 days. Ralph L. Cummins, a former official of the U.S. Department of Transportation, could have been sent to prison for 20 years for accepting $ 40,000 in bribes. Instead, his sentence was two to six years."[2]

The Cummins sentence prompted an unusual courtroom protest by nearly a dozen federal prosecutors in the district of Colombia who objected to the lenient treatment given to white-collar criminals. The District Court Judge Howard Corcoran, however, did not move by the protest. He chose to blame Cummins crimes on easy access to whiskey.[3]

The record or Federal Courts in America also support this contention that white-collar offenders generally have received more lenient treatment than other offenders. "The statistics compiled by the administrative office of the federal courts show that in the year 1975, some 1158 persons were sentenced for income tax fraud. The majority were released on probation, and 112 received fines. Of the 367 who were jailed, only 13 received sentences of five years or more; 154 were given sentences of six months or less, followed by probation. Of more than 3000 persons who were sentenced for all types of fraud went to jail, most of them for one year or less. Only 285 of the 1605 embezzlers received jail terms, and more than half were for one year or less. Persons convicted of Price-fixing and other violations of antitrust laws fared even better. Out of 112 antitrust offenders, only 8 were given jail terms, none of them for more than one year."[4]

---

2. Vetter and Silverman; *op. cit.*, p. 267.
3. *Ibid.*
4. *Ibid.*, p. 268.

On the contrary, federal judges sentenced 1853 bank robbers and sent all but 185 to Prison. Terms of five years or longer were handed out to 1313.[5] Thus, the contrast in implementation of law and execution policies of the courts is clearly visible on the face of records of these courts. These examples exhibit the evidence of class bias which has aggravated the incidences of white-collar crimes in the society.

An arrangement is generally advanced by white-collar criminals that damage to their reputation from conviction is sufficient punishment for their crimes. But this is not enough, as regard to their guilt. They don't deserve any judicial leniency. It is, therefore, contended that the use of criminal sanction against economic criminals is necessary for two-fold purpose, punishment and deterrence. Imposition of prison sentence accompanied with appropriate high fine, should be the rule in white-collar criminal cases. General Richard L. Thornburgh, Assistant Attorney General, once time head of the department of criminal division of a State in America observed, with regard to the economic criminals:

> "We must increase the costs to him of committing such crimes by ensuring his detection, quick prosecution, and punishment more severe than the mere loss of his reputation and community standing—It is hard to justify incarcerating the III ghetto youth for theft of a car, while at the same time putting on probation the corrupt government official or crooked attorney who has abused his position and milked the public for larger sums of money."[6]

It is, however, true that the use of criminal sanctions in the prosecution of economic crimes poses a number of problems. For example, the use of criminal law in cases of fraud suffers a great difficulty in identifying and holding responsible those individuals within corporations who are actually responsible for the criminal action. The stiff legal requirements for using criminal sanctions, i.e. problems of proof "beyond a reasonable doubt" and *mens-rea* are yet another problems in reluctance of judges to use criminal sanctions against white-collar offenders. So, the olden days maxims are not golden sayings to be followed by the courts in the present scenario. There is a need to change or modify the maxims so as to suit the present and future.[7]

Despite these problems, our courts and other law enforcement authorities are moving ahead with programmes that seek to supplement civil investigations and prosecutions of white-collar crimes with criminal

---

5. *Ibid.*
6. *Ibid.*
7. Prof. V. Narayana Swamy. Redefining in Penal Code; An urgent need; *Criminal Law Journal*, 2002, p. 94.

sanctions. It is the need of the day of shifting judicial attitude from being awarding civil penalties to criminal sentencing to the white-collar criminals.

In 1974, U.S. District Court Judge Charles B. Renfrew of San Francisco conducted an experiment in sentencing of economic criminals. He ordered a group of individuals convicted of Price-fixing to deliver a dozen speeches of contrition each other, rather than serve sentence in prison. He then queried judge, prosecutors, defence attorney, and the defendants themselves about the deterrent effect of his alternative to imprison.[8] The following are excerpts from some of the responses he received:

> **According to one defendant in the case:** "The Stigma of conviction had a strong impact on me and it has not died away with the termination of my sentence and probation. The year of probation in which I carried out the sentence with twelve speeches is some thing that I shall never forget. The consequences of the publicity on me and my family in our social and business relations was beyond anything I had expected. I'm determined never to be exposed to such a risk again through any of my own actions. Perhaps a jail sentence might have been more punitive and shocking; it could not possibly have been more effective as a deterrent for me."[9]
>
> **A defence Attorney said:** I am certainly in agreement with your decision not to send these defendants to jail. All of them were, I am sure, exemplary citizens for the most part who had spend years paying their "dues" to their communities and to society while building a good reputation. Once these defendants were convicted of felony, their general reputations were either destroyed or badly damaged. A mere conviction, therefore, is about as severe as any sentence which you can impose upon an individual of that type. This differentiates the normal anti-trust defendants from the normal defendant in non-white-collar crimes.[10]

But one of the judges expressed his views in a different way. He said that:

> "Jail for "white-collar" defendants is the only real deterrent. It carries a social obloquy and brands the offender for what he is.

8. An article entitled, "White-Collar Justice" (United State, Law Week, 1976); Vetter and Silverman, *op. cit.*, p. 271.
9. *Ibid.*
10. *Ibid.*

It is not appropriate if truly technical offences, but fraud is another thing and certainly many *per se* violations of the Sherman Act fall in the same category. We judges tend to forget the suffering of those who are victimized by such offences. My experience at the bar was that one jail sentence was worth 100 consent decrees and fines are meaningless because the defendant, in the end, is always reimbursed by the proceeds of his wrong doing or by his company down the line."[11]

White-collar crimes, thus, have been treated differently by the courts since their inception. The reason being the old established doctrine of criminal law which sets the limits of criminal law and criminals. Another reason has been the consensus idea of society as to what the people in a society disapprove of and find most unacceptable. Due process doctrine of criminal justice system requires the state to prove the guilt of a defendant beyond reasonable doubt. The need of proving *mens-rea* is very difficult in most of the cases of white-collar crimes and particularly in cases of corporate crimes.

Parliament generally lays down some essential conditions for criminal conduct and sets out maximum punishment. The courts through the judges set the limits, as to limits of mental intention and punishment to be awarded to the criminal, in any particular case. In this way the role of judges is very important in outcome of any criminal trial. Legally, judiciary tries to avoid to create new offences but in fact, judges always have played an important role in development of the law by the process of interpreting the will of the parliament.

The grading of the various offences in the opinion of the parliament is based on their gravity which is generally assessed in terms of social danger, alarm, social disapproval, harm and wickedness involved in it. Unfortunately, white-collar crimes could not attract a greater attention of legislature as well as of judiciary, so as to be taken and handle them on priority basis in comparison of the ordinary crimes. Though white-collar crimes are crimes under the law but most of them are still dealt with by administrative and quasi-judicial bodies. It is only in recent times that greater attention is being put on these white-collar economic crimes. The reasons of this change in attitude are primarily due to consumer advocacy, environmental awareness and growth in science and technology, etc. in the recent time.

From the above discussed examples, it is evident that the attitude of judiciary has been very lenient towards white-collar criminals since long back and courts have been giving differential treatment to these

11. *Ibid.*, pp. 271-72.

criminals. Some times, instead of punishing the guilty, the courts have used cease and desist orders in case of white-collar criminals, a technique which is not generally resorted to for ordinary criminals. It has been observed by the Taft and England: "we do not warn the burglar to desist we arrest him forthwith and send him to prison". But in recent times a change in judicial attitude is visible all over the world. For example, in U.S.A. this change in attitude, regarding these crimes is seen in a famous General Electric Case of the electrical equipment companies decided in the year 1961. In the words of Taft and England:

> "The plea of *nolo contendere* (no contest) by a person formally accused of a crime, is a backhanded plea of guilty. For decades, businessmen accused of violating anti-trust laws have pleaded *nolo contendere* when the evidence against them was clearly overwhelming. Never until 1959, did imprisonment follow such a plea. In that year, to their astonishment four Ohio businessmen were sentenced to jail for anti-trust violations. In February 1961, 44 executives of 29 electrical equipment companies, including general electric and westing house, pleaded guilty or *nolo contendere* to charges of price-fixing and rigging bids on $7 billion worth of heavy electrical equipment. In addition to fines ranging up to $12500, 23 executives, one of whom was a Westinghouse Vice-President, were variously sentenced to 30 and 60 day, jail terms. Most of these sentences were actually served. The extensive press coverage given to this incident was apparently based not upon the enormity of the crimes involved, but upon nation wide surprise at the jail sentences meted out and upon the verbal reprimands uttered by the sentencing judge."[12]

The trial courts in India some times fail to realise the gravity of white-collar crimes and award light or token punishments to white-collar criminals. The Law Commission was fully aware of this judicial leniency towards white-collar crimes and the dangers inherent in it. In its forty-seventh report the commission observed:

> "Suggestions are often made that in order that the lower magistracy may realise the seriousness of some of the social and economic offences, some methods should be evolved of making the judiciary conscious of the grave damage caused to the country's economy and health by such anti-social crimes. We hope that the higher courts are fully alive to the harm, and we have no

---

12. Taft and England Criminology; IVth edition, 1964, p. 203.

doubt that on appropriate occasions, such as judicial conferences, the subject will receive attention. It is of utmost importance that all State instrumentalities involved in the investigation, prosecution and trial of these offences must be oriented to the Philosophy which treats these economic offences as a source of grave challenge to the material wealth of the nation."[13]

The case of *M.H. Hoskot.* vs. *State of Maharashtra*,[14] illustrates the attitude of the lower judiciary towards white-collar criminals. Hoskot, a reader in Saurashtra university, was found guilty of an attempt to concoct degree certificates of the Karnataka University. The Sessions Court awarded him a single day's imprisonment.[15] The Court justified the token punishment on the basis of the background of the offender. The court found that the offender had no criminal record in past and unlikelihood of his indulging in criminal activities in future. On appeal by the State, the High Court enhanced the period of imprisonment to three years. The Supreme Court also uphold the sentence awarded by the High Court, and held the sentence awarded by the Session Court as 'incredibly indiscreet'. Censuring the sessions court for the wrong sentencing, the Supreme Court observed:[16]

> "It is surprising that the Public prosecutor has consented, on behalf of the State, to this unsocial softness to an anti-social offender on conviction for grave charges. Does the administration sternly view white-collar offenders, or abet them by agreeing to award of token punishment, making elaborate trials mere tremendous trifles?"

The court further said, "Social defence is the criminological foundation of punishment—That court, which ignores the grave injury to society implicit in economic: crimes by the upper-berth 'mafia,' ill serves social justice. Softsentencing justice is gross injustice where many innocents are the potential victim . While iatrogenic prison terms are bad because they dehumanise, it is functional failure and judicial pathology to hold out a benignly self-defeating non-sentence to deviants who endanger the morals and morale, the health and wealth of society."[17]

---

13. S.M.A. Qadri; Ahmad Siddique: Criminology, Fifth edition, 2005, p. 417.
14. (1978) 3 SCC, 544; 1978 SCC (Cri) 468.
15. An imprisonment upto 7 years is permissible under section 468 of the India Penal Code.
16. S.M.A. Qadri; *op. cit.*, p. 418.
17. *Ibid.*

The above observation of the Supreme Court of India is a clear indication of changed approach regarding white-collar crimes in recent time. This case was, however, not a fit case of white-collar criminality according to the definition of white-collar crimes because the forged document was not prepared by any officer of the university in the course of their occupation but even then it shows the grave concern and changed trend of our judiciary for these crimes, affecting the society.

This change in attitude is also visible in some specific areas discussed as under:

5.1 CORRUPTION CASES

Corruption in recent time is wide ranging and almost all the sectors, private or public and departments of government are infected by this virus. Indian judiciary has also taken a serious view regarding offences of corruption committed by public servants. In *Krishan Dayal* vs. *State*[18] the court outlined the dangers involved in corruption cases committed by public servants and made the following observations:

> "A corrupt official is a menace to the society and far from helping in the proper functioning of the government and implementing the laws, brings the government and society at large into disrepute— If such public servants are open to corruption and coerce the public into paying them illegal gratification the whole structure of the society would be upset and the policy of the government and the legislature, howsoever beneficial it may be, would generally suffer. A public servant, therefore, once he is found to be guilty of accepting or obtaining illegal gratification, deserves no soft corner or indulgence from the courts of law."

Public servants are the back-bone of any government and through this bureaucratic set-up government implements its policies of social welfare in society. If public servants are corrupt, then government cannot fulfil its constitutional promises and ultimately fails in achieving its goal. Our Supreme Court has taken this cause seriously and indicated its policy, regarding the punishment of white-collar crimes in the context of corruption by Public servants. In *Sam Prakash* vs. *State of Delhi,*[19] Supreme Court observed that severe punishment must be prescribed to root out such social menace. Though all-intensive efforts to track down bigger criminals were needed, the courts could not slow down because bigger criminals were to caught.[20]

18. (1958) Raj, L.W. 596.
19. (1974) 4 SCC, 84; 1974 SCC (Cri) 215.
20. Ahmad Siddiqui: Criminology; Problems and Perspectives; Fourth edition, Reprinted 2001, p. 357.

In *Suresh Chandra* vs. *State of Gujarat*[21] the Supreme Court held that in case of an officer accepting bribes, the considerations that he is a petty official caught for a small bribe or that deterrent punishment is not feasible do not warrant a lesser sentence.

It has, however, been experienced that courts in India, not only adopted lenient view in cases of white-collar criminals, but have always considered the various factors to mitigate the punishment to them. And whenever any such factor associated with the offender's sentence existed, they always reduced the punishment as part of their sentencing policy. Cases are not wanting when courts undertook various extenuating factors in sentencing policy of these crimes. For example, sufferings accompanying the conviction or where offence happened to be not illegal gratification but criminal breach of trust committed due to the pressure of influence of superior officers, have been considered as grounds for reduction in punishment. The loss of membership of the Municipal Board has been accepted as a factor for reduction in punishment.[22] In many cases the loss of the job consequent to the conviction has been found relevant in reducing the term of imprisonment. So as a part of judicial policy, various factors such as loss of job,[23] mental agony, imprisonment already gone,[24] etc. were taken into consideration, over a long period of time. In many cases, courts have been of the view that too lenient as well as too harsh sentences both lose their efficacy. One does not deter and the other may make one a hardened criminal and so they adopted a middle way in sentencing policy of these cases.

5.2 FOOD ADULTERATION CASES

In Food Adulteration offences, courts generally have taken a strict view. In *State of Maharashtra* vs. *Jathmal Himatmal Jain*,[25] the Bombay High Court found the Punishment of one year imprisonment and a fine of Rs. 2500 awarded to be too inadequate. The appellants were found guilty of stocking and adulterating life-saving drugs and selling medicines, meant for hospitals, in the open market. The court raised the fine of Rs. 2500 to Rs. 1,00,000 on each convict on each count. The enhancement of fine was based on the fact that in crimes against society, fines must be sufficiently heavy in order to be meaningful.[26]

21. (1976) 1 SCC, 654; 1976 SCC (Cri.) 145, *ibid.*
22. Prem Chand *vs.* State, AIR 1957 All 381.
23. Chakravarti *vs.* State of M.P. (1976) 1, SCC, 281: 1976 SCC (Cri.).
24. Munna Lal *vs.* State of U.P., AIR 1964 SC 28: (1964) 1 Cri. L.J. 11.
25. 1994, Cri. L.J. 2613.
26. Ahmad Siddiqui (2001); *op. cit.*, p. 353.

In another black-marketing case *Adamji Dmar* vs. *State,*[27] Supreme Court made the following observation:

> "The determination of the right measure of punishment is often a point of great difficulty and no hard and fast rule can be laid down—but the court has always to bear in mind the necessity of proportion between an offence and the penalty. In imposing a fine, it is necessary to have as much regard to the pecuniary circumstances of the accused persons as to the character and magnitude of the offence. It is no doubt true that the offence of black-marketing is generally prevalent in this country at the present moment and when it is brought home against a person, no leniency in the matter of sentence should be shown and a certain amount of severity may be very appropriate and even called for."

From the above observation of the Supreme Court, it is clear that in food adulteration and black-marketing cases, our judiciary and particularly the higher judiciary has adopted a tough line. It is, however, a matter of common experience that many times the punishment given by lower courts are very low. The Gujarat High Court has made strong observations against socio-economic offences and passed severe strictures against the lenient attitude of the lower judiciary in food adulteration cases.[28] The court observed that:

> "It is part of the function of the courts to create an ethical climate by their decisions. The decisions mould public opinion and create an appropriate ecology. If we are seriously and sincerely striving for a just socio-economic order in an egalitarian society, can we look upon such modes of adding to One's wealth—with indulgence? The offenders must be made to realise that the moving finger writes and having written moves on. And that the message is: Thy days are numbered: while the purpose of the sentencing policy is not to terrorise unwary persons, it certainly is to strike terror in the evil-eyed avaricious offenders to ensure that it has its desired deterrent effect. Unless it is brought home to the offenders that the courts take an extremely serious view, all those who play with the health and well-being of the people and with the economy of the nation by indulging in hoarding, profiteering, black-marketing and tax-evasion will be

27. AIR 1952 SC 14: 1953 Cri. L.J. 542.
28. (1974) 15 GLR 736.

> tempted to commit and re-commit those offences. The sentence of fine can have no meaning when it bears no relation with the profit that the offender can earn by taking a small risk of a fine by entering a plea of guilt. The frequency with which a plea of guilt is made in such cases and is visited with the deceptive sentence of tom-sized mini-fines makes one seriously doubt whether such cases should be tried by the subordinate judiciary at all."[29]

The Prevention of Food Adulteration Act, 1954 is brought into force by the government of India to check these social evils in the larger public interest and for ensuring public welfare in country. In certain cases, the act provides for imposition of penalty even without proof of a guilty mind. This shows a grater degree of concern exhibited by parliament in so far as public health and safety is concerned. It is because of this intention of legislature, that our judiciary has also adopted a strict view in interpretation of food laws. The courts, in India are of the view that the need for prevention of future injury is as important as punishing a wrong-door after the injury is actually inflicted by adulterated food stuffs. Merely because a person who has actually suffered in his health after consuming adulterated food would not be before court in such cases, courts should not be too eager to quash on slender grounds the prosecutions for offences, alleged to have been committed under the Act.[30]

Highlighting the gravity of the offence under the Act, the court held that adulteration of food is a menace to public health. The Prevention of Food Adulteration Act has been enacted with the aim of eradicating anti-social-evil and for ensuring purity in the articles of food. In view of this Act and intention of legislature as revealed by the fact that a minimum sentence of imprisonment for a period of six months and a fine of rupees one thousand has been prescribed, the court should not lightly resort to the provisions of the Probation of Offenders Act, in the case of persons above 21 years of age found guilty of offences under this Act.[31]

Rebutting the necessity of proving *mens-rea* in such offences, the Supreme Court in *Kisan Trimak Kathule* vs. *State of Maharashtra*,[32] held that adulteration of food is so dangerous and widespread and has so often led to large human tragedies, sudden or slow, insidious or open, that total

29. Ahmad Siddique; *op. cit.*, p. 359.
30. State of Punjab *vs.* Devinder Kumar, AIR 1983, SC 545, 1983 Cri. L.J. 980: (1983) 2 FAC 99.
31. Ishar Das *vs.* State of Punjab, AIR 1972 SC 1295: 1972 Cri. LJ 874.
32. AIR 1977 SC 435: (1976) 2 FAC 188.

defence compels casting of absolute liability on the criminal, even if the particular offence is committed with an unsuspecting mense. So, it is that, *mens-rea* is excluded and proof of *actus-reum* is often enough.

From the above discussion it is clear that courts in India have adopted a tough attitude as regard to the offences of food adulteration under The Prevention of Food Adulteration Act. Courts have observed that, the offences under The Prevention of Food Adulteration Act, are on an increase, and not a single article of food is available which is not adulterated. In fact, the adulteration has reached the saturation point and offenders are not entitled to any leniency.[33] It is due to seriousness of offences under this Act that higher judiciary passed a censure against lower judiciary, where it has adopted a lenient view. In *Pyarali K. Tejani* vs. *Mahadeo Ramchandra Dange*,[34] Supreme Court held that the Magistrate has completely failed to appreciate the gravity of food offences when he imposed a heavily negligible sentence of one hundred rupees fine. In a country where consumerism as a movement has not developed, the common man is at the mercy of the vicious dealers. And when the primary necessaries of life are sold with serious admixtures for making profit, his only protection is The Prevention of Food Adulteration Act and the court. If offenders can get away with it by payment of trivial fines, as is the present case, it brings the law in contempt and its enforcement a mockery.

Despite, the tough line adopted by the judiciary in food adulteration cases, instances are not wanting when various mitigating factors were also considered to reduce the punishment. In *Bala Bahera* vs. *Puri Municipality*,[35] the accused, a hawker was found guilty of selling adulterated milk. The court held that, being his first offence, substantive imprisonment was not needed to be imposed.

Supreme Court also adopted a lenient view where offence committed under Food Adulteration Act was different from selling adulterated food. In *Gurmukh Singh* vs. *State of Punjab*,[36] the appellant was found guilty of non-renewal of licence and was awarded imprisonment of 6 months and a fine of Rs. 1000. The Supreme Court found it unreasonable and reduced it to the imprisonment of 7 days already undergone and a fine of Rs. 250.

In *Ajaib Singh* vs. *State of Punjab*,[37] the court considered the nature and properties of the adulterated substance. The offender was found

---

33. Sita Ram *vs.* State of Haryana (1982) 2 FAC 222 (Pb.)
34. AIR 1974 SC 228, 1974 Cri. L.J. 313: FAC 74, Also Mohan Lal Chunnilal *vs.* K.M. Chauhan, Food Inspector, 1986, EFR 142.
35. (1973) CWR 744.
36. (1972) 4SCC 805: AIR 1972 SC 824: 1972 Cri. L.J. 634.
37. (1974) 76 PLR 45.

guilty of adulterating milk with Sucrose which is the major ingredient of Sugar. The High Court recommended a lenient sentence because Sugar was not injurious to health but rather nutritious.

Our Supreme Court has, thus, adopted a tough line to deal with white-collar crimes and favoured strict punishment, but in a number of cases it has adopted a liberal interpretation of penal laws which are dealing with social welfare legislation in order to see that the legislative object is not defeated. In *Murlidhar Meghraj Loya* vs. *State of Maharashtra*[38] the court observed that:

> "It is trite that the social mission of food laws should inform the interpretative process so that the legal blow may fall on every adulterator. Any narrow and pedantic literal and lexical construction likely to leave loopholes for this dangerous criminal tribe to sneak out of the meshes of the law should be discouraged. For the new criminal jurisprudence must depart from the old canons, which make indulgent presumptions and favoured constructions benefiting accused persons and defeating criminal statutes calculated to protect public health and the nation's wealth."

Similarly in *State of Maharashtra* vs. *Mohd Yaqub*,[39] the court adopted a liberal interpretation to suppress smuggling activities.

It is also with the tune of time that courts in India have given strict interpretation to the socio-economic statutes which do not require any *mens-rea* either in the form of intention or knowledge for committing an offence.[40] Dealing with a violation of the Foreign Exchange Regulation Act, 1947 the Court in *State of Maharashtra* vs. *George*[41] held that the very object and purpose of the Act and its effectiveness as an instrument for the prevention of smuggling activities would be entirely frustrated if conditions were to be read into section 8(1) or Section 8(1-A) of the Act qualifying the plain words of the enactment that the accused be proved to have knowledge that he was contravening the law, before he could be held to have contravened the provision.

In *State of M.P.* vs. *M/s Asian Drugs*,[42] the court observed that where a particular act is made statutorily penal, the question of *mens-rea* does not arise, if the act is proved. Manufacturing of drugs contrary to the terms of licence granted to the manufacturer is not only prohibited

38. (1976) 3 SCC 684: 1976: 1976 SCC (Cri.) 493
39. (1980) 3 SCC 57; 1980 SCC (Cri.) 513.
40. Ahmad Siddique (2001), *op. cit.* pp. 383-386.
41. AIR 1965 SC 722 (1965) Cri. L.J. 6-11.
42. 1990, Cri. L.J., 105.

but also made penal under The Drugs and Cosmetics Act, 1940. It is not open to court to insist for any proof of guilty mind on the part of the accused contravening the terms of licence. Acquittal based on such erroneous assumptions of law in not sustainable.

It is, thus, clear that our legislature has also shown its grave concern about these crimes and has amended various Acts and Statutes by rebutting the necessity of *mens-rea*, to bring them to the need of time. In *State of M.P.* vs. *Narayan Singh*,[43] a lorry driver who along with the cleaner was prosecuted under Fertilizer Movement Control Order for exporting fertilizer without a valid permit. The defence taken by the driver was that they were not aware of the contents of the document seized from them and that they were not engaged in exporting fertilizer. But the Supreme Court held the driver liable on the basis of factum of attempt to export by observing that section 7 of The Essential Commodities Act, 1955 includes the contravention done knowingly, intentionally and even unintentionally.[44]

The court in *Mis Shri Laxmi Trading Co.* vs. *Additional District Magistrate (C.S.S.), Rourkela*,[45] further added that section 10 of the Essential Commodities Act raises a presumption that culpable mental state exists, however, it is a rebuttable presumption and it would be open for the accused to prove that he had no such mental state with respect to the act charged. This section places heavy burden on accused to prove defence plea beyond reasonable doubts.[46]

Despite a strict attitude of our judiciary in economic and social offences, there are cases when courts' in India have always considered various mitigating factors to reduce punishment of such offenders. In *Bharat Prasad Gupta* vs. *State of Maharastra*,[47] the Supreme Court held that the factors that petitioner remained in custody during trial and that he was having a large family and case was going on for the last two decades, the sentence was reduced which was held already undergone.

Similarly, where the accused was alleged to have medicines for sale without licence and the defence taken by accused was that he is a research scholar and had kept medicines for research work, the accused was given benefit of doubt.[48]

It is, thus, evident from the above discussion that the legislature and courts in India are now serious to make the law effective regarding

---

43. AIR 1989 SC 1789.
44. Dr. B.K. Sharma, Dr. Vijay Nagpal, K.K. Khandelwal; A treatise on Economic & Social offences; First education, 2003, p. 228.
45. 1989, Cri. L.J., 659.
46. AIR 1996, SC 1043.
47. AIR 1996, SC 1043.
48. 1989, Cri. L.J. (NOC) 22.

white-collar crimes and its implementation so that the growing trend of these crimes may be curbed, if not completely checked. Judicial attitude is also very strict in this regard and they are contributing a lot to suppress this mischief and advance the cause of economic and social legislations. But at the same time cases are not wanting when quite unwanted lenient attitude has been shown by our judiciary towards white-collar criminals and various mitigating factors have been considered to reduce the punishment of these offenders. Consequently, all economic laws in India could not achieve their required objectives and growth of these crimes is going on unabated.

6

White-collar Crime and the Prevention of Corruption Act

Power always thinks it has a great soul and vest views beyond the comprehension of the weak and that it is doing God's service when it is violating all his laws.

—John Quincy Adams

There are certain anti-social activities which the persons of upper strata carry on in course of their occupation or business. These anti-social activities are called white-collar crime. These activities for a long time were accepted as a part of usual business tactics necessary for a shrewd professional man for his success in profession or business. *E.H. Sutherland* defined a white-collar criminal as a person of the upper socio-economic class who violates the criminal law in the course of his occupational or professional activities. White-collar crime was more dangerous to society than ordinary crimes because of greater financial losses and because of the damage inflicted on public morals.

White-collar crime is pervasive in almost all the professions and occu-pations in our society. The problem is quite acute, both in terms of variety and the extent of white-collar criminality. The report of *Santhanam Committee* in its findings gave a vivid picture of white-collar crimes committed by persons of respectability such as businessmen, industrialist, contractors and suppliers as also the corrupt public officials.

The white-collar crimes which are common to Indian trade and business world are hoardings, profiteering and black marketing. Violation of foreign exchange regulations (i.e. FERA) and import and export laws are frequently resorted to for the sake of huge profits. Further, adulteration of food-stuffs, edibles and drugs which causes irreparable damage to public health is yet another white-collar crime common in India.

The complexity of tax-laws in India has provided sufficient scope for the tax-payers to evade taxes. It is to be noted that tax-evasion is illegal, but tax-avoidance not. Tax-evasion implies non-payment of tax due to be paid, the tax-avoidance signifies arranging the spread over of one's income in such a way that it does not incur tax-liability legally and lawfully. In the profession of medicine, most common instances of white-collar criminality are illegal abortions, false medical certificates and unnecessary prolonged treatment in many cases. The usual legal and professional violations committed by lawyers are: advising organized criminals, aiding in performing false claims, engaging professional witness, fabricating false evidence, etc. In the engineering profession, understand dealing with contractors and suppliers, passing of sub-standard works and materials and maintenance of bogus records of work. Charged labours are some of the common examples of white-collar crime.

Corruption is also a well known white-collar crime. It is not limited to the concept of bribes of illegal gratification taken by public servants.

In its wider sense, corruption includes all forms of dishonest gains in cash, kind or position by persons in government and those associated with public and political affairs. The two government departments which have been traditionally notorious for corruptions in the country are those of police and public works.

There are some of the remedial measures for combating white-collar criminality, which are, creating public awareness against these crimes through the media of press, and other audio-visual aids and legal literacy programmes. Special Tribunals should be constituted with power to award sentence of imprisons upto 5 years for white-collar crimes. Convictions should result in heavy fines rather than arrest and detention of white-collar criminals. And public vigilance seems to be corner-stone of anti-white-collar crime strategy. Unless people strongly detest such crimes, it will not be possible to contain this growing menace.

In India there is need for strengthening of morals particularly in the higher strata and among the public services. It is further necessary to evolve sound group norms and services ethics based on the concepts of absolute honesty and integrity for the sake of national welfare. This is possible through character building at grass-root level and inculcating feeling of real concern for the motherland among youngsters so that they are prepared for an upright living when they enter real life.

From the foregoing discussion of the growing incidences of 'white-collar crimes' and 'social and economic crimes' in all directions, it is evident that the problem has assumed alarming dimensions in every walk of life. These crimes cause great financial loss to the government and public in comparison to the traditional blue-collar crimes. They also cause great injury to public health, public morale and general social and ethical values. I, therefore, feel that till the moral and ethical degradation of the social values is not checked/controlled or minimized, the incidence of white-collar crimes would go on increasing and their beneficiaries, the white-collar criminals, will flourish in the society.

These crimes have become a challenge to the law and enforcement machinery of the State and the country as a whole, because common man is the worst sufferer from these crimes. Therefore, measures of social defence are required to be made more prompt and effective to avert the potential danger of the collapse of democratic set-up of our national economy, because white-collar crimes are the problems of a democratic society and not of the totalitarian society. Unfortunately, our society and media have not shown much concern for this problem. Therefore, law enforcement agencies have a special responsibility in dealing effectively with such crimes. The press and mass media should also be utilised to create awareness about the grave social effects of these crimes.

One area which has also been ignored so far is the preparation of the annual report of these crimes. The subject is summarily dealt with and no serious effort is undertaken in formulating data of such crimes. So, there is a serious need of starting with the analysis of data to identify the status and background of white-collar criminals, the types of victims, the area of operation, their '*modus-operandi*', the financial implications and other relevant areas of study.

White-collar/economic crimes have been neglected by the criminal justice system from the very beginning, i.e., since their being noticed by Sutherland in 1930's. It is only in recent times that a great concern is made by our society towards these crimes. Ecology, environmental protection advocates and consumer advocacy have made substantial contribution towards increasing the public awareness of economic. But still the persons involved in these crimes are neither treated as ordinary criminals nor punished adequately, instend they move freely in the society like other respectable persons. This is because money and muscle power command everything including 'respect' and 'statuses'. The white-collar criminals, therefore, must be punished physically and monetarily. Mere public humiliation, at being caught, is momentary because public memory is very short.

There is a lack of social awareness, social consciousness and social education towards such type of crimes. Our media has failed to perform its duty in this regard because it is generally controlled by the upper section of the society. There is a class bias of the judicial tribunals, because such persons come from the more affluent section of the society. The consequences of these crimes are grave and far reaching. They have shattered the economic development of our society, adversely affected the health and happiness of the nation, demoralised people, degraded the public faith and belief, generated the feeling of distrust, caused moral degradation of the society and has created a feeling of disrespect towards the law and the enforcement machinery. Hence, it is high time to modify our traditional and conventional concept of crime, so as to make it suitable to the present and future criminal environment. The definition of crime should no longer be limited to the offences against human body, property and the State which are generally committed by the persons of lower class of society but must be wide enough, so as to include the illegal acts committed by the persons of upper class of the society. Time and tide wait for none. So, the law must change in line with the time. It is, therefore, an urgent need to redefine the law from time to time.

The olden day's maxims of criminal law should no longer be stretched to be followed in present time. There is a need to modify these old maxims, so as to suit the present and the future. The maxims like, the 'guilt of accused should be proved beyond all reasonable doubts', 'the guilt should be brought home to the accused' or 'benefit of doubt should go in favour of the accused' shall be given up in view of new trends. The doctrine of *mens-rea* and that 'let 100 guilty go unpunished but not an innocent', make a mockery of law and justice. In a group of smugglers, drug mafias, etc., if one of them is innocent and it is doubtful to identify who that one is, all the culprits are entitled to be acquitted, is a matter of laughter today. This is not proper in today's society, rather if one innocent is to be sacrificed in such circumstances, for the good of society; it is a great sacrifice of him. But if in order to save one innocent, other culprits are acquitted, the society will be full of offenders and that is, what is happening today. It is, therefore, necessary to give a fresh thinking to the subject and change the old laws and bring in new laws as required for today and tomorrow.[1]

At present, there are many Central Acts, besides State enactments to deal with social and economic offences, but there is a lack of uniformity in punishment, procedure and investigation techniques. The provisions and their implementation are also very complicated. There is a wide range of economic offences, some of them are cognizable and

1. V. Narayana Swami; Redefining Offence in Penal Code. An urgent necessity; Cr. L.J. 2002, p. 94.

some non-cognizable in nature. So, the police alone is not directly empowered nor are they equipped adequately to investigate and deal with white-collar offenders except in cognizable offences. On the other hand, there are many economic offences such as cheating, counterfeiting, criminal breach of trust, etc. which are dealt with by Indian Penal Code and regular police deals with these offences. So, in order to remove this obscurity in existing law relating to social and economic offences which is found in various statutes and to bring uniformity in their application, it is suggested to make a comprehensive unified criminal code to deal with these offences on scientific basis under a Central Act. This has become more urgent in modern time because of advanced technology and increasing reliance on computer. We are shifting from the world of electronics to the computer age, so, there is a need of advance planning to deal with these new kinds of crimes.

The main motive of white-collar economic offences is to earn wealth through illegal and illicit means. The emerging global trend to combat these crimes which is popularly known as 'Money Laundering' and 'Dealing in Proceeds of Crime' is by enacting legislations that could give power to attachment and seizure of the property illicitly achieved. Some of the existing legislations of our country are also enacted in this line and they provide for confiscation of the proceeds of crime and forfeiture of assets.[2] But these Acts are not so effective and many deficiencies are coming out in their effective implementation. So, in this area also, a new comprehensive legislation is urgently required to plug the existing loopholes and to make confiscation of properties and forfeiture of assets more effective, in the light of new legislations adopted in different countries.

The main object of punishment is to deter the accused from repeating the crime in future and a warning to other criminals. It is, therefore, necessary that the law should adopt a strict, not a lenient, attitude in awarding punishment to a white-collar or a socio-economic criminal. The purpose of the law will fail if it shows soft attitude to such criminals. Dr. Radhakrishnan, the second President of India, has expressed his views in this context. He said:

> "The Practitioners of this evil, the hoarders, the profiteers, the black-marketers, and speculators are the worst enemies of our society. They have to be dealt with sternly, however well placed,

---

2. Some of them are, Criminal Law (Amendment) Ordinance, 1944; Customs Act, 1962 (Secs. 119 to 122), Criminal Procedure Code, 1973) (Sec. 452); Foreign Exchange Management Act, 1999 (Sec. 13); Smugglers and Foreign Manipulators (Forfeiture of Property) Act, 1976; Narcotic and Psychotropic Substances Act, 1985; Terrorist and Disruptive Activities (Prevention) Act, 1981 (Secs. 8 to 21), etc.

important and influential they may be; if we acquiesce in wrong-doing, people will lose faith in us."[3]

Justice Krishna Iyer also made his deep concern about these crimes. He observed that:

> "The economic dacoits of the nation, who include the politico-economic delinquents and other white-collar offenders are the exploiters of the health and wealth of the country, and yet there is demonetizations of legislation, there is no stiff penal action against black marketers and hoarders and the worse, there is bearer bond mortality to bail out banians with varnish of innocence, with all their wealth accumulated by guilt."[4]

Accordingly, the penalty imposed for white-collar crimes should be more punitive and should vary according to the gravity of the offence. For example, in offences which affects health, like adulteration of food, drinks and drugs or the offences which adversely affect the economy of the country, such as smuggling, tax evasion, hoarding, black-marketing, etc., the penalty imposed must be harsh and more severe in order to control these grave offences.

Our existing criminal law and criminal justice system is deficient in many ways. In fact, our entire penal model was designed to deal with traditional criminals which has become outdated in cases of white-collar crimes, as they are the outcome of modem technological development. We have many laws on almost every aspect of public life of our country but it is observed that they are not seriously enforced. Our investigating officers with present training system and qualifications, have no such skill and knowledge so as to combat with these white-collar and professional criminals which are the product of modern complex society. With the development of science, technology and computer, many new kinds of offences are emerging which could not be foreseen or even dreamt of in 1860 when McCauley drafted our Indian Penal Code. What a computer is or what cyber crimes are, it was not known to the people 25 years ago. Hence, in view of rapid rise in magnitude and dimension of white-collar crimes, it is high time to draft a new comprehensive and complete criminal code to prevent and control white-collar crimes. It is also necessary that for proper and effective enforcement of legislations against white-collar crimes, there is a need to gear up the working of all agencies by providing them independence of action, freedom from

3. K.D. Gaur, Criminal Law and Criminology (2002), p. 289.
4. Justice Krishna Iyer; Indian Social Justice in Crisis (1983), p. 53.

political interference, more qualified and trained staff, waiving of the condition of prior sanction of government, etc.

In order to control the white-collar crimes, it is not enough to simply modernise the investigatory and prosecutorial machineries, but we have to look into the functioning of judiciary also. What is needed is the speedy disposal of these cases. For that purpose, it is suggested that a strict time limit of their judgment and appeal must be fixed and if necessary then special courts for trial of these cases must be established by treating these white-collar criminals as a "special class".

THE PREVENTION OF CORRUPTION ACT, 1988
[Act No. 49 of 1988 dated 9th September, 1988]

An Act to consolidate and amend the law relating to the prevention of corruption and for matters connected therewith.

BE it enacted by Parliament in the Thirty-ninth Year of the Republic of India as follows:

CHAPTER I

PRELIMINARY

1. Short title and extent

(1) This Act may be called the Prevention of Corruption Act, 1988.

(2) It extends to the whole of India except the State of Jammu and Kashmir and it applies also to all citizens of India outside India.

2. Definitions

In this Act, unless the context otherwise requires,—

(a) "election" means any election, by whatever means held under any law for the purpose of selecting members of Parliament or of any Legislature, local authority or other public authority;

(b) "public duty" means a duty in the discharge of which the State, the public or the community at large has an interest;

Explanation.—In this clause "State" includes a corporation established by or under a Central, Provincial or State Act, or an authority or a body owned or controlled or aided by the Government or a Government company as defined in section 617 of the Companies Act, 1956;

(c) "public servant" means—

(i) any person in the service or pay of the Government or remunerated by the Government by fees or commission for the performance of any public duty;

(ii) any person in the service or pay of a local authority;

(iii) any person in the service or pay of a corporation established by or under a Central, Provincial or State Act, or an authority or a body owned or controlled or aided by the Government or a Government company as defined in section 617 of the Companies Act, 1956;

(iv) any Judge, including any person empowered by law to discharge, whether by himself or as a member of any body of persons, any adjudicatory functions;

(v) any person authorised by a court of justice to perform any duty, in connection with the administration of justice, including a liquidator, receiver or commissioner appointed by such court;

(vi) any arbitrator or other person to whom any cause or matter has been referred for decision or report by a court of justice or by a competent public authority;

(vii) any person who holds an office by virtue of which he is empowered to prepare, publish, maintain or revise an electoral roll or to conduct an election or part of an election;

(viii) any person who holds an office by virtue of which he is authorised or required to perform any public duty;

(ix) any person who is the president, secretary or other office-bearer of a registered co-operative society engaged in agriculture, industry, trade or banking, receiving or having received any financial aid from the Central Government or a State Government or from any corporation established by or under a Central, Provincial or State Act, or any authority or body owned or controlled or aided by the Government or a Government company as defined in section 617 of the Companies Act, 1956;

(x) any person who is a chairman, member or employee of any Service Commission or Board, by whatever name called, or a member of any selection committee appointed by such Commission or Board for the conduct of any examination or making any selection on behalf of such Commission or Board;

(xi) any person who is a Vice-Chancellor or member of any governing body, professor, reader, lecturer or any other teacher or employee, by whatever designation called, of any University and any person whose services have been availed of by a University or any other public authority in connection with holding or conducting examinations;

(xii) any person who is an office-bearer or an employee of an educational, scientific, social, cultural or other institution, in whatever manner established, receiving or having received any financial assistance from the Central Government or any State Government, or local or other public authority.

Explanation 1.—Persons falling under any of the above sub-clauses are public servants, whether appointed by the Government or not.

Explanation 2.—Wherever the words "public servant" occur, they shall be understood of every person who is in actual possession of the situation of a public servant, whatever legal defect there may be in his right to hold that situation.

3. Power to appoint special Judges

(1) The Central Government or the State Government may, by notification in the Official Gazette, appoint as many special Judges as may be necessary for such area or areas or for such case or group of cases as may be specified in the notification to try the following offences, namely:

(a) any offence punishable under this Act; and

(b) any conspiracy to commit or any attempt to commit or any abetment of any of the offences specified in clause (a).

(2) A person shall not be qualified for appointment as a special Judge under this Act unless he is or has been a Sessions Judge or an Additional Sessions Judge or an Assistant Sessions Judge under the Code of Criminal Procedure, 1973.

4. Cases triable by special Judges

(1) Notwithstanding anything contained in the Code of Criminal Procedure, 1973, or in any other law for the time being in force, the offences specified in sub-section (1) of section 3 shall be tried by special Judges only.

(2) Every offence specified in sub-section (1) of section 3 shall be tried by the special Judge for the area within which it was committed, or, as the case may be, by the special Judge appointed for the case, or where there are more special Judges than one for such area, by such one of them as may be specified in this behalf by the Central Government.

(3) When trying any case, a special Judge may also try any offence, other than an offence specified in section 3, with which the accused may, under the Code of Criminal Procedure. 1973, be charged at the same trial.

(4) Notwithstanding anything contained in the Code of Criminal Procedure, 1973, a special Judge shall, as far as practicable, hold the trial of an offence on day-to-day basis.

5. Procedure and powers of special Judge

(1) A special Judge may take cognizance of offences without the accused being committed to him for trial and, in trying the accused persons, shall follow the procedure prescribed by the Code of Criminal Procedure, 1973 for the trial of warrant cases by Magistrates.

(2) A special Judge may, with a view to obtaining the evidence of any person supposed to have been directly or indirectly concerned in or privy to, an offence, tender a pardon to such person on condition of his making a full and true disclosure of the whole circumstances within his

knowledge relating to the offence and to every other person concerned, whether as principal or abettor, in the commission thereof and any pardon so tendered shall, for the purposes of sub-sections (1) to (5) of section 308 of the Code of Criminal Procedure, 1973, be deemed to have been tendered under section 307 of that Code.

(3) Save as provided in sub-sections (1) or sub-section (2), the provisions of the Code of Criminal Procedure, 1973, shall, so far as they are not inconsistent with this Act, apply to the proceedings before a special Judge; and for the purposes of the said provisions, the Court of the special Judge shall be deemed to be a Court of Session and the person conducting a prosecution before a special Judge shall be deemed to be a public prosecutor.

(4) In particular and without prejudice to the generality of the provisions contained in sub-section (3), the provisions of sections 326 and 475 of the Code of Criminal Procedure, 1973, shall, so for as may be, apply to the proceedings before a special Judge and for the purposes of the said provisions, a special Judge shall be deemed to be a Magistrate.

(5) A special Judge may pass upon any person convicted by him any sentence authorised by law for the punishment of the offence of which such person is convicted.

(6) A special Judge, while trying an offence punishable under this Act, shall exercise all the powers and functions exercisable by a District Judge under the Criminal Law Amendment Ordinance, 1944.

6. Power to try summarily

(1) Where a special Judge tries any offence specified in sub-section (1) of section 3, alleged to have been committed by a public servant in relation to the contravention of any special order referred to in sub-section (1) of section 12A of the Essential Commodities Act, 1955 or of an order referred to in clause (a) of sub-section (2) of that section, then, notwithstanding anything contained in sub-section (1) of section 5 of this Act or section 260 of the Code of Criminal Procedure, 1973, the special Judge shall try the offence in a summary way, and the provisions of sections 262 to 265 (both inclusive) of the said Code shall, as far as may be, apply to such trial:

Provided that, in the case of any conviction in a summary trial under this section, it shall be lawful for the special Judge to pass a sentence of imprisonment for a term not exceeding one year:

Provided further that when at the commencement of, or in the course of, a summary trial under this section, it appears to the special Judge that the nature of the case is such that a sentence of imprisonment for a term exceeding one year may have to be passed or that it is, for any other reason, undesirable to try the case summarily, the special Judge shall, after hearing the parties, record an order to that effect and thereafter recall any witnesses who may have been examined and proceed to hear or re-hear the case in accordance with the procedure prescribed by the said Code for the trial of warrant cases by Magistrates.

(2) Notwithstanding anything to the contrary contained in this Act or in the code of Criminal Procedure, 1973, there shall be no appeal by a convicted person in any case tried summarily under this section in which the special Judge passes a sentence of imprisonment not exceeding one month, and of fine not exceeding two thousand rupees whether or not any order under section 452 of the said Code is made in addition to such sentence, but an appeal shall lie where any sentence in excess of the aforesaid limits is passed by the special Judge.

CHAPTER III

OFFENCES AND PENALTIES

7. Public servant taking gratification other than legal remuneration in respect of an official act

Whoever, being, or expecting to be a public servant, accepts or obtains or agrees to accept or attempts to obtain from any person, for himself or for any other person, any gratification whatever, other than legal remuneration, as a motive or reward for doing or forbearing to do any official act or for showing or forbearing to show, in the exercise of his official functions, favour or disfavour to any person or for rendering or attempting to render any service or disservice to any person, with the Central Government or any State Government or Parliament or the Legislature of any State or with any local authority, corporation or Government company referred to in clause (c) of section 2, or with any public servant, whether named or otherwise, shall be punishable with imprisonment which shall be not less than six months but which may extend to five years and shall also be liable to fine.

Explanations.—(a) "Expecting to be a public servant." If a person not expecting to be in office obtains a gratification by deceiving others into a belief that he is about to be in office, and that he will then serve them, he may be guilty of cheating, but he is not guilty of the offence defined in this section.

(b) "Gratification." The word "gratification" is not restricted to pecuniary gratifications or to gratifications estimable in money.

(c) "Legal remuneration." The words "legal remuneration" are not restricted to remuneration which a public servant can lawfully demand, but include all remuneration which he is permitted by the Government or the organisation, which he serves, to accept.

(d) "A motive or reward for doing." A person who receives a gratification as a motive or reward for doing what he does not intend or is not in a position to do, or has not done, comes within this expression.

(e) Where a public servant induces a person erroneously to believe that his influence with the Government has obtained a title for that person and thus, induces that person to give the public servant, money or any other gratification as a reward for this service, the public servant has committed an offence under this section.

8. Taking gratification, in order, by corrupt or illegal means, to influence public servant

Whoever accepts or obtains, or agrees to accept, or attempts to obtain, from any person, for himself or for any other person, any gratification whatever as a motive or reward for inducing, by corrupt or illegal means, any public servant, whether named or otherwise, to do or to forbear to do any official act, or in the exercise of the official functions of such public servant to show favour or disfavour to any person, or to render or attempt to render any service or disservice to any person with the Central Government or any State Government or Parliament or the Legislature of any State or with any local authority, corporation or Government company referred to in clause (c) of section 2, or with any public servant, whether named or otherwise, shall be punishable with imprisonment for a term which shall be not less than six months but which may extend to five years and shall also be liable to fine.

9. Taking gratification, for exercise of personal influence with public servant

Whoever accepts or obtains or agrees to accept or attempts to obtain, from any person, for himself or for any other person, any gratification whatever, as a motive or reward for inducing, by the exercise of personal influence, any public servant whether named or otherwise to do or to forbear to do any official act, or in the exercise of the official functions of such public servant to show favour or disfavour to any person, or to render or attempt to render any service or disservice to any person with the Central Government or any State Government or Parliament or the Legislature of any State or with any local authority, corporation or Government company referred to in clause (c) of section 2, or with any public servant, whether named or otherwise, shall be punishable with imprisonment for a term which shall be not less than six months but which may extend. to five years and shall also be liable to fine.

10. Punishment for abetment by public servant of offences defined in section 8 or 9

Whoever, being a public servant, in respect of whom either of the offences defined in section 8 or section 9 is committed, abets the offence, whether or not that offence is committed in consequence of that abetment, shall be punishable with imprisonment for a term which shall be not less than six months but which may extend to five years and shall also be liable to fine.

11. Public servant obtaining valuable thing, without consideration from person concerned in proceeding or business transacted by such public servant

Whoever, being a public servant, accepts or obtains or agrees to accept or attempts to obtain for himself, or for any other person, any valuable thing without consideration, or for a consideration which he knows to be inadequate, from any person whom he knows to have been, or to be, or to be likely to be concerned in any proceeding or business transacted or about to be transacted by such public servant, or having any connection with the official functions of himself or of any public servant to whom he is subordinate, or from any person whom he knows to be interested in or related to the person so concerned, shall be punishable with imprisonment for a term which shall be not less than six months but which may extend to five years and shall also be liable to fine.

12. Punishment for abetment of offences defined in section 7 or 11

Whoever abets any offence punishable under section 7 or section 11 whether or not that offence is committed in consequence of that abetment, shall be punishable with imprisonment for a term which shall be not less than six months but which may extend to five years and shall also be liable to fine,

13. Criminal misconduct by a public servant

(1) A public servant is said to commit the offence of criminal misconduct,—

(a) if he habitually accepts or obtains or agrees to accept or attempts to obtain from any person for himself or for any other person any gratification other than legal remuneration as a motive or reward such as is mentioned in section 7; or

(b) if he habitually accepts or obtains or agrees to accept or attempts to obtain for himself or for any other person, any valuable thing without consideration or for a consideration which he knows to be inadequate from any person whom he knows to have been, or to be, or to be likely to be concerned in any proceeding or business transacted or about to be transacted by him, or having any connection with the official functions of himself or of any public servant to whom he is subordinate, or from any person whom he knows to be interested in or related to the person so concerned; or

(c) if he dishonestly or fraudulently misappropriates or otherwise converts for his own use any property entrusted to him or under his control as a public servant or allows any other person so to do; or

(d) if he,—

(i) by corrupt or illegal means, obtains for himself or for any other person any valuable thing or pecuniary advantage; or

(ii) by abusing his position as a public servant, obtains for himself or for any other person any valuable thing or pecuniary advantage; or

(iii) while holding office as a public servant, obtains for any person any valuable thing or pecuniary advantage without any public interest; or

(e) if he or any person on his behalf, is in possession or has, at any time during the period of his office, been in possession for which the public servant cannot satisfactorily account, of pecuniary resources or property disproportionate to his known sources of income.

Explanation.—For the purposes of this section, "known sources of income" means income received from any lawful source and such receipt has been intimated in accordance with the provisions of any law, rules or orders for the time being applicable to a public servant.

(2) Any public servant who commits criminal misconduct shall be punishable with imprisonment for a term which shall be not less than one year but which may extend to seven years and shall also be liable to fine.

14. Habitual committing of offence under sections 8, 9 and 12

Whoever habitually commits—

(a) an offence punishable under section 8 or section 9; or

(b) an offence punishable under section 12,

shall be punishable with imprisonment for a term which shall be not less than two years but which may extend to seven years and shall also be liable to fine.

15. Punishment for attempt

Whoever attempts to commit an offence referred to in clause (c) or clause (d) of sub-section (1) of section 13 shall be punishable with imprisonment for a term which may extend to three years and with fine.

16. Matters to be taken into consideration for fixing fine

Where a sentence of fine is imposed under sub-section (2) of section 13 or section 14, the court in fixing the amount of the fine shall taken into consideration the amount or the value of the property, if any, which the accused person has obtained by committing the offence or where the conviction is for an offence referred to in clause (e) of sub-section (1) of section 13, the pecuniary resources or property referred to in that clause for which the accused person is unable to account satisfactorily.

CHAPTER IV

INVESTIGATION INTO CASES UNDER THE ACT

17. Persons authorised to investigate

Notwithstanding anything contained in the Code of Criminal Procedure, 1973, no police officer below the rank,—

(a) in the case of the Delhi Special Police Establishment, of an Inspector of Police;

(b) in the metropolitan areas of Bombay, Calcutta, Madras and Ahmedabad and in any other metropolitan area notified as such under sub-section (1) of section 8 of the Code of Criminal Procedure, 1973, of an Assistant Commissioner of Police;

(c) elsewhere, of a Deputy Superintendent of Police or a police officer of equivalent rank, shall investigate any offence punishable under this Act without the order of a Metropolitan Magistrate or a Magistrate of the first class, as the case may be, or make any arrest therefor without a warrant:

Provided that if a police officer not below the rank of an Inspector of Police is authorised by the State Government in this behalf by general or special order, he may also investigate any such offence without the order of a Metropolitan Magistrate or a Magistrate of the first class, as the case may be, or make arrest therefor without a warrant:

Provided further that an offence referred to in clause (e) of sub-section (1) of section 13 shall not be investigated without the order of a police officer not below the rank of a Superintendent of Police.

18. Power to inspect bankers' books

If from information received or otherwise, a police officer has reason to suspect the commission of an offence which he is empowered to investigate under section 17 and considers that for the purpose of investigation or inquiry into such offence, it is necessary to inspect any bankers' books, then, notwithstanding anything contained in any law for the time being in force, he may inspect any bankers' books in so far as they relate to the accounts of the persons suspected to have committed that offence or of any other person suspected to be holding money on behalf of such person, and take or cause to be taken certified copies of the relevant entries therefrom, and the bank concerned shall be bound to assist the police officer in the exercise of his powers under this section:

Provided that no power under this section in relation to the accounts of any person shall be exercised by a police officer below the rank of a Superintendent of Police, unless he is specially authorised in this behalf by a police officer of or above the rank of a superintendent of Police.

Explanation.—In this section, the expressions "bank" and "bankers' books" shall have the meanings respectively assigned to them in the Bankers' Books Evidence Act, 1891.

19. Previous sanction necessary for prosecution

(1) No court shall take cognizance of an offence punishable under section 7, 10, 11, 13 and 15 alleged to have been committed by a public servant, except with the previous sanction,—

(a) in the case of a person who is employed in connection with the affairs of the Union and is not removable from his office save by or with the sanction of the Central Government, of that Government;

(b) in the case of a person who is employed in connection with the affairs of a State and is not removable from his office save by or with the sanction of the State Government, of that Government; and

(c) in the case of any other person, of the authority competent to remove him from his office.

(2) Where for any reason whatsoever any doubt arises as to whether the previous sanction as required under sub-section (1) should be given by the Central Government or the State Government or any other authority, such sanction shall be given by that Government or authority which would have been competent to remove the public servant from his office at the time when the offence was alleged to have been committed.

(3) Notwithstanding anything contained in the code of Criminal Procedure, 1973,—

(a) no finding, sentence or order passed by a special Judge shall be reversed or altered by a Court in appeal, confirmation or revision on the ground of the absence of, or any error, omission or irregularity in, the sanction required under sub-section (1), unless in the opinion of that court, a failure of justice has in fact, been occasioned thereby;

(b) no court shall stay the proceedings under this Act on the ground of any error, omission or irregularity in the sanction granted by the authority, unless it is satisfied that such error, omission or irregularity has resulted in a failure of justice; and

(c) no court shall stay the proceedings under this Act on any other ground and no court shall exercise the powers of revision in relation to any interlocutory order passed in any inquiry, trial, appeal or other proceedings.

(4) In determining under sub-section (3) whether the absence of, or any error, omission or irregularity in, such sanction has occasioned or resulted in a failure of justice the court shall have regard to the fact

whether the objection could and should have been raised at any earlier stage in the proceedings.

Explanation.—For the purposes of this section,—

(a) error includes competency of the authority to grant sanction;

(b) a sanction required for prosecution includes reference to any requirement that the prosecution shall be at the instance of a specified authority or with the sanction of a specified person or any requirement of a similar nature.

20. Presumption where public servant accepts gratification other than legal remuneration

(1) Where, in any trial of an offence punishable under section 7 or section 11 or clause (a) or clause (b) of sub-section (1) of section 13 it is proved that an accused person has accepted or obtained or has agreed to accept or attempted to obtain for himself, or for any other person, any gratification (other than legal remuneration) or any valuable thing from any person, it shall be presumed, unless the contrary is proved, that he accepted or obtained or agreed to accept or attempted to obtain that gratification or that valuable thing, as the case may be, as a motive or reward such as is mentioned in section 7 or, as the case may be, without consideration or for a consideration which he knows to be Inadequate.

(2) Where in any trial of an offence punishable under section 12 or under clause (b) of section 14, it is proved that any gratification (other than legal remuneration) or any valuable thing has been given or offered to be given or attempted to be given by an accused person, it shall be presumed, unless the contrary is proved, that he gave or offered to give or attempted to give that gratification or that valuable thing, as the case may be, as a motive or reward such as is mentioned in section 7, or, as the case may be, without consideration or for a consideration which he knows to be inadequate.

(3) Notwithstanding anything contained in sub-sections (1) and (2), the court may decline to draw the presumption referred to in either of the said sub-sections, if the gratification or thing aforesaid is, in its opinion, so trivial that no inference of corruption may fairly be drawn.

21. Accused person to be a competent witness

Any person charged with an offence punishable under this Act, shall be a competent witness for the defence and may give evidence on oath in disproof of the charges made against him or any person charged together with him at the same trial:

Provided that—

(a) he shall not be called as a witness except at his own request;

(b) his failure to give evidence shall not be made the subject of any comment by the prosecution or give rise to any presumption against himself or any person charged together with him at the same trial;

(c) he shall not be asked, and if asked shall not be required to answer, any question tending to show that he has committed or been convicted of any offence other than the offence with which he is charged, or is of bad character, unless—

(i) the proof that he has committed or been convicted of such offence is admissible evidence to that he is guilty of the offence with which he is charged, or

(ii) he has personally or by his pleader asked any question of any witness for the prosecution with a view to establish his own good character, or has given evidence of his good character, or the nature or conduct of the defence is such as to involve imputations on the character of the prosecutor or of any witness for the prosecution, or

(iii) he has given evidence against any other person charged with the same offence.

22. The Code of Criminal Procedure, 1973 to apply subject to certain modifications

The provisions of the Code of Criminal Procedure, 1973, shall in their application to any proceeding in relation to an offence punishable under this Act have effect as if,—

(a) in sub-section (1) of section 243, for the words "The accused shall then be called upon", the words "The accused shall then be required to give in writing at once or within such time as the Court may allow, a list of the persons (if any) whom he proposes to examine as his witnesses and of the documents (if any) on which he proposes to rely and he shall then be called upon" had been substituted;

(b) in sub-section (2) of section 309, after the 'third proviso', the following proviso had been inserted, namely:

"Provided also that the proceeding shall not be adjourned or postponed merely on the ground that an application under section 397 has been made by a party to the proceeding";

(c) after sub-section (2) of section 317, the following sub-section had been inserted, namely:

"(3) Notwithstanding anything contained in sub-section (1) or sub-section (2), the Judge may, if he thinks fit and for reasons to be recorded by him, proceed with inquiry or trial in the absence of the accused or his pleader and record the evidence of any witness subject to the right of the accused to recall the witness for cross-examination";

(d) in sub-section (1) of section 397, before the Explanation, the following proviso had been inserted, namely:

"Provided that where the powers under this section are exercised by a Court on an application made by a party to such proceedings, the Court shall not ordinarily call for the record of the proceedings—

(a) without giving the other party an opportunity of showing cause why the record should not be called for; or

(b) if it is satisfied that an examination of the record of the proceedings may be made from the certified copies."

23. Particulars in a charge in relation to an offence under section 13(1)(c)

Notwithstanding anything contained in the Code of Criminal Procedure, 1973, when an accused is charged with an offence under clause (c) of sub-section (1) of section 13, it shall be sufficient to describe in the charge the property in respect of which the offence is alleged to have been committed, and the dates between which the offence is alleged to have been committed, without specifying particular items or exact dates, and the charge so framed shall be deemed to be a charge of one offence within the meaning of section 219 of the said Code:

Provided that the time included between the first and last of such dates shall not exceed one year.

24. Statement by bribe giver not to subject him to prosecution

Notwithstanding anything contained in any law for the time being in force, a statement made by a person in any proceeding against a public servant for an offence under sections 7 to 11 or under section 13 or section 15, that he offered or agreed to offer any gratification (other than legal remuneration) or any valuable thing to the public servant, shall not subject such person to a prosecution under section 12.

25. Military, Naval and Air Force or other law not to be affected

(1) Nothing in this Act shall affect the jurisdiction exercisable by, or the procedure applicable to, any court or other authority under the Army Act, 1950, the Air Force Act, 1950, the Navy Act, 1957, the Border Security Force Act, 1968, the Coast Guard Act, 1978 and the National Security Guard Act, 1986.

(2) For the removal of doubts, it is hereby declared that for the purposes of any such law as is referred to in sub-section (1), the court of a special Judge shall be deemed to be a court of ordinary criminal justice.

26. Special Judges appointed under Act 46 of 1952 to be special Judges appointed under this Act

Every special Judge appointed under the Criminal Law Amendment Act, 1952, for any area or areas and is holding office on the commencement of this Act shall be deemed to be a special Judge appointed under section 3 of this Act for that area or areas and, accordingly, on and from such commencement, every such Judge shall continue to deal with all the proceedings pending before him on such commencement in accordance with the provisions of this Act.

27. Appeal and revision

Subject to the provisions of this Act, the High Court may exercise, so far as they may be applicable, all the powers of appeal and revision conferred by the Code of Criminal Procedure, 1973 on a High Court as if the court of special Judge were a court of Session trying cases within the local limits of the High Court.

28. Act to be in addition to any other law

The provisions of this Act shall be in addition to, and not in derogation of, any other law for the time being in force, and nothing contained herein shall exempt any public servant from any proceeding which might, apart from this Act, be instituted against him.

29. Amendment of the Ordinance 38 of 1944

In the Criminal Law Amendment Ordinance, 1944,—

(a) in sub-section (1) of section 3, sub-section (1) of sector 9, clause (a) of section 10, sub-section (1) of section 11 and sub-section (1) of section 13, for the words "State Government", wherever they occur, the words "State Government or, as the case may be, the Central Government" shall be substituted;

(b) in section 10, in clause (a), for the words "three months", the words "one year" shall be substituted;

(c) in the Schedule,-

(i) paragraph 1 shall be omitted;

(ii) in paragraphs 2 and 4,-

(a) after the words "a local authority", the words and figures "or a corporation established by or under a Central, Provincial or State Act, or an authority or a body owned or controlled or aided by Government or a Government company as defined in section 617 of the Companies Act, 1956 or a society aided by such corporation, authority, body or Government company" shall be inserted;

(b) after the words "or authority", the words "or corporation or body or Government company or society" shall be inserted;

(iii) for paragraph 4A, the following paragraph shall be substituted, namely:—

"4A. An offence punishable under the Prevention of Corruption Act, 1988";

(iv) in paragraph 5, for the words and figures "items 2, 3 and 4", the words, figures and letter "items 2, 3, 4 and 4A" shall be substituted.

30. Repeal and saving

(1) The Prevention of Corruption Act, 1947 and the Criminal Law Amendment Act, 1952 are hereby repealed.

(2) Notwithstanding such repeal, but without prejudice to the application of section 6 of the General Clauses Act, 1897, anything done or any action taken or purported to have been done or taken under or in pursuance of the Acts so repealed shall, in so far as it is not inconsistent with the provisions of this Act, be deemed to have been done or taken, under or in pursuance of the corresponding provision of this Act.

31. Omission of certain sections of Act 45 of 1860

Sections 161 to 165A (both inclusive) of the Indian Penal Code shall be omitted, and section 6 of the General Clauses Act, 1897, shall apply to such omission as if the said sections had been repealed by a Central Act.

Bibliography

Ahmad Siddique: Criminology, IVth edition (1997), Reprinted, 2001.

Aristotle: Politics, Macmillan, London, Book-II.

August Bequai: White-collar Crime—A 20th Century Crisis, (Lexington Books Toronto, 1978).

B.K. Sharma, Vijay Nagpal, K.K. Khandelwal: A Treatise on Economic and Social Offences, First edition, 2003.

Barnes and Tetters: New Horizons in Criminology, 3rd edition.

Brihaspati Smriti: Published by Sacred Books of East Series, Vol. LXXXV (1965 Reprint).

C.H. McCaghy: Deviant Behaviour, New York, The Macmillan Co. 1964.

Crime in India (1994): Published by National Crime .Record Bureau (M.H.A.)

Dharma Kumar (ed.): The Cambridge Economic History of India, Vol. II (UP), 1982.

E.H. Sutherland: White-collar crime, New York, Dryden Press (1949).

Edwin H. Sutherland: Principles of Criminology, VIth edition.

E. Kintner: An Antitrust Primer, New York, The Macmillan Co. 1964.

Friedman: Law in a Changing Society (1951).

G.S. Karkara: Environment Law, 1st edition (1999).

Gharpure, Smriti Chandrika: Gilbert Geis and Robert F. Meher (Eds); White-collar Crime, Offences in Business, Politics and Professions, (New York, Free Press, 1977).

Girish Mishra and Braj Kumar Pandey: White-collar Crimes (1998).

Hargovind Shastri: Manu Samriti (Hindi) (The Kashi Sanskrit Series-114), IIIrd ed. (1982).

Hari Narayana Apte: Yajnavalkya Smriti (1904).

Hermann Mannheim: Comparative Criminology, Boston, Houghton Mifflin (1965).

I.A. Khan: Environmental Law, 1st edition (2000).

Ilbert: Legislative Methods and Forms (1901).

James and Wilson: Thinking about Crime, (New York! Basic Books, 1975).

Justice V.R. Krishna Iyer: Indian. Social Justice in Crisis (1983).

K.D. Gaur: Criminal Law and Criminology (2002).

Kamal Nayan Kabra: Financial Sector Scam—Fruits of Liberalisation, New Delhi (1992).

Katherine S. Williams: Criminology, 3rd edition, First Indian reprint-2001.

L. Srinivasacharya (ed.), Translated by J.R. Gharpure; Smriti Chandrika of Devanna Bhatta (1914).

M. Hidayatullah: Constitutional Law of India, Volume I, First Published, 1984.

M. Rama Jois: Legal and Constitutional History of India, Volume I and II (Second Printing 1990).

Mahendra P. Singh: V.N. Shukla's Constitution of India, 8th edition (Reprint 1992).

Michael Conaut: Antitrust in Motion Picture Industry (Berkeley, University of California Press, 1972).

N.V. Paranjape: Criminology and Penology, XIth edition, reprinted 2002.

Narada Smriti: SHE Publication, Vol.-XXXIII (1965 Reprint).

P.M. Bakshi: Public Interest litigations, Edition 1998(Oct.).

P.R. Rajgopal: Violence and Response.

P.V. Kane: Katyanana Smriti, Sanskrit to English Translation (1933).

R.H. Tawney: The Acquisitive Society, Sussex (1982).

R.K. Suri and T.N. Chhabra: Cyber Crime, Reprint 2003.

R. Rama Shastri: Saraswati Vilasa (1927).

R. Shama Shastry: Kautilya Arthasastra (Eng. ed.) (1967).

Rohiriton Mehta: Crime and Criminology, 1st edition (1999), Published by Snowwhite Publication, Bombay.

S.D. Satvalekar (ed.): Mahabharata Shanti Parva (Sanskrit to Hindi translation) (1952).

S.M.A. Quadri: Ahmad Siddiqu: Criminology, Fifth edition (2005).

S. Venugopal Ra: Facets of crime in India, Second revised edition (1967).

Taft and Ralph W. England: Criminology, VIth ed. (1969).

T.K. Tope: Constitutional Law of India, IInd edition, 1992.

Vetter and Silverman: The Nature of Crime (1978). Published by Saunder's Company Philadelphia /London/ Toronto.

Walter Reckless: The Crime Problem.

Articles

Ajit Kumar Sahu: "Lajya" Published in Oriya "Praharee" 21.10.1996.

C.S. Lewis: The Screw Tape Letters and Screw Tape Purpose (New York: Macmillan, 1961).

Donald J. Newman: Corporate and Business White-collar Crime; Gilbert Geis (1968).

Edward Alsworth Ross: The Criminaloid, Gilbert Geis and Robert F. Meher (1977).

Edwin H. Sutherland: Crime of Corporations, Karl Schuessler ed. Analyzing Crime (1973), Gilbert Geis and F. Meher (1977).

Edwin H. Sutherlan: The Professional Thief (Chicago, University of Chicago Press, 1937).

E.H. Sutherland: White-collar Criminality; Gilbert Geis and Robert F. Meher eds. (1968).

E.H. Sutherland: White-collar Criminality; American Sociological Review (February, 1940).

E.H. Sutherland: Is White-collar Crime—Crime? American Sociological Review (10th April, 1945), Gilbert Geis and Robert F. Meher (1977).

Gulshan Rai, R.K. Dubash, A.K. Chakravarti: Computer-related Crimes; Government of India, Department of Electronics, New Delhi.

Gurpal Singh: Problems of White-collar Crime in India and its Control, Punjab University Law Journal (1977).

John Lobo: White-collar crime—A social Malaise, CBI Bulletin, March, 1982.

Justice Prasun Kumar Deb: High Court Patna, White-collar Crime—Crime committed by a person of respectability and high social status in course of his occupation, Criminal Law Journal, 2000.

K.K. Birla: Midway to Elections, An article published in 'The Hindustan Times' late city edition (New Delhi) dated 7.8.2002, p.8.

M.P. Mehani: Financial Crimes and Frauds in Banking Industry, CBI Bulletin, Vol. VI, No. 9, September 1998.

N. Narayana Swami: Redefining Offences in Penal Code—An Urgent Necessity, Criminal Law Journal, 2002.

Parank E. Hartung: White-collar offences in the whole-sale meat industry in Detroit, American Journal of Sociology, 56 (1950-51).

Paul W. Tappan: Who is criminal? American Sociological Review, 12.

Prabhat Chandra Tripathi: The Menace of White-collar Crimes and Need for a New Code, Criminal Law Journal/3-III (1997).

Robert E. Lane: Why Businessmen Violate the Law, Gilbert Geis & Robert F. Meher (1977).

T.N. Ashok: White-collar Crime, "Lawyer" (1983).

U. Sieber (Prof): Computer Crime and Criminal Information Law.

Winifred Bose: The Trader in 'opinion', quoted by N.R. Menon in his unpublished thesis, A socio-legal study of white-collar crime in India (1968).